The Lawyer's Guide
to Social Networking

*Understanding Social Media's
Impact on the Law*

John G. Browning

ASPATORE

Project Manager, Kristen Lindeman; edited by Eddie Fournier; proofread by Melanie Zimmerman

Aspatore books may be purchased for educational, business, or sales promotional use. For information, please e-mail West.customer.service@thomson.com.

ISBN 978-0-314-27350-5

For corrections, updates, comments, or any other inquiries, please e-mail TLR.AspatoreEditorial@thomson.com.

First Printing, 2010
10 9 8 7 6 5 4 3 2 1

Mat #41105137

ASPATORE

Aspatore Books, a Thomson Reuters business, exclusively publishes C-Level executives (CEO, CFO, CTO, CMO, Partner) from the world's most respected companies and law firms. C-Level Business Intelligence™, as conceptualized and developed by Aspatore Books, provides professionals of all levels with proven business intelligence from industry insiders—direct and unfiltered insight from those who know it best—as opposed to third-party accounts offered by unknown authors and analysts. Aspatore Books is committed to publishing an innovative line of business and legal books, those which lay forth principles and offer insights that, when employed, can have a direct financial impact on the reader's business objectives, whatever they may be. In essence, Aspatore publishes critical tools for all business professionals.

Dedication and Acknowledgements

Dedication

To my father, Walter W. Browning, Jr., for his unwavering support of my writing from a very early age; to my wife Lisa, without whose love, patience, and encouragement this book would never have happened; to my late brother Michael, whose courage and grace during the worst ravages of cancer taught me more than I can acknowledge and inspires me always; and to my little girl Bo, who will forever be the angel on my shoulder.

Acknowledgements

This book benefited tremendously from the input of friends and colleagues too numerous to list, especially my partners at Thompson, Coe, Cousins & Irons LLP. I have judges like the Honorable Gena Slaughter and the Honorable Susan Criss to thank for generously providing insight into judicial perspectives on social media. Finally, the skillful help of my assistants Vena Hamje and Kathy Brennan, as well as Kristen Lindeman and the editorial staff at Thomson Reuters, helped this work transcend my sometimes random scribblings.

CONTENTS

Foreword

Well over a century ago, the United States Supreme Court wrote that:

> Perhaps the most remarkable invention of modern times, in the influence which it has had, and is yet to have, on the affairs of the world, as well as in its total change of all the elements on which land transportation formerly depended, is the railroad system. It is not strange, then, that when we are called to construe a statute relating to this class of subjects, passed before a steam engine or a railroad was thought of, in its application to this modern system, we should be met by difficulties of the gravest character.

Bridge Proprietors v. Hoboken Co., 68 U.S. 116, 146-47 (1864).

Like the advent of the steam engine, the Internet has transformed our society, as it has crept its way into the courtroom. The results, as revealed in this book, range from the quirky to the innovative, whether from the perspective of a personal injury lawyer who requires that his clients refrain from social networking, or from a criminal judge who monitors juveniles on probation by "friending" them on Facebook. Browning's take on the role of social networking neither condemns nor exalts it, but rather examines the myriad ways in which it affects the legal world. The advice and caution he gives will be of immense utility to practitioners and judges alike.

Courts occupy a delicate position regarding the law and the Internet. In addition to ethical considerations, the judge must balance evolving notions of privacy with laws that were often codified decades before the Internet promised instant communication. For an elected judge in particular, the rise of social networking further complicates the precarious relationship between voters and the goal of impartial administration of justice. On the one hand, the Internet—and social networking in particular—provides a convenient tool for campaigning; but the judge who engages in electronic networking heightens the risk of inappropriate communication with potential litigants. Internet postings, even once deleted, have lasting perpetuity, thanks to widespread dissemination and "downloadability."

What may seem like an innocent "tweet" one moment can force a judge's recusal or worse, as Browning recounts with stark anecdotes.

Browning underscores that social networking is at once the medium of our age and a minefield for those engaged in the legal profession. Practitioners will find useful tips on how to market their firms on social media outlets, how to capitalize on the evidentiary value of online postings, and how to protect clients from damaging their own credibility through ill-considered electronic revelations. Importantly, Browning reminds us that "social networking is an invaluable tool to educate yourself and others, and to initiate and maintain contact—but it's no substitute for face to face interaction."

In 1864, when Justice Miller of the U.S. Supreme Court spoke of the "remarkable invention" of the steam engine, he foresaw the challenges that technology would bring to the judiciary as "difficulties of the gravest character." Nuclear and solar energy have replaced coal and steam; pen and paper no longer drive the courts. As we in the judiciary, and lawyers at the bar, adapt to this new world, we must maintain our adherence to the rule of law. Browning has given us the building blocks to continue our great mission to maintain justice and impartiality in a wired society.

Chief Justice Wallace B. Jefferson
Supreme Court of Texas
September 2010

1

Introduction

"The Internet has opened new channels of communication and self-expression... Countless individuals use message boards, date matching sites, interactive social networks, blog hosting services and video sharing websites to make themselves and their ideas visible to the world. While such intermediaries enable the user-driven digital age, they also create new legal problems."

Fair Housing Council of San Fernando Valley v. Roommates. Com LLC, 489 F.3d 921, 924 (9th Cir. 2007)

There is no greater proof of the truth of the Ninth Circuit's observation than social networking sites like MySpace and Facebook. What your teenager has known about social networking sites "for, like forever" is only recently becoming apparent to attorneys: they are virtual treasure troves of information. Lawyers on both the plaintiff and defense sides of the bar, in specialties ranging from personal injury and employment law to criminal defense and family law, are rapidly becoming aware of the increasing importance of having a working knowledge of sites like Facebook and MySpace. On what Professor Daniel Solove described as the "permanent chronicle of our private lives" that social networking sites represent, attorneys can find useful and sometimes startling information on other parties, key witnesses, and even their own clients. These sites allow users to post comments, photos, and videos, build an online network, and share information with others. Evidence from social networking sites can help defend a murder case, pressure a settlement in a medical malpractice trial, negate a sexual harassment claim, and even provide insight into prospective jurors. Simply put, social networking sites are valuable weapons that should be a standard feature of any litigator's arsenal.

The explosive growth in and sheer pervasiveness of social networking is one reason why the legal profession will continue to be shaped by this phenomenon for years to come. Nearly 60 percent of Internet users in the United States have a profile on a social networking site; according to a September 2009 Nielsen online survey, social networking is now the fourth most popular online activity. Internet users spend 17 percent of their online time on social networking, a figure that represents a usage rate increase that is growing at three times that of overall Internet usage.

MySpace, founded in 2003, has more than 250 million users worldwide, while Facebook (started in 2004 by Mark Zuckerberg) has swelled to more than 500 million users internationally. If "Facebook Nation" were indeed its own country, it would be the third most populous on Earth. The social networking/micro-blogging site Twitter only began in 2006, but it too has enjoyed remarkable growth, with more than 75 million users sharing information instantaneously and sending out messages, or "tweets," of 140 characters or less. Three years ago, Twitter handled 5,000 tweets a day. Today, that figure is a staggering 50 million per day, with 600 tweets being sent out every second.

Given the sheer magnitude of such numbers, as social networking's cultural tsunami shapes society, its impact on the legal profession should not come as much of a surprise. However, social networking's influence is being felt not just in more predictable fashion, such as providing new sources of evidence for cases, but also in ways that are as of yet impossible to fully appreciate. As this book will demonstrate, social networking's prevalence is altering the way we look at existing bodies of law like defamation, and changing our perception of concepts like service of process. In the coming years, social networking will not only continue to affect how lawyers pursue discovery and introduce evidence, but it will also have an even greater impact on how attorneys market themselves to prospective clients and conduct themselves officially.

Simply put, what Jimmy Buffett might have characterized as a digital "permanent reminder of a temporary feeling" has far-reaching implications for the legal professional, and will continue to do so well into the future. Besides providing an overview of social networking, this book will examine real-world examples of how social networking evidence is being used in various types of cases; look at discovery and evidentiary issues raised by social networking; analyze how basic notions like jurisdiction and service of process are being changed by social media; and consider the ethical issues raised by social networking. This book will also discuss social networking's implications for such subjects as legal ethics, the role of judges, attorney marketing, how the phenomenon is influencing juror behavior, and how social media may shape the notion of duty in the near future.

Why are understanding and utilizing social media critical for lawyers? You can't avoid it; it permeates virtually every layer of our culture. It's no passing fad, but instead is a paradigm shift overtaking society at large, and those who view such a shift as generational in nature are not seeing the complete picture: Facebook reports that its fastest-growing demographic is the thirty-five to fifty-four age range. Lawyers who dismiss social networking as a waste of time do so at their own peril.

The Internet, and by extension the information-sharing avenues presented by social media, have transformed consumer society. People not only find everything from restaurant reviews and movie times online in a way that is faster and cheaper than ever, but they also invest a high level of trust in that information. A Pew Internet study in 2009 found that nearly 40 percent of Americans doubted a doctor's opinion or diagnosis because it conflicted with information they discovered online. It's not surprising, then, that corporate giants like Coca-Cola (with 5.5 million fans on Facebook) and McDonald's (2.3 million fans) have embraced social networking as a vital element in their marketing strategy. Even the government has gotten into the act, with the White House issuing a memo on April 7, 2010, announcing that "interactive meeting tools—including but not limited to public conference calls, webinars, blogs, discussion boards, forums, message boards, chat sessions, social networks, and online communities—to be equivalent to in-person public meetings." Open government, consequently, is more open than ever.

Being a part of society in which more and more people seem to be living their lives online comes with a price. Sometimes the revelations on social networking sites can have national security implications—such as the recent Wikileaks circulation of tens of thousands of pages of information about U.S. operations in Afghanistan, or the Israeli soldier court-martialed for divulging details of an upcoming West Bank raid on Facebook. British newspapers widely reported the details about England's head of MI-6 (the British intelligence service) that were publicly available thanks to his wife's postings on Facebook. While it may not have compromised national security to reveal that Sir John Sawers wears blue Speedos and enjoys a brisk game of Frisbee, photos posted by his wife about their travels could have breached England's strict intelligence protocols.

Social media can be a powerful force for good, and it was instrumental in organizing and focusing world attention on protests in Pakistan and Iran against authoritarian regimes. In July 2010, a message written on Facebook led police in Nevada to a couple who had been eluding authorities for months in the case of a nine-year-old girl who was found dead in May. Social networking sites have even helped locate missing or kidnapped children. The power of social media has also been harnessed to help coordinate donations and relief efforts in areas devastated by natural disasters, such as when Haiti was rocked with earthquakes.

Unfortunately, social networking is often used for more nefarious purposes. "Cyber-bullying," such as the online tormenting by classmates that led to the January 2010 suicide of fifteen-year-old Phoebe Prince in Massachusetts, has become a topic of national discussion. And in 2008, Aimee Sword of Michigan used Facebook to track down the fourteen-year-old son she had given up for adoption shortly after delivery, only to later engage in incestuous sex with him after finding him (Sword pleaded guilty, and is serving a nine- to thirty-year prison sentence). Frequently, those engaging in criminal acts are as prone as the rest of society to living their lives online, to the point of documenting their transgressions. Examples like the thirty-six-year-old Maine resident who decided not only to set fire to a car, but also to post photos of the act on Facebook, could fill a whole chapter of this book. Everyone, it seems, wants his or her digital fifteen minutes of fame.

Efforts to address many of the issues presented by social media within the confines of a legal system that has not kept pace with technology often lead to unsatisfying results or difficult dilemmas. Is a student who creates a fake MySpace profile derogatory of his teacher guilty of defaming the educator, or are his activities protected by freedom of speech? Has an estranged spouse who "pokes" her partner on Facebook violated a domestic violence protective order prohibiting all contact between the two? Can a statement made on a social networking site be admissible to impeach or exculpate a witness? An Arkansas mother probably thought she was within the bounds of responsible parenting earlier this year when she accessed her son's Facebook page, didn't like what she saw, and so posted statements about him on his profile and changed his password. Unfortunately, the court disagreed and convicted her of harassment for the actions. Will such a ruling make it "open season" on parents who try to supervise their children's Internet activities? Only time will tell.

Social networking is here to stay. As its presence and influence continue to be felt across our system of justice, as well as in the profession itself, lawyers need to keep up with what many once dismissed as a passing fad or a drain on productivity. Hopefully, this book will provide useful guidance and information to those navigating their way through the digital maelstrom.

2

Social Media 101

"Social media," also known as "social networking," is the term used to describe any type of social interaction using technology (primarily the Internet, but also including modern smartphone and PDA innovations) with some combination of words, photos, video, and/or audio. Unlike the earlier days of the Internet, the interactivity of "Web 2.0" sites enables users to communicate and connect with each other, as well as to share user-generated content like video, music, and written postings. Do a search of "John Browning" on Facebook, and you'll find not only the lawyer who authored this book and numerous articles on legal topics, but also a different individual, a rap artist who goes by "J Bigga" and who shares his music and philosophical outlook on life. You'll encounter online journals or "blogs" (short for weblog) where individuals discuss various topics, provide news or editorial content, and invite readers to comment (a blog written by a lawyer or devoted to a legal topic is called a "blawg").

Social networking sites actually originated in the mid-1990s, but only started exploding across the web in recent years. The concept itself is a relatively simple one: just as with a network of roads that enables you to see that Dallas is connected via highways to St. Louis, which in turn is connected with yet another city, a network of people exists as well. While on a personal level, you may know a friend who in turn knows a friend who works in an industry and knows of a job for you, this type of connection isn't widely known. Social networking sites help you see connections that you otherwise wouldn't see. Essentially, you begin by filling out a profile (most of these sites are free). Afterward, you look for people you know. When you find someone, you click to add him or her as a friend; once you do this, you and that person have a connection that others can see. He or she is a member of your network, and vice versa. You can see whom your friends know, whom your friends' friends know, and so on. Since you're no longer a stranger, you can contact them more easily.

There are social networking sites for every conceivable interest, from NASCAR (Infield Parking) to fine wines (Vinorati). There are also sharing sites, where people share everything from photos (Flickr) to video (the very popular YouTube); Amazon.com is actually one of the original sharing sites, with book reviews and recommended lists that people can contribute. And yes, there is even LawLink, "the first online network exclusively for attorneys." There are blogs, where one can write a personal journal or a newsletter, featuring separate posts organized by date. In addition, there are micro-blogs (if blogs take the form of essays, think of micro-blogs as instant messages); well-known micro-blog sites include Twitter (which bills itself as "a global community of friends and strangers answering one simple question: what are you doing?") and Pownce. Finally, there are blog/social network hybrids like Xanga or LiveJournal. These are online communities where the user's "home base" is a blog with date-stamped entries rather than a page featuring posted information. Such hybrids are organized around blogs, but fulfilling the same functions as social networking sites— meet friends, form groups, post photos and videos, etc.

Lawyers are rapidly becoming familiar with the benefits of social networking sites like LinkedIn, which is geared toward businesspeople and professionals. On LinkedIn (where "relationships matter"), you have "connections" as opposed to "friends." With more than 75 million users (a growing number of whom are lawyers), LinkedIn offers many of the same functions and features as other social networking sites. LinkedIn is a contact management system as well as a social network, and has a question-and-answer feature similar to Yahoo! Answers.

However, the two biggest social networking sites are MySpace (with more than 250 million members) and Facebook (with more than 500 million active users worldwide). MySpace was started in 2003. Facebook, founded by Mark Zuckerberg in 2004 as a social networking site for Harvard students, spread rapidly through the university ranks and down into high school as well. It was opened to the public in 2006 and has continued its phenomenal growth.

At a social networking site, one creates a profile using a valid e-mail address; first and last names; personal password; country; postal code; date of birth (one must be over the age of thirteen, although there doesn't appear to be a way to validate such information before a page can be created); and gender. When a profile is created, the user also creates his or her own URL (e.g., www.myspace.com/bobthelawyer). Someone can type in this URL and pull up the user's social networking page, depending on the privacy settings. You do not have to be a registered user to browse social networking profiles. You can also search for an individual through categories such as "full name," "display name," "registered e-mail address," "school," or "career interests." You may also narrow down results using categories for "country," "postal code," "miles within postal code," "city," and "gender."

Social networking sites have various privacy settings. "Online status" controls whether visitors can see when a user is online. "Birthday" controls whether individuals who are friends will receive reminders when a user's birthday is approaching. "Profile viewable by…" is a control that enables a user to remit his or her profile to "viewable by everyone," "viewable by everyone age 18 and older" (which actually will block not only registered users under eighteen, but also any member of the public from viewing the profile), and "viewable by friends only" (which allows an individual on the "friends" list to view the profile). There are additional privacy controls that determine whether photos can be e-mailed or shared, that block users by age, and that block individual users.

Social networking sites are highly customizable, and offer a plethora of choices. Users can search for friends, blog, discuss topics in message forums, explore new music, view film trailers and comedy clips, join groups, plan events, advertise a business, and many more activities.

Facebook has continued to tweak its privacy settings to permit users to exert greater control over which of their friends are allowed to see personal details that they post. Now, Facebook users who upload racy photos or list information like cell phone numbers or personal e-mail addresses on their Facebook page can ban some people on a list of friends from viewing such details. Prior to such changes, the only way Facebook users could block such information was to deny friend requests outright, or to create a limited profile that would keep entire groups of people from accessing much of the page's content. With proper use of privacy settings, Facebook makes it possible to funnel certain information only to certain parties—factor to certainly keep in mind when conducting discovery into an individual's online alter ego.

Privacy has been a subject of ongoing debate in the world of social networking. Consider this: a relatively complete Facebook profile contains more than forty pieces of recognizable personal information, including name; date of birth; educational and employment history; sexual preference and relationship status; online and offline contact information; political and religious views; tastes in music, books, and movies; and of course, photos (Facebook remains the largest photo-sharing application on the web, with more than 14 million photos uploaded daily). In completing a typical social networking profile, a person will have constructed a fairly detailed database of information—not only about who he or she is, but also who he or she knows.

Facebook has been criticized by many for its privacy policies, even after adjusting their privacy settings in early 2010. Despite the fact that the social networking site now claims that 35 percent of users who had never before engaged with their privacy settings took the initiative to do so after Facebook updated its privacy options, Facebook still faces official concerns both inside and outside the United States. Senator Charles Schumer of New York has called on the Federal Trade Commission to step up and draft guidelines for how social networking sites use and share their users' personal information. Schumer maintains that Facebook's new privacy policies "have limited the ability of users to control the information they share and keep private… These changes can adversely affect users and, currently, there is little guidance on what social networking sites can and cannot do and how disclosure is provided." Meanwhile, a Canadian law firm is pursuing a potential class action suit against Facebook, contending that the site "intentionally or negligently designs its privacy policies…in such a fashion as to mislead and induce users into putting their personal information and privacy at further risk." The suit contends that Facebook has retroactively purported to make public material that was previously private, including profile photos and lists of friends. And in Germany, the Hamburg data protection office is pursuing legal proceedings against

Facebook for allegedly violating German privacy laws by saving third-party non-user personal information without permission.

It's no secret that keeping things private on a site like Facebook requires considerable effort. Opting out of full disclosure of most information requires a user to click through more than fifty privacy buttons and choose from more than 170 different options. No small wonder, then, that Facebook's privacy policy (5,830 words long) dwarfs the U.S. Constitution (a paltry 4,543 words long by comparison). For those who are concerned about their privacy, at a bare minimum you should pay particular attention to three settings: who can see the things you share (such as status updates or photos), who can see your personal information (the default setting is "Everyone"), and what Google can see (in order to keep your data off the search engine).

Facebook founder and chief executive Mark Zuckerberg, however, points to a generational shift in expectations of privacy, saying that people no longer want "complete privacy." He says, "Our core belief is that one of the most transformational things in this generation is that there will be more information available."

The result of all this information being online, of course, is that lawyers have more data than ever before at their fingertips, data that can literally make or break a case.

3

The Long Arm of the Cyber Law: Social Networking and Jurisdictional Issues

Any understanding of how the advent of social media has affected jurisdictional issues hinges on a grasp of jurisdictional requirements in general, as well as a sense of how notions of jurisdiction have been refined in recent years to account for the Internet and how it has transformed the ways people now conduct business. As one court noted, the Internet "makes it possible to conduct business throughout the world entirely from a desktop." *Jones v. Beech Aircraft Corp.*, 995 S.W.2d 767, 772 (Tex. App. 2009) (pet. dism'd w.o.j., mand. denied).

In a series of landmark decisions, the U.S. Supreme Court established the requirements for a court in one state to lawfully exercise jurisdiction over a citizen from another state. Foreseeability is crucial, with the defendant's conduct and connection to the forum state being such that he or she should reasonably expect to be haled into court there. *World Wide Volkswagen v. Woodson*, 444 U.S. 286 (1980). In addition, a defendant must have sufficient "minimum contacts" with the forum state, the claim asserted against the defendant must arise out of those contacts, and the exercise of jurisdictions must be reasonable. *Burger King Corp. v. Rudzewicz*, 471 U.S. 462, 475 (1985). The minimum contacts must be continuous and systematic, not just an isolated incident or happenstance, so as not to run afoul of due process concerns. *Helicopteros Nacionales de Colombia, S.A. v. Hall*, 466 U.S. 408 (1984). Key questions in examining the nature of the defendant's contacts with the forum state include whether the defendant purposefully availed him or herself of the privilege of conducting activities within that state, such that he or she would be invoking the benefits and protections of that state's laws; and whether the exercise of jurisdiction would comport with "traditional notions of fair play and substantial justice." *International Shoe Co. v. Washington*, 326 U.S. 310, 316 (1945).

But with the Internet came radically new notions of what constituted doing business, and the nature of e-commerce demanded a reexamination of how traditional principles of jurisdiction would apply to situations where a consumer in New York could, with a few keyboard clicks, transact business with a company in California. The seminal decision on whether minimum contacts exist in a party's operation of an Internet-based business came with *Zippo Manufacturing Co. v. Zippo Dot Com Inc.*, 952 F. Supp. 1119 (W.D. Pa. 1997). In this case, Zippo filed suit in its home state, Pennsylvania, against a California Internet news service, Zippo Dot Com, alleging that it was wrongfully capitalizing on the lighter manufacturer's name and reputation in the marketplace. The trial court held that Pennsylvania did have jurisdiction over the California company, pointing out that Zippo Dot Com delivered news to approximately 140,000 subscribers worldwide, of whom roughly 3,000 were residents of Pennsylvania.

More importantly, the *Zippo* decision established a sliding scale test to evaluate the "nature and quality of commercial activity that an entity conducts over the Internet." This analysis categorizes Internet use on a three-point spectrum:

1. At one end of this spectrum, a defendant "merely establishes a passive website that does nothing more than advertise on the Internet." Basing personal jurisdiction on such a "passive website" would be inappropriate.
2. At the opposite end of the spectrum are those defendants who are clearly doing business over the Internet by entering into contracts with residents of other states, such that they "involve the knowing and repeated transmission of computer files over the Internet." Under these circumstances, exercising personal jurisdiction over the non-resident defendant would be proper.
3. In between those two extremes lie cases in which a defendant's website allows a visitor to exchange information with a host

computer. In this middle ground, according to the *Zippo* court, "the exercise of jurisdiction is determined by the level of interactivity and commercial nature of the exchange of information that occurs on the [w]ebsite."

Again, a critical part of this inquiry will be whether the contacts suggest that the non-resident defendant purposefully availed him or herself of the privilege of conducting activities in the forum state.

Since *Zippo*, there have been a significant number of cases in Texas and elsewhere that analyze whether the Internet activity has been sufficient to constitute minimum contacts and thus support jurisdiction. They include cases involving everything from breach of contract allegations to patent infringement to defamation. However, an examination of this case law is beyond the scope of this chapter. Suffice to say, most of the analysis in these cases revolves around a determination of the situations that fall under the *Zippo* decision's "middle ground," and which examine the degree of interactivity of a particular site.

Given the relatively recent phenomenon that is social networking, discussion of social media in a jurisdictional context has been limited to say the least. In one such case, Allison Chang (a minor child, suing through her mother) and photographer Justin Ho-Wee Wong sued Australian-based Virgin Mobile Pty. Ltd., alleging a number of tort claims, including wrongful use of young Allison's likeness and misappropriation of her right of publicity. *Chang v. Virgin Mobile USA, LLC,* 2009 WL 111570 (N.D. Tex. Jan. 16, 2009). Apparently, Wong took a photo of Allison, uploaded it to the photo-sharing site Flickr (attaching a creative commons license to it), and Virgin got the photo off Flickr and used it in an Australian advertising campaign. Virgin moved to dismiss the case for lack of jurisdiction, arguing that it lacked minimum contacts with the forum state of Texas.

The court agreed, and dismissed the case. It found that Chang had failed to establish that the downloaded photo was on a server located in Texas; while Flickr does maintain servers in Texas, the photo could have been on another server in Virginia. The court also rejected Chang's argument that because Virgin had directed its conduct to Flickr.com, it should reasonably expect to be haled into court whenever Flickr servers may be. Similarly, the court noted that Virgin used the photo only in Australia, and therefore didn't perform any acts or obligations in Texas.

In many instances, courts will look at the terms of service found on websites in order to establish jurisdiction and venue, since such terms often spell out the governing law that will apply and fix jurisdiction and venue for disputes. This doesn't always happen, however. When the virtual world Second Life took away virtual property belonging to Marc Bragg, he brought a very real lawsuit in his home state of Pennsylvania. *Bragg v. Linden Research, Inc.* 487 F.Supp.3d 593 (E.D. Pa., May 30, 2007). Linden Research (parent company of Second Life) argued that its terms of use mandated that all disputes be resolved in California via binding arbitration. The court disagreed, holding that since Second Life's founder, Phillip Rosedale, had held a virtual town hall meeting on Secondlife.com and invited Pennsylvania residents to attend, Rosedale and his company had "purposely availed" themselves of Pennsylvania law. Consequently, the court reasoned, they should reasonably have expected that they might be haled into a Pennsylvania court.

Perhaps the most interesting example of social media influencing a court's analysis of jurisdiction came in a case of alleged threats of domestic violence made by a resident of one state against the resident of another, via the popular site YouTube. Stacy Rios left North Carolina and Christopher Fergusan (the father of her four-year-old child) in early 2008 for Connecticut. Rios claimed that Fergusan had threatened her. Shortly after her move, Fergusan posted the first of multiple videos on YouTube, in which he rapped about wanting to shoot the mother of his child and "put her face on the dirt until she can't breathe no more"; in the videos, Fergusan brandishes a handgun and makes other threats against Rios. Rios sought a restraining order against Fergusan in New Haven Superior Court.

In a case of first impression, Judge Stephen F. Frazzini granted Rios the six-month restraining order, ruling in December 2008 that the Connecticut court *did* have jurisdiction over Fergusan. Acknowledging that "content on the Internet that some may find offensive or harmful has also created new and challenging issues" for the legal system, Frazzini tackled the thorny issue of whether the court could exercise jurisdiction over a non-resident defendant who had threatened a Connecticut resident using a computer in

North Carolina and posting videos that anyone worldwide could access. Frazzini reasoned, "Even though there is no allegation that Fergusan ever stepped foot in Connecticut, the court can exercise personal jurisdiction over him without violating the principles of due process."

The court noted that Fergusan's video was not simply uploaded to YouTube for consumption by a wide and random viewing audience, but instead was actually directed at Rios in Connecticut. Frazzini said, "Fergusan's YouTube video is more than the mere posting of a message upon an open Internet forum. The evidence shows here that he specifically targeted his message at Rios by threatening her life and safety," and therefore his actions constituted a tortious act committed in Connecticut. Frazzini noted Connecticut's "strong interest in protecting its citizens from domestic abuse," and said it "should have been foreseeable to Fergusan that by placing a video on YouTube threatening Rios in Connecticut he could be haled into this state to answer an application seeking a restraining order against him." The restraining order application was granted in December 2008.

4

Served through Facebook: Social Networking and Service of Process

It's a familiar refrain to many litigators: your usually reliable process server has had no luck serving an evasive defendant at his or her last known address, and you're about to file a motion for substituted service. But is there some other means of dragging this party into court than attaching the summons and suit papers to his or her front door or publishing a legal notice in the local newspaper, perhaps some method more in keeping with twenty-first century lifestyles and technology? A growing number of jurisdictions outside the United States are allowing parties to be served via popular social networking sites like Facebook. After all, the odds are pretty good that the person you're looking for will have a social networking presence of one kind or another: Facebook (created by Mark Zuckerberg in 2004 as a way for Harvard students to stay in touch) has more than 500 million users worldwide, while MySpace has approximately 250 million and the recent but rapidly growing micro-blogging site Twitter has more than 77 million users sharing information instantaneously and sending out messages, or "tweets," of 140 characters or less. Almost half of Facebook's users visit the site every day. According to a September 2009 Nielsen online survey, social networking is now the fourth most popular online activity. Internet users spend 17 percent of their online time on social networking sites; such usage is growing at a rate of three times that of overall Internet usage.[1]

---

[1] David DiSalvo, "Are Social Networks Messing with Your Head?" *Scientific American Mind*, January 2010.

Australia was the first country to permit service via social networking, but it didn't come easily. Rule 116(1) of the Australian Uniform Civil Procedure Rules permits substituted service "where, in effect, there is a practical impossibility of personal service and that the method of service proposed is one which in all reasonable probability, if not certainty, will be effective in bringing knowledge or notice of the proceedings to the attention of the defendant."[2] In effect, attorneys seeking court approval to serve someone via a social networking site would have to demonstrate both (1) an inability to serve the defendant through a more traditional medium, and (2) that service through Facebook offered a reasonable chance of success. The Queensland District Court had rejected a previous request in another case to serve documents via Facebook, in part because of the concern about fake social networking profiles. In that decision, Judge Ryrie said, "I am not so satisfied in light of looking at the uncertainty of Facebook pages, the facts that anyone can create an identity that could mimic the true person's identity and indeed some of the information that is provided there does not show me with any real force that the person who created the Facebook page might indeed be the defendant, even though practically speaking it may well indeed be the person who is the defendant."[3]

In the face of such concerns, it would be an uphill battle for the next attorneys seeking service via Facebook, but that same year the opportunity presented itself. In *MKM Capital v. Corbo*, Australian couple Carmel Corbo and Gordon Poyser defaulted on a six-figure loan to purchase a home.[4] After the default, mortgage lender MKM Capital filed suit and obtained a default judgment allowing seizure of the property when the defendants failed to appear. However, efforts at serving the judgment on Corbo and Poyser using traditional methods of service proved fruitless. The defendants weren't at either their residence or their last known place of employment, having moved and changed both jobs and phone numbers. Personal service was unsuccessful, as was mail; even hiring private investigators and advertising in *The Canberra Times* led nowhere for the lender's attorneys. Corbo and Poyser, however, didn't count on the tech-savviness of Mark McCormack and MKM Capital's other lawyers.

---

[2] *Citigroup Party Ltd. v. Weerakoon* (2008) QDC 174, 1 (Austl).
[3] Id. at 3-4.
[4] *MKM Capital v. Corbo* (2008) ACTCA _____ (Austl).

Using Corbo's e-mail address, the MKM legal team was able to locate her Facebook page. Because Corbo and Poyser had "friended" each other on the social networking site, and because neither defendant had chosen to use Facebook's various privacy settings to prevent others from seeing their information, the attorneys were able to match up personally identifiable information on the defendants' Facebook profiles (birth dates, lists of "friends," and e-mail addresses) with information disclosed in Corbo's and Poyser's loan applications. Armed with the evidence of names, birth dates, and e-mail addresses listed on Facebook matching the information from the applications, McCormack was able to make the required showing under Australian law and assuage any concern of the court's that they indeed had the right people and that delivery via Facebook would be sufficient notice to the defendants. Master David Harper of the Australian Capital Territory Supreme Court approved MKM Capital's request and ordered that service could be perfected by sending a private electronic message, with the legal documents attached, to each defendant's Facebook page alerting them to the entry of the default judgment and disclosing its terms.

When the decision came down in December 2008, it was the shot heard 'round cyberspace, making international news. Facebook itself praised the decision. A spokesman for the site said, "We're pleased to see the Australian court validate Facebook as a reliable, secure and private medium for communication. The ruling is also an interesting indication of the increasing role that Facebook is playing in people's lives."[5] Rather understandably, Carmel Corbo and Gordon Poyser were less enthusiastic about the novel method of serving a foreclosure notice: following the widespread publicity about the court order, the couple implemented privacy restrictions that removed their Facebook profiles from public view. Mark McCormack, on the other hand, viewed the ruling and subsequent attempt via Facebook as vindicating his client's position that all reasonable steps had been taken to serve Corbo and Poyser, characterizing it as "a valid method of bringing the matter to the attention of the defendant."[6]

---

[5] See Rod McGuirk, "Australia OKs Facebook for Serving Lien Notice," Dec. 16, 2008, http://news.yahoo.com/s/ap/20081216/ap_on_re_as/as_australia_facebook (last visited 12/17/2008).
[6] Id.

Although this Australian case made legal history as the first time service via a social networking site was allowed, it would not be the last. In a Canadian case, a judge entered an order for "substitutional service," ruling that the plaintiff could serve one of the multiple defendants by publication, by forwarding a copy of the statement of claim to the human resources department where the defendant had formerly worked, and *by sending notice to the defendant's Facebook page.*[7] The next month, in March 2009, the New Zealand High Court allowed an individual to be served with process via Facebook in commercial litigation over some failed business dealings. Arguing that more conventional efforts at service had been fruitless since the defendant's exact whereabouts were unknown, the New Zealand plaintiff's counsel pointed out that the defendant maintained a profile on Facebook. The court was persuaded.[8]

The trend has spread to the United Kingdom, where—in another first—the High Court in September 2009 permitted an injunction against an anonymous blogger to be served via Twitter.[9] Prominent British lawyer and conservative blogger Donal Blaney sought the injunction after an unknown blogger began impersonating Blaney on the Internet. The imposter set up a Twitter account using Blaney's own blog photo and links to Blaney's own blog posts, and then "tweeted" in a writing style similar to Blaney himself. While parody can be legally permissible, Blaney took the position that the Twitter account was calculated to make readers think it was Blaney himself tweeting, and that the impersonator was infringing Blaney's copyrighted materials. Rather than wait for Twitter's California-based site administrators to take down the offending account, Blaney and his barrister Matthew Richardson went directly to court to obtain permission to serve the injunction through Twitter. They were fortunate enough to find a tech-savvy judge familiar not only with Twitter but also with the December 2008 Australian court's ruling allowing service by Facebook.

---

[7] *Knott v. Sutherland* (Feb. 5, 2009) Edmonton 0803 002267 (Alta.Q.B.M.) (emphasis added).
[8] Ian Llewellyn, "NZ Court Papers Can Be Served Via Facebook, Court Rules," March 16, 2009, www.nzherald.co.nz/nz/news /article (last visited 3/23/09).
[9] See Martha Neil, "UK's High Court OKs Serving Injunction on Anonymous Blogger Via Twittter," Oct. 2, 2009, www.abajournal.com/news/uk_high_court_uses_twitter_to_serve-Injunction_on_an (last visited 10/2/2009).

Another country may soon join the ranks of nations permitting service via social media. In August 2010, the Singapore High Court circulated a consultation paper for public comment that included a proposal that lawyers could use sites like Facebook and Twitter to serve legal documents. The proposal indicated that service by social media could be done when personal service could not be accomplished, in conjunction with other forms of substituted service. The high court also envisioned lawyers using social networking sites for ordinary service of documents pursuant to contractual agreements specifying such an alternative. As the Singapore High Court acknowledged in its paper, the use of social media "is a phenomenon that has become virtually impossible to ignore. Given that other jurisdictions have used social media effectively for substituted service of documents, there is no reason why we should not consider doing so." In its paper, titled "Impact of Social Media on Civil Litigation," the court cited a number of the cases and ethics opinions described in this book.

Courts abroad may be starting to embrace the potential of social networking sites as an alternate avenue for service of formal court documents, but here in the United States no court has yet followed suit. Certainly, some of the factors accounting for even the Australian courts' initial reluctance constitute grounds for equal concern here. For example, few controls exist to guarantee that a person registering for a social networking profile truly is who he or she claims to be. Celebrities have fallen prey to pranksters setting up fake Twitter accounts in their names, and nationally litigation has raged over fake MySpace and Facebook pages set up to defame others (many of which have involved students creating unflattering profiles of teachers or school administrators).[10] Another potential hurdle is whether "service by Facebook" will provide actual notice to the defendant, given the uncertainty of determining how frequently an individual uses his or her social networking page. While such service is reasonably calculated to reach a regular user, someone who checks his or her Facebook page more sporadically may not receive timely notice; in default judgment situations and others where timeliness of the notice is an issue, this can pose due process concerns.

---

[10] See, *Draker v. Schreiber*, 271 S.W.3d 318 (Tex.App. 2008).

Nevertheless, the concept of "service by Facebook" may catch on in the United States sooner than one might think. Much has been written about how lawyers in various practice areas have mined the social networking sites of litigants and witnesses for valuable, often incriminating information.[11] Courts across the country have been admitting evidence (such as photos and blog postings) gleaned from sites like MySpace and Facebook in a wide variety of proceedings—everything from divorce and custody matters to sexual harassment litigation, insurance coverage disputes, and murder cases.[12] Viewed in the context of an age in which digital intimacy is rapidly becoming the social norm, those with due process concerns about the efficacy of service via social networking would do well to keep in mind the observations of Justice Sandra Day O'Connor. In dissenting from a Supreme Court opinion that neither notice by publication nor public posting provided actual notice to a mortgagee, Justice O'Connor[13] wrote that "notice is constitutionally adequate when the practicalities and peculiarities of the case…are reasonably met…Whether a particular method of notice is reasonable depends on the outcome of the balance between the 'interest of the State' and 'the individual interest sought to be protected by the Fourteenth Amendment.'" In other words, she noted, "notice will vary with the circumstances and conditions."[14] Certainly, as courts in Australia, New Zealand, Canada, and the United Kingdom have recognized, circumstances can exist in which "service by Facebook" is the most likely avenue for ensuring actual notice.

Some courts already seem to acknowledge that social networking sites are viable avenues for communication and are as subject to judicial oversight as their more traditional counterparts. In October 2009, Shannon Jackson was charged with violating a Sumner County (Tennessee) General Sessions Court protective order to refrain from "telephoning, contacting, or otherwise communicating" the petitioner when she "poked" the other

---

[11] See, for example, John Browning, "From Lawbooks to Facebook: What You Need to Know about Using Social Networking Sites," *Voir Dire*, Vol. 16, Issue 1 (Spring 2009), at p. 6-13.

[12] See, for example, *Mann v. Dept. of Family and Protective Services* 2009 WL 2961396 (Tex.App. 2009); *Hall v. State*, 283 S.W.3d 137 (Tex.App. 2009); *Mackelprang v. Fidelity National Title Agency* 2007 U.S. Dist. LEXIS 2379 (D. Nev. Jan. 9, 2007); *Wolfe v. Fayetteville*, 2009 U.S. Dist. LEXIS 15182 (D. Ark. Feb. 26, 2009).

[13] *Mennonite Bd. of Missions v. Adams*, 462 U.S. 791, 801 (1983).

[14] Id. at 802 (quoting *Walker v. City of Hutchinson*, 352 U.S. 112, 115 (1956).

woman on Facebook (a "poke" is a quick message sent by one Facebook user to another).[15] In July 2009, a Providence, Rhode Island, judge imposed a gag order ordering Michelle Langlois not to post comments about a bitter child custody case involving her brother and his ex-wife (the complaint that prompted the order was later dismissed after the American Civil Liberties Union contested it on free speech grounds).[16]

And in a case of first impression, a Staten Island (New York) family court judge ruled that a MySpace "friend request" can constitute a violation of a temporary order of protection. Judge Matthew Sciarrino Jr. noted, "While it is true that the person who received the 'friend request' could simply deny the request to become 'friends,' that request was still a contact," and that using MySpace as a "conduit for communication" was prohibited by the court's mandate that "Respondent shall have 'no contact' with Sandra Delgrosso."[17]

Another compelling reason for the coming acceptance of service through social media is the fact that many jurisdictions already acknowledge the potential need for alternative methods of serving a defendant. In New York, for example, service by e-mail was permitted (along with standard and registered international mail) in a case where the defendant was employed in Saudi Arabia.[18] Another New York decision also upheld service by e-mail, so long as other, more conventional methods were employed as well (it is worth noting here that prior to allowing service via social networking, courts in both Australia and the United Kingdom had permitted service by electronic mail).[19] The Federal Rules of Civil Procedure explicitly approve of service of documents via e-mail (except for initial pleadings), provided the opposing party agrees in advance to this manner of service. In addition, the local rules in a number of Texas

---

[15] See Martha Neil, "Did Court Order Ban Facebook 'Poke'?" Oct. 13, 2009, www.abajournal.com/news/did_court_order_ban_facebook_poke (last visited 10/14/2009).

[16] See Associated Press "ACLU Fights Judge's Facebook Comments Ban," July 23, 2009, www.msnbc.com (last visited 1/4/2010).

[17] *People v. Fernino*, No. 07RI0073222 (Staten Island Family Court, February 2008).

[18] *Hollow v. Hollow*, 747 N.Y.S.2d 704 (N.Y. Sup. Ct. 2002).

[19] *Snyder v. Energy Inc.*, 847 N.Y.S.2d 442 (N.Y. 2008).

counties have been amended to permit parties to electronically serve legal documents other than citation.[20]

The Texas Family Code already allows service of citation by publication, provided the person to be served "cannot be notified by personal service or registered or certified mail and to persons whose names are unknown."[21] Tex.R.Civ.P. 102 also provides for substituted service when the serving party can show the court that attempts at personally serving someone have been unsuccessful and that routine service would be improbable. Although it is virtually impossible for the law to keep pace with technological innovation, the rapid spread and ubiquitous nature of social networking sites, coupled with growing acceptance of them abroad as alternative means of serving parties with legal documents, may soon alter the notion of just what constitutes valid service here in the United States. People who previously regarded their social networking presence as just a source of entertainment or a means of staying in touch with friends and family may soon find that membership in sites like Facebook or Twitter come with an unexpected and dubious "privilege"—being more accessible to the legal system.

---

[20] See, for example, Bexar County Local Rules of the District Courts concerning the Electronic Filing of Court Documents, Rule 5.1(b) ("Documents may be electronically served upon a party only where that party has agreed, in writing, to receive electronic service in that case.").

[21] Tex. Fam. Code Ann. § 102.010 (Vernon 2008).

5

The Facebook Divorce: Social Networking and Family Law

Few areas of the law have been affected by the social networking revolution quite like the realm of family law. Worldwide, the newly discovered resource for connecting—and in many cases, reconnecting—with others has fueled not only the development of new relationships, but also the disintegration of existing ones. The Australian Family Relationships Clearing House noted that marriage counselors in that country were reporting a rise in social networking sites like Facebook contributing to separations and divorce, as the Internet makes it easier than ever for bored or troubled spouses to reconnect with former flames. While conceding that social networking sites don't make people have affairs, relationship experts there observed that relationships tend to develop more quickly online because of lowered inhibitions and the fact that technology enables people to find their ex-loves from the past. Divorce-Online, a British firm specializing in divorce law, even did a study that concluded that one out of every five petitions they processed cited Facebook or another social networking site. According to Mark Keenan, Divorce-Line's managing director, "the most common reason seemed to be people having inappropriate sexual chats with people they were not supposed to."

For some people, the revelation that a relationship was over has even come via social media. Event planner Emma Brady learned the devastating news when she saw that her husband had updated his Facebook status to read, "Neil Brady has ended his marriage to Emma Brady." For some, cheating in cyberspace only has been reason enough for divorce. Twenty-eight-year-old Amy Taylor filed for divorce from David Pollard after discovering that he was sleeping with an escort in the game/virtual world Second Life, despite the fact that her husband had never met this virtual love interest. Even more disturbing, thirty-four-year-old Briton Wayne Forrester stabbed his wife to death after learning she had changed her Facebook status to "single." The fifteen-year marriage, described in court as "volatile," was headed for divorce when Emma Forrester insisted that her husband move out of their home. The day before the murder, Forrester called his wife's parents, accusing her of cheating and claiming that the new Facebook entry "made her look like a fool" and had "devastated and humiliated" him. Forrester pleaded guilty, and was sentenced to fifteen years to life in prison.

Many commentators have addressed the ways the Internet, online dating services like Match.com or eHarmony, or social networking sites like Facebook have altered the relationship landscape, enabling people to turn dating into a supermarket or window shopping experience—"Facebook trolling," if you will. But the flipside to the Facebook hookup, of course, is the Facebook breakup, or as the *New York Times* characterized it, "breaking up in a digital fishbowl." Social media has ensured that couples who previously only ran into each other's friends at social gatherings now have twenty-four/seven access to their erstwhile significant other's confidants thanks to Facebook. In addition, the digital age has redefined the meaning of trust, with sharing passwords to e-mail accounts, photo-sharing sites, etc. serving as the new yardstick of intimacy. According to the Pew Internet and American Life Project, one in five teenagers report sharing online passwords as a way of building trust and fostering romance. The time-honored tradition of literally cutting an ex out of photos is also a little tougher when digital images of a once-happy couple abound on the web. With a labyrinthine set of online strings connecting so many of us, severing them when the relationship is over becomes more challenging than ever.

In addition, social networking sites can provide the confused, the angry, and the distraught with a nearly irresistible venue for airing their gripes and working through their feelings. Spurned spouses are usually not at a loss for personal opinions, leading to the creation of such Facebook groups as "I Hate My Ex-Husband" and "I Hate My Ex-Wife." When one man told his wife he wanted a divorce, she posted angry, hurt messages on his Facebook wall. Concerned that clients, colleagues, family, and friends were now privy to his marital woes, the husband deleted her comments and blocked her access to this page. Days later, two Facebook friends alerted him that his estranged wife had used a mutual friend's account to view his wall and to contact several women with whom he'd been in touch. High-profile relationships aren't immune to this either; when Chelsea Davy ended her five-year relationship with England's Prince Harry, the relationship's demise was publically marked by her changing her Facebook status to "single." As one Salon.com commentator describes this new frontier in online etiquette, "Facebook is the theater where some of life's most chaotic, catastrophic and bewildering moments are now being played out."

Given such tendencies to allow human dramas to play out online, divorce lawyers have a digital treasure trove of information to work with in preparing their cases, and to contend with when it comes to their own clients. In a February 2010 survey by the American Academy of Matrimonial Lawyers, an astonishing 81 percent of the nation's top divorce attorneys reported seeing an increase in the number of cases featuring social networking evidence in the past five years. Among the social networking sites cited by the study's respondents, Facebook was the overwhelming favorite source of such online evidence, with 66 percent of the attorneys responding citing it as the primary source for helpful or incriminating information. MySpace was a distant second at 15 percent, while 5 percent reported finding evidence on Twitter. Another 14 percent listed other sources, such as Flikr. Marlene Eskind Moses, president of the American Academy of Matrimonial Lawyers, explains the obvious importance of these sites to divorce lawyers: "If you publicly post any contradictions to previously made statements and promises, an estranged spouse will certainly be one of the first people to notice and make use of that evidence. As everyone continues to share more and more aspects of their lives on social networking sites, they leave themselves open to much greater examinations of both their public and private lives in these sensitive situations."

Whether you consider them cautionary tales to pass on to clients, or examples of what to look for from your adversaries, divorce lawyers across the country point to real-life examples of cases where social networking evidence proved to be crucial. Consider the following:

- A woman in the midst of a divorce from an alcoholic husband and seeking custody of their children had to contend with her estranged spouse's insistence to the judge that he had found religion and sworn off alcohol. Her soon-to-be ex inadvertently helped her cause when recent photos of him appeared on Facebook, depicting him with a beer in each hand and a joint in his mouth.

- In a custody fight, the ex-wife claimed to be engaged, and therefore more capable of providing a stable home environment for the children. But thanks to a friend of the ex-husband who remained "Facebook friends" with the estranged wife, the former husband received some very helpful information—a posting on Facebook that the wife had broken up with the fiancé (who was allegedly abusive), and that she was seeking friends of hers to fix her up with "a rich friend."

- In a Louisiana custody case, the ex-husband's lawyer did some digital digging, and found some sexually explicit boasts and graphic pictures posted by the ex-wife on the MySpace page of her new boyfriend. The court awarded custody to her ex-husband.

- In a dispute over alimony payments, the ex-husband initially claimed in a deposition to have no real job prospects after getting laid off. However, the enterprising attorney for his ex-wife found Twitter messages in which the husband had tweeted about a new job offer (sites such as LinkedIn can also be useful in disputes over support payments, for their evidence of earning capacity or job prospects).

- In another custody matter, a father was denying drug use. His protests might have proven more convincing if the background of his MySpace page hadn't prominently featured marijuana leaves.

- A wife who had kicked out her husband, changed the locks, and cleaned out bank accounts overlooked one crucial item: it's not enough to "de-friend" your ex when he can access your profile when it's open to "Friends of Friends," thanks to mutual acquaintances. Despite her denials of infidelity, her husband found her celebration of the three-month "anniversary" with her new boyfriend—only one month after the split. Other gems uncovered by the ex-husband's online sleuthing included messages from the wife to friends of hers about how good the husband was to her, as well as proof that trips taken prior to the separation to see her sick father were actually romantic getaways with the new boyfriend.

- One husband in Florida had a habit of frequently posting on Facebook his frustrations over everything, including parenting. His ex-wife's lawyers made liberal use of these statements during the fight over custody.

- A man in the middle of a divorce cried poor when it came to child support. Researching his Facebook profile showed photos of him in a Ferrari, on a cruise, and also contained statements by him referring to selling a piece of real estate that he owned.

- In one custody battle, a mother carried on a Facebook dialogue with a friend after posting photos of her children on her page. When the friend commented that the children didn't look like the estranged husband, the mother replied, "That's because they're not his." That statement came back to haunt her.

- Lynn France was suspicious of her husband John possibly having an affair, so she searched for the "other woman" on Facebook. Imagine her shock when she discovered photos from a wedding at Disney World, complete with "Sleeping Beauty" theme featuring her husband in a Prince Charming costume! France made the rounds of television shows like *Today* with her Facebook revelation of her husband's alleged bigamy; John France, meanwhile, contended that his marriage to Lynn wasn't valid in the first place, and that she was using this Facebook discovery as a ploy during their contentious child custody proceedings.

Because of the wealth of information available through social networking sites, family lawyers not only have to take steps to investigate the incriminating photos or statements from the other side, but they also need to police their own clients. According to Joseph Cordell of the national domestic relations firm Cordell & Cordell, "It's now just routine for us to go over with clients whether they have an active presence on the Web and if they Twitter, or have a MySpace page." Rick Robertson of Texas's Koons, Fuller, Vanden Eykel & Robertson P.C. goes a step further. "When it comes to social media, just shut it down prior to getting a divorce. Shut it down because it can be used in court," he says. He points to a 2009 custody case he handled on behalf of a husband, in which the wife had argued that her ex should have only minimal contact with the child due to alcoholism and the risk of exposing the child to "unhealthy relationships." Robertson cross-examined the wife, using photos of her and her new fiancé drinking in various bars that were posted on her newly created Facebook page, along with statements that convinced the court she had engaged in extramarital affairs. According to Robertson, "The bottom line is that Facebook was the critical piece of evidence that got my client fifty-fifty possession of his child."

So what lessons can family lawyers take from these battles in the trenches of social media? The first is to make clients or prospective clients aware that anything they do online can and will likely be used against them—an electronic Miranda warning, if you will. From e-mails and texts to lovers (a lá Tiger Woods), to tweets from your girlfriend about the new jewelry you bought her, to vacation photos from Disney World when your custody agreement specifies you won't take the kids out of the state, what goes online can come back to haunt you.

Next, do some pre-emptive damage control. As soon as you engage a client, have a frank discussion about their Internet presence, what they've posted, etc. Charleston, South Carolina, domestic relations specialist Melissa Brown has her legal assistants scour social networking sites for mentions of her clients, and she obtains clients' authorization to bolster their privacy settings or delete online photo albums. "At first, some clients thought I was overreaching, but when I explain how a photo could be blown up and it could look inappropriate, they will take the site down immediately," says Brown. Some attorneys even document their insistence that a client end his or her social media presence with a clause in their engagement agreement. If a client is unwilling to cancel his or her social media accounts, you should at a minimum insist that they stop posting to them, as it could later become evidence in the case. If he or she maintains a blog, the client shouldn't discuss the case, anything related to the divorce, or any personal information that could be used against them. All too often, Facebook becomes, alternatively, the new confessional or an avenue for retaliation after an estranged spouse posts something about the ex. Tampa attorney Chris Ragano, who estimates that over half of his new cases involve social media evidence, compares such Facebook postings to "gasoline on the fire. One side posts something nasty and the other can't help but retaliate, and we're off to the races. It's World War III."

Another good piece of advice is not to overlook the basics. If your client shares a computer with a spouse, consider the possibility of having the hard drive mirror-imaged; it may contain relevant information, or proof that the soon-to-be ex installed spyware on the computer. Counsel clients to create a new web-based e-mail address, with a new password, to ensure that the ex doesn't have access.

Also, don't forget about the children. Remember that children—frequently more tech-savvy than their parents—may be texting, e-mailing, or posting on social networking sites about the divorce proceeding. Make sure your client monitors what his or her children are doing online and with cell phones. A child's Facebook page may contain references to problem issues like drugs or alcohol that could become pivotal in a custody battle. Along the same lines, don't overlook the potential evidence from what friends, relatives, co-workers, and others may have posted online about your client or your client's ex. Mentions of affairs, money spent on gifts or lavish trips, or photos of a parent smoking or drinking may not necessarily wind up on a spouse's social networking page, but they just might be available on the publicly accessible Facebook page of a third party.

Of course, this works both ways. In the age of social networking, a client's complaints about the ex are no longer the province of a neighbor or friend with a shoulder to cry on. That "shoulder" may be 600 Facebook friends, or Twitter followers who re-tweet.

Finally, advise clients to avoid online references to finances. Discussions about an expensive vacation, a bonus or raise at work, or a planned purchase can serve as evidence in a subsequent alimony or child support proceeding. They can even expose clients to charges of marital waste (spending community or marital assets on another party).

Although I'm not a family law practitioner, I've tried to bring some of these social networking lessons to the occasional domestic relations cases I've handled. For example, in a 2009 child custody dispute, my client (the mother) filed suit against the estranged father, who failed to answer and had a default judgment entered against him. To set it aside he had to show that he wasn't "consciously indifferent" to the lawsuit, but rather that his failure to answer was the result of a mere mistake or accident. To demonstrate this, he filed an affidavit in which he testified about working long hours virtually every day, and that he was confused about the process and didn't know that he needed to file an answer. Unbeknownst to him, we were aware that his tweets on Twitter and his posts on MySpace told a very different story. He posted during that timeframe about leaving work early to go to the gym, taking long lunches with his new girlfriend, enrolling in classes during work hours, volunteering at a local Halloween "haunted house," and even taking multiple days off as sick days. Additionally, the estranged father exchanged multiple e-mails with my client during this timeframe, in which she repeatedly reminded him about the necessity of filing an answer to the suit. He not only acknowledged this, but even went as far as to say he had an attorney already and was "working on it." Needless to say, the erstwhile "baby daddy's" posts and admissions were news to his lawyer. Upon being made aware of the social networking evidence, the opposing counsel was only too happy to get the matter resolved—quickly, quietly, and on very favorable terms for my client.

For an example of how courts have treated social networking evidence in family law cases, consider the 2009 Texas case of *Mann v. Department of Family and Protective Services*, 2009 WL 296-1396 (Tex. App. September 17, 2009). In this case, Stephanie Mann was challenging a trial court's decree terminating her potential rights to her minor child, and naming the Department of Family and Protective Services as the child's sole managing conservator. The department had removed the child from Ms. Mann's care originally because of a risk of abuse, and the trial court had ordered Ms. Mann to complete a drug and alcohol assessment and to refrain from criminal activity. On appeal, Ms. Mann challenged the sufficiency of evidence supporting the court's findings that she had endangered the well-being of her child, including through underage drinking. The appellate court noted that there was ample evidence that Ms. Mann had continued to engage in underage drinking while her child was in the care of the Department of Family and Protective Services, and in particular pointed to evidence from Mann's own MySpace page. The court stated in its opinion that pictures of Mann drinking, accompanied by such helpful captions as "At Ashley House Dranking it Up (sic)," "Me Dancing My Ass Off, I Can Dance When I Drunk (sic)," and "Yall see how much we Dranked plus the one's that dropped on the floor (sic)," "could lend a reasonable fact finder to firmly believe that appellant engaged in underage drinking."

Consequently, with the aid of social networking evidence, the trial court's appointment of the Department of Family and Protective Services as the child's sole managing conservator was affirmed.

Social media evidence has proven pivotal in other ways. Take the immensely popular video-sharing site YouTube, for example. In July 2008, Broadway mogul Philip Smith was granted a divorce and had his prenuptial agreement upheld, in part because of his wife's lashing out on YouTube. Tricia Walsh Smith, a former actress, uploaded a YouTube video in which she makes embarrassing claims about the couple's sex life, calls her husband's office to repeat these claims to one of his assistants, and goes through their wedding album making disparaging remarks about family members. The video went viral, resulting in more than 3 million hits. Manhattan judge Harold Beeler was not among those amused. He referred to the video stunt as "a calculated and callous campaign to embarrass and humiliate her husband" to pressure him into settling the case on terms more favorable than the prenuptial would've allowed. He granted Mr. Smith a divorce on grounds of cruel and inhuman treatment.

YouTube was also at the heart of another domestic matter. In 2008, Stacy Rios left North Carolina and an allegedly abusive relationship with Christopher Fergusan, the father of their four-year-old child. Ms. Rios then moved to Connecticut, where she sought a restraining order against Fergusan in New Haven Superior Court. The reason? After she moved out, Fergusan posted first one, then another video on YouTube in which he threatened to harm Rios. Among other things, Fergusan is shown brandishing a handgun, rapping about wanting to shoot Rios, and "put her face on the dirt until she can't breathe no more."

In a case of first impression, Judge Stephen F. Frazzini ruled in December 2008 that even though there was no allegation that Fergusan had ever set foot in Connecticut, the court could still exercise personal jurisdiction over him without violating due process. Frazzini noted, "The Internet has transformed our ways of communicating and sharing information, but content on the Internet that some find offensive or harmful has also created new and challenging issues." In his order, Frazzini explained why it was fair to assert jurisdiction over Fergusan, saying, "It should have been foreseeable to Fergusan that by placing a video on YouTube threatening

Rios in Connecticut he could be haled into this state to answer an application seeking a restraining order against him." He also noted that Rios's interest in protecting herself from domestic violence outweighed any burden on Fergusan and that Connecticut had a strong interest in protecting its citizens from domestic abuse. Judge Frazzini also pointed out that this was no mere posting of a message on an open Internet forum available to a wider audience, but a specific threat that constituted a tortious act committed in the state of Connecticut. Judge Frazzini observed, "The evidence shows here that he specifically targeted his message at Rios by threatening her life and safety." As a result, a six-month restraining order was entered.

However, social networking has affected other aspects of family law as well. With emotions running high in an arena marked by custody disputes and the dissolution of once intimate relationships, judicial intervention—in the form of orders of protection and similar decrees—is frequently necessary. In an era in which communication via social networking takes place so casually and spontaneously, though, is a "poke" or a "friend request" or a "tweet" the sort of statement or communication that should come under court purview? So far, in the limited instances in which courts have tackled this issue, the answer seems to be "yes."

Shannon Jackson of Tennessee found this out the hard way in October 2009. The thirty-six-year-old was subject to an order of protection issued by the Sumner County General Sessions Court, which called for her to refrain from "telephoning, contacting, or otherwise communicating with the petitioner." After sending the female petitioner a "poke" via Facebook, Jackson was arrested and charged with violating the protective order, an act punishable by up to one year in jail and a fine of $2,500. Poking is unique to Facebook, and is a form of deliberate interaction that is frequently subjective: some regard it as synonymous with "hello" or as innocuous as a nudge for attention, while some recipients view it as analogous to flirting. While Jackson's lawyer professed shock at the charge against his client, he shouldn't have. A poke, which requires a conscious decision to reach out and (virtually) touch a specific person, who is on one's friend list, is certainly a form of communication, albeit fleeting. Therefore, it would appear to be encompassed by the court's prohibition against contact.

In a similar case of first impression in Staten Island, New York, Judge Matthew Sciarrino Jr. ruled that a MySpace friend request could constitute a violation of an order of protection. In *People v. Fernino*, sixteen-year-old Melissa Fernino was the subject of an order barring her from contacting either forty-three-year-old Sandra Delgrosso or her two minor daughters (a romantic relationship between Delgrosso and Fernino's father had apparently ended badly). Yet on July 26, 2007, Fernino allegedly sent separate friend requests to Delgrosso and each of her two daughters. Delgrosso reported the contacts to the police, and Fernino was charged with three counts of second-degree criminal contempt for allegedly violating the judge's order. Fernino moved to dismiss the charges, and Judge Sciarrino denied it.

In his order, Judge Sciarrino pointed out that whether the contact took place in cyberspace or not, it still violated the clear terms of the protective order. He wrote, "While it is true that the person who received the 'friend request' could simply deny the request to become 'friends,' that request is still a contact, and 'no contact' was allowed by the order of protection. It is no different than if the defendant arranged for any agent to make known to a claimant, 'Your former friend wants to communicate with you. Are you interested?'" Judge Sciarrino compared the fact pattern with a 1994 case involving an unsolicited communication to a victim in response to a personal ad. In this case, the protective order was clear, and MySpace was simply a different conduit for the forbidden communication.

In August 2010, fifty-four-year-old Harry Bruder of Florida was arrested for violating a protective order by contacting his soon to be ex-wife through Facebook. Bruder was jailed on a $5,000 bond after admitting that he violated the order by twice sending his wife friend requests (the two had been separated for two years); Bruder was allegedly upset over having to go to court-ordered counseling sessions.

But what about an instance where the communication via social media is made by a third party who isn't subject to the court's order? In July 2009, Rhode Island family court judge Michael Forte was presiding over a bitter custody dispute between two former spouses. During the case, Michelle Langlois (sister of the estranged husband) began posting comments and public information about the custody proceeding on her Facebook page.

The ex-wife, Tracy Martin, alleged that the comments traumatized the couple's children and revealed intimate details about the marriage. She filed a complaint and sought a court order banning Ms. Langlois from posting any information about the case on the Internet; in June 2009, Judge Forte signed such a gag order.

Some family court judges may be finding more positive uses for social media, such as online visitation. A judge in New York has already ordered that a Long Island mother make her two children available for conversations with their father via Skype, the online video conferencing service. The order, made a condition of permitting the mother's move to Florida to seek out work, is the first of its kind in New York. A number of states already allow for "virtual visitation," in which judges can provide a mechanism for non-custodial parents to stay in touch with their children through e-mail, text messaging, and even webcams. Social networking sites give judges an additional option to provide for such real time communications.

Langlois reached out to the American Civil Liberties Union, which filed a motion challenging the constitutionality of the order, and seeking to have it rescinded as a violation of Langlois's First Amendment right to freedom of speech. Shortly before a hearing on this motion, Ms. Martin voluntarily dismissed her harassment complaint and Judge Forte dismissed the gag order. As a result, Langlois was free to resume posting about the case. As she put it, "I do not believe the truth was coming out in Family Court. I was simply using the Internet to publicize my brother's plight."

6

Foiled by Facebook: Use of Social Networking Evidence in Criminal Matters

Social networking sites such as MySpace and Facebook have hit society with the force of a juggernaut. With more than 500 million users worldwide, if Facebook were a country, it would be the fourth most populous in the world. Almost half of its users visit the site everyday. A September 2009 Nielsen survey revealed that time spent on social networking sites is growing at three times the rate of overall Internet usage, making social networking now the fourth most regular online activity. Fortunately for law enforcement personnel and prosecutors everywhere, the criminal element seems to be just as addicted to Facebook and similar sites as everybody else.

Generally, if you're going to do something illegal, it's really stupid to go on a social networking site with evidence of the misdeed—sort of a "Don't post about the crime if you can't do the time" principle.

Vanessa Palm and Alexander Rust, two twenty-something Americans vacationing in the Bahamas in February 2009, decided to catch and eat an iguana—a species protected under Bahamian law. Unfortunately for them, they also decided to post pictures on Facebook of their illicit meal. Bahamian authorities were alerted to the photos, and they promptly proceeded to track down and arrest the two tourists for killing and eating a protected iguana. Perhaps they used the jail time to debate whether it tasted like chicken.

Similarly, a twenty-year-old employee of a Petland pet store in Ohio not only drowned rabbits from the store, but she also creepily bragged about it on her Facebook "wall." Someone from People for the Ethical Treatment of animals learned of this, and she was soon charged with two counts of animal cruelty.

Meanwhile, it wasn't enough for thirty-eight-year-old Jacob Rehm of Morrisville, Vermont, to steal a tour bus from his former employer, Lamoille Valley Transportation, and take it on a joyride. No, he had to go and make a four-minute video of his little adventure (complete with a tour of the $500,000 bus itself) and post it on YouTube. After the bus was recovered in another town and Rehm was charged with the theft, the prosecutors found that video very helpful when they went to court.

Police in Austin were wondering how to prove that Robert Fitzgerald was in fact the notorious graffiti "artist" who scrawled the tag "KUDOS" on more than forty-four structures in the city in 2009. Fortunately, the ever-thoughtful "tagger" had made sure to leave examples of the distinctive writing throughout his MySpace page, and police matched photos from that page to samples on local buildings. Just in case that wasn't overwhelming enough, Fitzgerald had also left samples on the wall and mirror of his cell from a previous stay at the Travis County Jail. He might want to get comfortable and order some art supplies, since he faces up to two years in state jail if convicted.

And in Cedar Rapids, Iowa, Gamaliet Figueroa might have to find a new hobby. In 2009, Figueroa was on probation for gun charges from back in 2007, and one condition of the probation sentence was not to possess any firearms. Not only did he disregard that, but he actually posted pictures of himself on MySpace holding a rifle and shotgun. His probation officer discovered the photos and tipped off police. In October 2009, Figueroa was sentenced to prison by a federal district court judge. I guess he'll have a lot of time to think about updating his MySpace page.

For the criminally inclined, it's a good idea to remember that you never know who's watching social networking sites. Radford, Virginia, clothing boutique owner Stacey Price suspected that someone was shoplifting from her store, but she was without any clues about the suspect until a tipster let her know that a student from nearby Radford University had a seemingly inexhaustible wardrobe. Unfortunately for the culprit, Price was not merely a mild-mannered merchant, but also a media studies professor at Radford who regularly discussed with her students the impact of social networking sites on the business world. Price looked up the student on Facebook, and a link led her to another suspect. Photos posted on the sites for both young women featured them in various social settings wearing items that Price recalled being stolen from the store. Price printed out the incriminating photos, along with the purchasing history of both students in her store, and turned them over to the Radford police department. Police questioned Alison Robertson and Hedi Chantry, both twenty years old, and both confessed that same day to having stolen the merchandise. According to Officer Bryon Mayberry, "The Facebook pictures were invaluable to making the case."

Twenty-six-year-old Maxi Sopo will probably be reconsidering the wisdom of his "friend" requests for a long time. The Cameroon native moved to the United States in 2003, and after a stint selling roses in Seattle nightclubs, he apparently moved on to bank fraud. When he got wind of federal agents investigating the fraudulent activities, Sopo headed off to Cancun, Mexico. There he apparently lived the dream of fugitives everywhere, relaxing on the sunny beaches by day and partying in the clubs at night.

Sopo was having so much fun that he regularly posted Facebook updates about what he was doing "living in paradise," as he put it. A Secret Service agent saw a photo of the happy fugitive, but was unable to do anything about it because Sopo's profile was set to private. His list of Facebook "friends," however, was not. An assistant U.S. attorney helping with the investigation, Michael Scoville, pored over the list and found one such "friend" who had been a Justice Department official. The official had moved to Mexico and met Sopo in a Cancun nightclub, after which the hard-partying fugitive "friended" him. Upon learning that Sopo was wanted by the law, this Justice Department "friend" found out where Sopo was living and provided that information to Scoville. Shortly thereafter, Mexican authorities paid Sopo a visit, and he was taken to a Mexico City prison to await extradition to the United States. Presumably, his Facebook status has changed to "sitting in jail."

Among criminals addicted to social networking, you would think nineteen-year-old Jonathan Parker of Fort Loudoun, Pennsylvania, is in a class by himself. Parker was arrested in connection with the burglary of a home on August 28, 2009. What led police to Parker? Outstanding forensics work? Eyewitness testimony? Actually, it seems that when the victim returned home to find her home ransacked and items such as two diamond rings missing, she also noticed that her computer was on and someone's Facebook account was still open—Jonathan Parker's Facebook account, that is. Believe it or not, Parker had apparently stopped in mid-burglary to check his Facebook page. Police tracked him to another residence in the vicinity of the victim's home, where they spoke with someone Parker had approached about helping with the crime. Parker was arrested, and now faces one to ten years in prison. His Facebook status: "busted."

As incredible as Parker's case may seem, it's not an isolated incident—which speaks volumes about either Internet addiction or the questionable intelligence of the criminal element. In March 2010, a seventeen-year-old boy allegedly broke into Bella Office Furniture in Kennewick, Washington, and stole a number of items. But ill-gotten gains were not the only thing on this young man's mind. He apparently spent approximately five hours on the store's computer, looking at pornography, attempting to sell some of the stolen items, and, yes, checking his MySpace account. That gave investigating officers all the clues they needed to track down and arrest the teenager on first-degree burglary charges.

In Albano Laziale, a town near Rome, Italy, a fifty-two-year-old homeowner returned to his residence in October 2009 to find that it had been ransacked, with cash and jewelry missing. He noticed something else that was amiss: the computer was still on, and when he touched the keyboard, the homepage for Facebook came on. The only problem was, this homeowner wasn't a Facebook user. He alerted police, and they followed the burglar's digital footprints and arrested a twenty-six-year-old suspect (he had written several messages on his wall) and recovered the missing cash and valuables. Carabinieri Major Ivo DiBlasio stated, "He was tempted to log on during the break-in and it led to his arrest—it was a silly mistake to make, and we were onto him very quickly…he did not expect us at all and was very surprised when we told him how we had tracked him down. He has a history of break-ins and will now go before a judge."

Criminals don't seem to grasp that while there may be a time and a place for social networking, mid-crime is not it. After robbing a bank in North Augusta, South Carolina, of $3,924, twenty-seven-year-old Joseph Wade Northington was thoughtful enough to update his MySpace page status to "Wanted." He also posted the message, "One in the head still ain't dead!!!!!! On tha run for robbin a bank. Love all of yall." A friend recognized Northington from surveillance photos that were posted, and police arrested the bank robber for the January 2009 heist. The incriminating statements Northington posted online led to his conviction.

A twenty-six-year-old Canadian man will also probably think twice about what he puts on Facebook. After his infant son was taken into the custody of the Children's Aid Society, the distraught father allegedly threatened to suicide bomb the child welfare agency and kill the nurse who in November 2007 had notified authorities; he posted this threat on Facebook. The message on the man's Facebook page read: "When I find out what nurse called the CAS, may God have mercy on my soul because I'm going straight to hell with a 25-year pit stop in prison." Another post said that the man was "going to suicide bomb the CAS." Authorities learned of the threatening posts, and the angry father has now pleaded guilty to a weapons charge and making a death threat.

The long-running television show "The Fugitive" probably wouldn't have lasted long in the age of social media. Dr. Richard Kimble would have been too tempted to post Facebook updates in his quest for the one-armed man. At least, he would if he were anything like Joseph Luebke, Craig Lunch, or Alfred Hightower.

The Florida Fish and Wildlife Conservation Commission may made surfing social media sites mandatory for their game wardens, after their investigation of twenty-one-year-old William Buchanan and twenty-eight-year-old Tara Anne Carver. Fish and Wildlife officials received a tip about the two Citrus County residents allegedly possessing deer taken illegally and the key evidence came in the form of photos on Carver's Facebook page of the two hanging and skinning a deer that had allegedly been killed in May— well outside of hunting season. The commission, recognizing the utility of social media, has set up a special Internet Crimes Unit to monitor and collect evidence in wildlife crimes.

And even the famous can be "foiled by Facebook." After Paris Hilton was recently charged with felony drug possession, she quickly claimed that neither the cocaine nor the designer purse in which it was found were hers. Alert observers pointed out that just one month before her arrest, Hilton had tweeted "Love my new Chanel purse I got Today," and included a "TwitPic" photo of a Chanel purse looking suspiciously like the one she later claimed at the time of her arrest belonged to "a friend."

Facebook has even been blamed for certain crimes. Police investigating a murder-suicide in North Carolina believe that Karen Ann Rooney's changing her relationship status on Facebook to "engaged" may have been what prompted her ex-boyfriend Peter Moonan to shoot her before killing himself in August 2010. And a Chicago woman was charged with felony aggravated battery and aggravated assault after allegedly stabbing another woman over "ugly baby" comments that the victim's daughter had made on Facebook. Eighteen-year-old Briana Smith contacted her former friend Natia Robinson over comments Robinson made online about Smith's four day-old baby, and wound up allegedly stabbing Robinson's mother during the ensuing scuffle.

In March 2010, nineteen-year-old Joseph Luebke was just months away from paying his debt to society after being convicted of burglary. He was finishing up, working a day job as a telemarketer, and spending his nights at a halfway house in Dixmoon, Illinois. Then, on March 17, Luebke lost his job "selling rich people vacations," and fearing he'd be sent from the halfway house back to prison, he went on the lam. Despite having seemingly more important things on his mind, Luebke felt compelled to discuss his fugitive status on Facebook, posting "On da run" just minutes after leaving. He tried to reassure his 526 Facebook friends, "It's all good imma be fine jusfine don't trip! Im jus gettin some fresh air before I go bakk to the clinker lol." He even responded to concerned friends and family, telling his mother, "Ma, i need u to get my property plz. ill get an outfit from u some how." Within a few hours, Luebke's sojourn into freedom came to an abrupt halt when he was taken into custody. Law enforcement authorities declined to reveal if the Facebook postings assisted them in apprehending Luebke. He is now spending his time in a Joliet, Illinois, prison, presumably without Internet access.

Few criminals on the run can match the sheer bravado of Craig "Lazie" Lynch of Great Britain. In September 2009, the twenty-eight-year-old escaped from Hollesley Bay prison near Suffolk in eastern England while serving a seven-year term for aggravated burglary. For months, he taunted police with postings, including photographs, on his Facebook page. In photo after photo, the smiling Lynch is depicted giving the finger, holding up a "wanted" sign, and even enjoying a Christmas turkey. He updated regularly on everything from the sumptuous meals he was enjoying to the women he planned to date. While Facebook disabled various accounts or otherwise provided data to law enforcement, Lynch constructed an elaborate web of personal profiles and fan pages with varying degrees of privacy (at one point, he had 7,300 fans and 1,300 friends). At times, Lynch's updates revealed the more paranoid side of life on the run—"Oh no sirens! It's happening," read one close call. Not long before he was ultimately apprehended, Lynch waxed philosophical. He posted, "Well what can I say fellow friends. The run is nearly over. Sorry some of you had to find out like this. I know some of you might take offense that I never told you personally. But you know me. I Trust No One. It's the only way to be." Lynch was finally caught (police hinted that they used clues from Lynch's posts) and taken back into custody, at which point cyberspace got a lot less interesting than it had been.

Addiction to online role-playing gaming spelled doom for Alfred Hightower. On the run since an arrest for drug dealing in 2007, Hightower fled to Canada. An intrepid sheriff's deputy from Howard County, Indiana, Matt Roberson, received a tip that Hightower was an avid player of the game World of Warcraft, an online role-playing game with more than 14 million devotees worldwide. Roberson obtained Hightower's IP address, online screen name, billing address, and other account information from Blizzard Entertainment, the game's owners. He provided the fugitive's information to the Canadian Mounted Police, who apprehended Hightower and deported him. That just goes to show that being a Level 80 shaman who wields a magical sword may be great online, but it won't help you escape the long arm of the law.

It's kind of hard to deny engaging in criminal activity when photographic evidence of it exists, and it's even harder to deny when you yourself have created and disseminated such evidence. Twenty-two-year-old Paul Crowell of Waukesha, Wisconsin, and his father had quite an adventure after the younger Crowell drove his car into a ditch on New Year's Day. While being arrested by police, Crowell stole a Taser from the officer's squad car. Several hours later, father and son were tasing each other for fun. It apparently was so much fun that they decided to immortalize the hijinks on video, and then share it with countless others on YouTube. The younger Crowell boasted of the "shocking" video to a teenage girl, including the fact that he and his father were zapping each other with a stolen Taser. She then reported this to police, who easily tracked down Crowell and his father using the YouTube clip. After finding the weapon in Crowell's home, police charged Paul Crowell with "possession of an electric weapon." Faced with the video evidence he himself had created, and already on probation for previous crimes, Crowell pleaded guilty and was sentenced to two years in prison. Somewhere out there, physicists are probably busy formulating the "YouTube theorem": the more incriminating the video is, the greater the gravitational pull of YouTube will become.

YouTube and other social networking sites have proven to be a fertile ground for law enforcement officials. When police in Suffolk, Virginia, arrived at the scene of a large street brawl on December 14, 2009, the suspects had already scattered and witnesses weren't talking. But hours later, cell phone videos of the fighting began surfacing on YouTube. Investigators monitoring the video-sharing website were able to pick out the suspects, and soon seven people identified in this matter were awaiting trial.

As Jack Rinchich, president of the National Association of Chiefs of Police, has observed, "Technology has revolutionized law enforcement in many ways. Sometimes people are pretty liberal about what they put on [social networking sites]." After riots marred the aftermath of the June 2009 NBA Championship in Los Angeles, police there used footage from YouTube and the photo-sharing site Flickr to identify and apprehend rioters. In January 2010, police in Chattanooga, Tennessee, discovered an online forum where individuals were discussing illegal drag racing. Acting on the information, officers staked out the site of the drag race and ticketed a number of racers who were caught red-handed. In November 2009, police in Minneapolis and St. Paul arrested four people for assault after observing videos the suspects had posted online. Police use of such sites is becoming routine enough that criminal defense attorneys like Nashville's David Raybin are giving their new clients advice that wouldn't have been necessary (or possible) a decade ago: "The first thing I tell them is, 'You are shutting down your Facebook account,'" says Raybin.

For some observers, such monitoring of cyberspace has overtones of Big Brother. Adam Bauer, a student at the University of Wisconsin-LaCrosse, didn't think much of the friend request he received in the fall of 2009. "She was a good-looking girl. I usually don't accept friends I don't know, but I randomly accepted this one for some reason," said the nineteen-year-old. The good-looking girl on Facebook turned out to be affiliated with the LaCrosse police, who cited Bauer and at least seven other students for underage drinking based on photos posted on their Facebook pages. LaCrosse police officer Al Iverson was unapologetic, pointing out that the students were not only caught in an illegal act, but one that they had felt comfortable enough about to immortalize with photos on the Internet, thus glamorizing binge drinking. Iverson also points out that such online surveillance has helped nab sexual predators, like the child-rape suspect caught by Massachusetts authorities in December 2009 after they learned of his whereabouts on Facebook.

In upstate New York, police have found social networking evidence posted by suspects particularly helpful. In January 2009, Niagara Falls police were attempting to convince a judge to revoke bail or raise it substantially for Spencer Bomberry, the purported leader of the "8 Trey Gangster Crips." Judge Matthew Murphy raised bail from $5,000 to $50,000, giving particular "credence to a MySpace page that gives clear evidence of gang membership." The ten-page printout from Bomberry's social networking site showed him wearing gang clothing, giving Crips hand signs, and even posing with his children and other family members in gang colors. Also in upstate New York, police in Lockport were pleased with the evidence that thirty-nine-year-old Christopher Crego had featured on his Facebook page. Crego had filled his profile with a wealth of information, including photos with guns, descriptions of alleged criminal activities, and even a newspaper article that named him one of the area's "Ten Most Wanted" (hey, criminals have egos too). He also provided information about his most recent employment at an Indiana tattoo parlor, where police were able to arrest him. He now faces charges including assault, driving while intoxicated, and animal cruelty. Police Captain Richard Rodgers couldn't resist posting a comment on Crego's Facebook page thanking him for detailing his activities, saying, "It was due to your diligence in keeping us informed that now you are under arrest."

Facebook has proven to be a helpful tool for crime victims as well. In September 2009, a nineteen-year-old Georgetown University student was attacked by an assailant yelling homophobic slurs during the assault. After the incident, the victim was on Facebook when he saw the profile of the person who he believed was his attacker. Police investigated, and created a photo lineup of possible suspects. The victim picked out the photo of the person located via Facebook, Georgetown sophomore Phillip Cooney. Cooney was charged with simple assault with a bias/hate crime specification, which means that if convicted he could face a stiffer maximum sentence. Lieutenant Alberto Jova of the Metropolitan Police said he'd never before heard of a crime victim using Facebook to help police catch a suspect before.

Online investigations have paid off for police in surprising ways. On January 11, 2005, fifty-five-year-old Gurdeep Kaur was struck and killed at 9:00 p.m. while crossing the street near her home in Lafayette, California. She had just been dropped off from her job as a cook at a restaurant owned by her family. The driver who hit her left the scene. There were no skid marks. Police investigators believed the vehicle involved was a red or burgundy Jaguar XJ6 or XJ8, built between 1995 and 2003. They based this on debris recovered at the crime scene, including a hood ornament broken off because of the impact.

The police investigation led them to Lee Harbert, a San Francisco Bay-area investment banker with three convictions for driving while intoxicated. A search of Harbert's garage revealed a black 2000 Jaguar Vanden Plas. Despite its recent cleaning, there was body damage and a particularly damning piece of evidence: one of Kaur's earrings was found in the windshield well. Although Harbert had clearly hit the woman, his defense to the charge of failing to stop and render aid was his professed belief that he had hit a deer. He claimed that, returning home after imbibing several drinks at a business meeting that day, he had no idea that he had struck a person: "whether it was a large animal or…not…I didn't know," Harbert maintained. But a crucial piece of evidence—Harbert's Internet searches—would prove pivotal in determining what Harbert's actual knowledge was.

A police examination of Harbert's computer revealed evidence of Google searches a few days after the accident. These included search terms such as "auto glass reporting requirements to law enforcement," "auto glass, Las Vegas," "auto parts," "auto theft," and the Moraga, California, police department. Harbert's alleged searches also included one for hit-and-runs, which led to a news web page dealing with Kaur's death. After being convicted and sentenced to three years in prison, Harbert appealed, claiming there was no evidence that he had actual knowledge that a person was hit, and that the prosecutor's comments about the Internet searches amounted to misconduct.

The California appeals court rejected those arguments and upheld the conviction on January 14, 2009, concluding that "there was abundant evidence from which the jury could conclude that defendant did indeed have knowledge—actual or constructive—that he had collided with a human being on the evening of January 11, 2008, on Moraga Boulevard." The court also found that Harbert's Internet searches were "inextricably linked to his state of knowledge on January 11," and were thus an appropriate subject for argument by the prosecutor. Harbert's case isn't the only one in which Google searches have proven to be the working of criminal suspects. In a 2005 murder case, the defendant's use of search terms like "neck," "snap," and "break" were introduced, and in a 2008 case, a woman accused of murdering her husband had a hard time explaining a Google search about "decomposition of a body in water."

Federal law enforcement has also gotten into the social networking act. The training manual for the Department of Justice's Computer Crime and Intellectual Property Section, for example, now includes an entire section on social networking. It addresses such subjects as undercover operations witnesses and social networks, and the dangers of social networking by jurors or "friending" judges and defense counsel. The manual admonishes federal law enforcement officers to research *all* witnesses on social networking sites, and to advise government witnesses not to discuss cases on such sites. As the manual states, "Knowledge is power." Federal agents, like their state counterparts, are using social networking sites to identify a suspect's friends or relatives; using online photos of suspects posing with jewelry, guns, or fancy cars, to link them to crimes; and comparing suspects' alibis or accounts given to police with tweets and Facebook updates made around the same time regarding their whereabouts.

Of course, police internationally have found social networking sites to be useful tools as well. After several incidents in which British inmates had used Facebook to plot with criminal associates and intimidate victims, the U.K. justice minister prevailed upon Facebook to delete the pages of thirty U.K. prisoners. (Generally, inmates are banned from using such sites, but some have nonetheless been able to update their personal pages either through family members on the outside or through the use of cell phones smuggled into jail.) In Scotland, nineteen-year-old Anthony Bowman pleaded guilty in 2008 to violating anti-violence laws by posting photos of himself with a sword on the popular social networking site Bebo. Bowman's charge came as part of Operation Access, a police crackdown on "youth violence and anti-social behavior." Police Superintendent Bill Fitzpatrick hailed such "creative investigative techniques," saying, "Youngsters who use social networking sites irresponsibly should be warned that their activities are being monitored and they may get a visit from the police."

In Melbourne, Australia, Facebook helped police assist a victimized restaurant owner after five customers "dined and ditched" after an expensive meal, leaving him with an unpaid $323 bill. The owner recalled one of the diners asking about a former waitress; an examination of that employee's list of Facebook friends helped the restaurateur spot a photo of one of those who ate and ran. Meanwhile, in Queenstown, New Zealand, police turned to Facebook to nab a would-be burglar. The hopeless thief broke into a pub through the roof and tried to crack open a safe. Because of the enclosed space and the heat, the suspect took off his gloves and mask. When he finally gave up and got ready to leave, the formerly masked man turned and looked right into a surveillance camera. Police posted the surveillance camera photos on Facebook, and by the next day had the suspect in custody—identified by people who recognized him on Facebook.

In Russia, where traditional media is under government control and the rule of law is frequently perceived as weak, social media sites are increasingly taking on the role of government watchdog, with fed-up citizens broadcasting their grievances for all to see. In 2009, an unusual outburst of whistle-blowing occurred on YouTube, as Russian police officers like Major Alexei Dymovksy began posting pleas on the video-sharing site in which he accused higher-ups of corruption and forcing officers like himself to falsely report the cracking of unsolved cases. Dymovsky's posts received over 700,000 hits, even as he was being fired. More officers threatened to post their own reports of corruption and abuses, prompting an Interior Ministry investigation.

Don't Post About the Crime if You Don't Want To Do the Time

For many criminal defendants, being "foiled by Facebook" has happened when they were actually on probation or seeking probation, achingly close to dodging the bullet of jail time. Not surprisingly, a number of these offenses involved alcohol use. After Jessica Binkerd drove under the influence and was involved in a January 2007 auto accident in Santa Barbara, California, that killed her passenger, her defense attorney Steve Balash fully expected his client to get probation, given her lack of prior offenses. Then the prosecutor produced photos from Binkerd's MySpace page depicting the young woman partying with friends.

One photo even showed her wearing an outfit featuring a bandoleer of shot glasses and a tequila company's T-shirt. Although Balash tried to argue that the outfit was part of a Halloween costume, the damage was done. Stating that Binkerd had not learned her lesson from the tragedy and had shown no remorse, the judge sentenced her to five years and four months in prison. Interestingly enough, Balash had asked Binkerd if she had a MySpace page when he originally met with her. Although he instructed her to take it down, she apparently did not do so.

MySpace evidence played a pivotal role in a similar case in Santa Barbara. Twenty-two-year-old Lara Buys pleaded to vehicular manslaughter charges in a case where her passenger, like Ms. Binkerd's, was killed. Senior Deputy District Attorney Darryl Perlin submitted printouts from Ms. Buys's MySpace profile, including a photo of her smiling while holding a glass of wine and comments she had posted about binge drinking. As a result, in April 2007 she was sentenced to two years in prison. According to Perlin, "from all these statements in her account, we realized that she continued to be a danger to the community. So the case went from being a probation case to a prison case, and it was all a result of her MySpace account."

According to Rhode Island prosecutors, twenty-year-old Bryant University junior Joshua Lipton was drunk and speeding in Smithfield, Rhode Island, in October 2006 when he allegedly caused a three-car collision that left twenty-year-old Jade Combies in a hospital for weeks. Jay Sullivan, the prosecutor handling Lipton's drunk-driving case, received copies of photos from another victim of the crash. They were photos from Lipton's Facebook page, taken a mere two weeks after the near-fatal crash. They depicted Lipton attending a Halloween party dressed in an orange jumpsuit labeled "Jail Bird," and including an image of Lipton smiling and clutching a can of Red Bull with his arm around a young lady in a sorority shirt. Sullivan incorporated the photo into a PowerPoint presentation for Lipton's sentencing (including one with the sarcastic caption "Remorseful?"), depicting Lipton as an unrepentant partier who thought nothing of partying while his victim languished in a hospital bed. Lipton's attorney, Kevin Bristow, felt the photos didn't accurately portray his client or Lipton's level of remorse, pointing out that Lipton had written apologetic letters to the victim and her family, and was so despondent that he left school. "The pictures showed a kid who didn't know what to do two weeks after this accident. He didn't know how to react," Bristow insisted.

But Superior Court Judge Daniel Procaccini was offended by the presentation, calling the pictures "depraved" before sentencing Lipton to two years in prison. According to Judge Procaccini, "I did feel that gave me some indication of how that young man was feeling a short time after a near-fatal accident, that he thought it was appropriate to joke and mock about the possibility of going to prison."

On May 30, 2009, seventeen-year-old Ashley Sullivan of North Tonawanda, New York, was going fifty-six miles per hour in a thirty miles per hour zone and was drunk when she crashed her car into a bridge pillar in front of the Deerwood Golf Course. Her blood-alcohol level was measured at 0.13 percent (0.08 is legally intoxicated in New York). Her boyfriend and passenger, twenty-year-old Alex Rozicki of Niagara Falls, was killed. Sullivan sought to be treated as a youthful offender rather than as an adult, and she was seeking probation after pleading guilty on November 18, 2009, to criminally negligent homicide and misdemeanor driving while intoxicated.

But then Judge Matthew Murphy learned that Sullivan went to Florida a month after the crash and apparently lived it up, posting a photo on her Facebook page with the caption "Drunk in Florida." Murphy not only denied the request for youthful offender status, but he sentenced her to six months of jail time and five years probation. "I'm troubled by your conduct since the crash, and that's the reason for the jail sentence," he said. He also emphasized, in reading the terms of Sullivan's probation, that she isn't allowed to consume alcohol for five years, saying, "You're seventeen years old. You're not old enough to drink."

Sometimes, those already on probation forget that what gets posted on Facebook doesn't necessarily stay on Facebook. In June 2009, Erika Scoliere of Illinois was awaiting trial on charges of reckless homicide and aggravated drinking under the influence stemming from a 2007 accident. As a condition of bail, she was ordered not to drink or to be around those who were consuming alcohol. Unfortunately for the twenty-year-old Scoliere, she not only violated the terms of her bail, but she also chronicled her drinking exploits on Facebook. Kane County Judge Thomas Mueller reviewed photos from her Facebook page, noting, "It appears the defendant is having a grand old time drinking tequila." One of the photos taken by a friend of Erika's bore the caption "Erika passed out in my bed. Ha ha." Judge Mueller ordered Scoliere to be fitted with an alcohol-monitoring ankle bracelet at her expense; Scoliere left the courtroom in tears.

In another case, defendant Pressley was subject to a lifetime probation, the terms of which did not allow him to possess or have access to a computer without his probation officer's permission, and did not permit him "to consume or drink any substance containing alcohol." When Pressley's probation officer made a surprise visit in July 2007, he not only found a laptop with icons bearing Pressley's name, but he also found a partially empty vodka bottle. Among the evidence admitted in the proceedings to revoke Pressley's probation: a photo of Pressley holding a beer (Pressley testified that the photo was from her MySpace page, and indeed the photo was accompanied by the caption "Me and my wife"). Pressley was sentenced to ten years in prison and appealed, claiming that the MySpace photo shouldn't have been admitted. The appellate court disagreed with him and affirmed the sentence, holding that the photo was relevant to the issue of whether Pressley had violated probation.

In yet another probation violation case, Christopher Leon of South Elgin, Illinois, probably wishes he never had a MySpace page. The twenty-year-old had been convicted for his role in a 2005 Plato Township brawl that involved more than fifty people and left Nicholas Swanson dead. Seventeen young men, including Leon, were convicted of taking part in the brawl. As conditions of his probation, Leon was not allowed to drink and was restricted from contact with the other sixteen defendants. But then Leon's probation officer came across his client's MySpace page, which featured a photo of him—beer mug in hand—crouching in front of a group of scantily clad young women. The page also contained photos of Leon with bottles of alcohol, as well as messages he posted to his fellow defendants. Circuit Judge Grant Wegner could've sentenced Leon to up to five years in jail, but in October 2006 opted instead for a year of "intensive probation" and sixty days of electronic home monitoring.

Social Networking and Other Crimes

While Facebook photos of drinking and partying can come back to haunt defendants facing alcohol-related crimes, social networking evidence has been put to effective use with other types of offenses as well, and by both prosecutors and defense attorneys. In Pensacola, Florida, a defense attorney was able to contradict a woman's claims of continual harassment by a former boyfriend by using her own MySpace page against her. In support of his client's assertions that he had cut off all contact and that, in fact, it was the complainant who was contacting him, the attorneys produced a number of messages she had sent her ex-boyfriend via MySpace. And in Tucson, Arizona, defense attorney D. Jesse Smith won an acquittal for a client accused of assault. When a witness for the state testified, Smith showed the jury video from the witness's own MySpace page showing him beating up different people, thus impeaching the witness and proving that someone other than Smith's client was the aggressor who had started the brawl.

In Pima County, Arizona, Deputy County Attorney Jonathan Mosher prosecuted Matthew Cordova for aggravated assault with a deadly weapon after the nineteen-year-old was accused of holding up a University of Arizona student with a Tec-9 semiautomatic weapon. According to Mosher, "at sentencing they are trying to portray (Cordova) as a guy who had found religion and was very peaceful," hardly the gun-toting type. Mosher then introduced printouts from Cordova's MySpace page, including photos of him holding a gun that looked just like a Tec-9, along with comments Cordova had posted about the gun. Cordova was sentenced to five years in prison.

Meanwhile, in Florida, attorney Leo Thomas used social networking evidence in defending Brandon Ward, an ex-Marine accused of stabbing Joseph Hall to death. To show that his client feared for his life and acted in self-defense, Thomas showed the jury Hall's extremely violent MySpace profile, which the late Mr. Hall had thoughtfully titled "joehallwillkillyourfamily." However, prosecutor Bobby Elmore responded with a little online evidence of his own. Elmore showed the jury a MySpace message to the victim from Ward's girlfriend, inviting him to a party the two were hosting—not exactly the sort of behavior consistent with Ward's "I was afraid of him" defense. Ward was convicted, and is seeking a new trial.

Conclusion

Social networking sites have not only become new sources of evidence, both incriminating and exonerating, in criminal law—they have inadvertently inspired criminal acts. People who can't resist posting about their vacation plans and business trips on Facebook or tweeting on Twitter have returned to find their homes burglarized. And in South Wales, thirty-one-year-old Brian Lewis allegedly killed his girlfriend Hayley Jones in March 2009 after becoming suspicious of her activities on Facebook.

Social networking sites are more than just sources of photos or statements capable of undermining or exculpating a defendant. Many state criminal proceedings, for example, permit "victim statements" during the penalty phase of a trial. In one vehicular homicide case where the prosecutor did not have family members' letters of live testimony to use in explaining to the jury how the victim's relatives had suffered, the prosecutor took a different approach. She read from the victim's social networking profile, sharing the decedent's "Random Things About Me," including her love of chocolate milkshakes and Disneyland, her goal of learning to play the piano, and wanting a butterfly tattoo.

Even one's "mood indicator" on Facebook has proven helpful in a criminal case. Gary Walters, a paroled burglar, faced changes of carrying a loaded weapon following an altercation with New York police officer Vaughan Ettienne. Officer Ettienne claimed that when he arrested Walters in 2006, the defendant had been carrying a loaded 9mm pistol. But Walter's attorney, Adrian Lesher, sought to convince the jury that the gun had been planted on his client as an excuse for breaking Walter's ribs during the arrest. Lesher wanted to portray officer Ettienne, a bodybuilder who'd been disciplined in 2007 after testing positive for steroids, as a cop filled with "roid rage" trying to emulate Denzel Washington's corrupt narcotics officer character in the movie "Training Day."

Lesher had some help, courtesy of Ettienne's own social networking profile. On the day before the arrest, Ettienne's mood on the page was set to "devious," complete with an angry red emoticon being licked by flames. And in the days leading up to the trial, the hulking policeman had even set his status to read "Vaughan is watching 'Training Day' to brush up on proper police procedure." Lesher's digital sleuthing also turned up incriminating comments Ettienne had made on the UselessJunk video sharing site, under his screen name "Blakryno." These included comments supportive of police who had beaten a handcuffed suspect (and then videotaped doing it), saying that "if you were going to hit a cuffed suspect, at least get your money's worth 'cause now he's going to get disciplined for a…love tap."

In the end, the defense worked, and Waters was acquitted of the more serious charges and his conviction was downgraded to resisting arrest—all because the jury was convinced by the evidence of Ettienne's social networking activities. Ettienne himself, while denying that his Internet self reflects his true character as a police officer, recognized the permanence of online miscues. "You have your Internet persona, and you have what you actually do on the street…what you say on the Internet is all bravado talk, like what you say in a locker room. I'm not going to say it was the best of things to do in retrospect…stupidity on the Internet is there for everyone to see for all times in perpetuity. That's the case for me."

Such observations apply to all of those who have been in a criminal case, only to be "foiled by Facebook."

7

Who Are You Going to Believe, Me or My Facebook Page? Social Networking and Personal Injury Cases

A colleague of mine in Dallas who practices plaintiffs' personal injury law is so concerned about the chance of cases being undermined by contradictory statements or photos from the Internet that he doesn't just insist that clients take down their social networking profiles—he incorporates this requirement into his attorney-client engagement agreements. Plenty of horror stories about how a decent personal injury case was ruined or a witness's credibility was destroyed by incriminating Facebook evidence have circulated among members of the personal injury bar. They've inspired articles with titles like "Will Your Client's Facebook Page Sink Your Case?" and "One Tweet Can Tank Your Personal Injury Case." One such blog by a personal injury lawyer warned would-be clients, "You may think you can't live without Facebook or Twitter, but if you are in the middle of a personal injury suit, you should consider it... If you say you are hurt, but tweet about hitting in the winning run at the company softball game or are posting photos of your latest ski vacation on Facebook, you can be sure that the insurance companies will use that against you... So while your injury case is outstanding, take a break from social media so you don't jeopardize your chances for a positive settlement or victory in the courtroom." Even if liability isn't the issue, a good damages case can be torpedoed by online evidence. Consider, for example, a recent case in which the plaintiff sued the federal government under the Federal Tort Claims Act following a 2006 automobile accident. The plaintiff, riding a bicycle, was struck by a Post

Office vehicle. In a bench trial, even though U.S. Magistrate Judge Elizabeth LaPorte found that the plaintiff had established liability, she awarded less in damages ($297,624.66) than the plaintiff sought. In her "Findings of Fact and Conclusions of Law Following Court Trial," Judge LaPorte explained that this was the direct result of social media evidence uncovered by defense counsel:

> Other evidence also undermines the extent of plaintiff's general damages… For example, plaintiff's online writings show that his life was not constantly "hell on earth" as he claimed. Plaintiff maintained his pages on MySpace and Facebook since the accident, and as of January 12, 2010, his MySpace page listed various activities and hobbies, and friends of plaintiff. Plaintiff wrote entries on his MySpace page, including one on June 3, 2007, in which he described painting as a frustrating activity when his arm hairs would get caught in paint. Yet painting was on the list of activities that plaintiff claims were adversely affected by the accident. Plaintiff also testified that he had not done any painting since the accident, but the MySpace entry was written in the present tense at a time just prior to his microdiscectomy. Plaintiff testified that the MySpace entry was a joke, but the Court did not find the testimony credible.

> *Sedie v. United States*, No. C-08-04417, 2010 WL 1644252 (N.D. Cal. April 21, 2010)

In another example of a personal injury case undercut by social networking evidence, a federal judge in Cleveland dismissed a case in January 2010 brought by Ernest Ray. Ray, a welder from Columbia, South Carolina, had filed suit in 2004 against Lincoln Electric Holdings Inc. and several other welding equipment companies, claiming to have suffered physical and psychological damage (including neurological damage) because of exposure to the chemical manganese from welding fumes. The suit was one of dozens brought in multi-district litigation in federal court in Ohio against the welding industry. But shortly before trial was due to start, Ray's claims of being totally disabled were devastated by photos from Facebook of Ray competing in high-speed boat races, and his lawyers dropped the case. According to defense attorney Stephen Harburg, "This is the sixth trial-ready case plaintiffs have been forced to dismiss due to fraud uncovered by the defendants."

Similarly, in a product liability case involving severe carbon monoxide exposure, defense attorneys took great interest in the young male plaintiff's MySpace page after he claimed that the poisoning led to recurring headaches, serious cognitive deficits, and problems with walking. The young man's MySpace profile, it seems, was full of depictions of the plaintiff performing "Jackass"-style athletic stunts and displaying a quick wit while engaged in trivia drinking games. This social networking evidence contradicted his claims of limited cognitive and physical liabilities, and the result was a quick settlement.

Sometimes, it's not the content of one's social networking page that can undermine a personal injury case, but the mere use of it that hurts. Mary Mack, corporate technology counsel for the e-discovery company Fios Inc., was involved in a case with a plaintiff claiming personal injuries that left him incapable of using his hands beyond a token amount. While searching the Internet for evidence, defense counsel learned not only that the plaintiff maintained a blog and social media profile, but that he posted and blogged frequently as well—*very* frequently, as it turns out. The defense team downloaded all the blog posts and calculated exactly how many keystrokes would have been required to write them all. The lawyers confronted the plaintiff with that number at trial, impeaching his credibility.

But defense lawyers aren't the only ones finding support for their personal injury cases in cyberspace. Although my practice is primarily defense-oriented, I recently found myself as co-counsel for the plaintiffs in a wrongful death lawsuit. I represented the grieving parents of a young college student who was struck and killed by a commercial vehicle in an auto-pedestrian collision. Under Texas law, one of our causes of action involves the loss of society, companionship, and comfort provided by the victim to his surviving parents. As with any wrongful death case, it is always a challenge to illustrate, in a manner that hits home with the jury, the impact this young man had on people during his lifetime, as well as the void left by his death. How does one convey this effectively to twelve strangers in a jury box who never met the decedent?

The answer, oddly enough, came in an offhand remark by one of the parents, who noted the friends of their son who would to this day call, stop, or post messages on his MySpace page. Yes, there on his MySpace page were photos of Tommy with friends, discussions about his taste in music and other subjects, and postings by friends, classmates, ex-girlfriends, and so on. As I read the posting from a former girlfriend about how it helps her to "talk" to him this way, together with the reminiscing of friends about milestones reached that Tommy would never share except in spirit, it struck me that the photos and comments on this young man's MySpace page could paint a far richer, more complete picture for the jury of who this young man was and where he was going in his life before tragedy interrupted.

Sometimes, coverage issues arise in personal injury matters. Yet even here, evidence from social networking sites can be a factor. In two recent insurance coverage cases in federal court in New Jersey, U.S. Magistrate Judge Patty Shwartz allowed Horizon Blue Cross Blue Shield of New Jersey to pursue a cyber investigation into postings made about children suffering from eating disorders like anorexia or bulimia. At issue was a New Jersey state law that requires coverage of "biologically based" mental illnesses, and a suit brought by parents of children with eating disorders brought against Horizon for declining coverage. Horizon argued that discovery into postings made by the children on social networking sites like MySpace and Facebook could support Horizon's position that the disorders have emotional causes, and are not biologically based.

After Judge Shwartz initially ordered the plaintiffs on October 30, 2007, to provide "emails, journals, diaries and communications concerning the [children's] eating disorder(s) or manifestations/symptoms thereof," the parents moved for reconsideration, asserting that compelling such disclosure of the children's private writings "will be harmful to their health, negatively impact their recovery and place them at risk for relapse." The parents also argued that "No parent should have to sacrifice their child's health and the sanctity of trust within their parent-child relationship in order to maintain the right to legally fight for their contractual rights to insurance coverage to treat their child."

Not so, countered Judge Shwartz. In denying the motion to reconsider on December 12, 2007, she pointed out that any decision in balancing privacy concerns was made "when the plaintiffs decide to file an action which required them to disclose information concerning their children's eating disorders, something that they have described as an extremely sensitive topic." Judge Shwartz then went on to order the production "of entries on webpages such as 'MySpace' or 'Facebook' that the beneficiaries shared with others. The privacy concerns are far less where the beneficiary herself chose to disclose the information. In addition, journals or writings that have been shared with other health professionals who have treated the beneficiaries shall be provided to the defendants' experts as they would be part of their medical records." The court also ordered the plaintiffs to ensure the preservation of writings like diaries and journals that had not yet been shared with others. In essence, the need for the information outweighed the concerns over privacy.

Indeed, privacy and relevance concerns are often the most significant points of contention in personal injury cases featuring social media evidence. In Washington state, auto giant Chrysler defended a product liability suit brought on behalf of twenty-one-year-old Marissa Schneider. Once an aspiring art student, the young woman was confined to a nursing home—the result of injuries sustained when her car was struck by an oncoming vehicle that crossed the center line. Schneider's family sued Chrysler, alleging a design flaw in her Dodge Spirit. Chrysler's attorneys issued a subpoena to get full access to the young woman's MySpace account and private blogs from before the accident—at issue were admissions on Marissa's MySpace page that she smoked. That justification infuriated the Schneiders' attorney, Karen Koehler, who maintained that being under the influence was not an issue in the case. "To say that anything posted on MySpace is gospel is ludicrous and it really paves the way for you to say, 'I can never post anything on this site because it's going to be used against me,'" said Koehler. A Chrysler spokesperson countered, "We believe information on Marissa's MySpace page may lead to evidence relevant to this case."

In *Ledbetter v. Wal-Mart Stores Inc.*, the plaintiff's alleged personal injuries resulted from an electrical shock at Wal-Mart. These injuries allegedly included bilateral hearing impairment, skin burns, headaches, fatigue, chronic neck and wrist pain, sleep disturbance and anxiety, as well as "cognitive inefficiencies and depression." The wife of one plaintiff also asserted a loss of consortium claim. Plaintiff's counsel objected to the defense's subpoenas seeking the claimants' records from Facebook, MySpace, and Meetup.com on privacy grounds, and claimed that both physician-patient and spousal privileges applied, asking the court to conduct an *in camera* inspection of the information requested. The court found that the plaintiffs had waived any physician-patient privilege by virtue of bringing the lawsuit, and that asserting a loss of consortium claim "injected the issue" of the marital relationship into the case. It rejected the applicability of either privilege, and ruled that the social networking evidence was reasonably calculated to lead to the discovery of admissible evidence. An already-existing protective order, the court held, was sufficient to protect any privacy interests. *Ledbetter, et al. v. Wal-Mart Stores Inc.*, 2009 WL 1067018 (D. Col. April 21, 2009).

In a 2007 New Jersey Superior Court case involving a teenager sexually assaulted by a fellow middle school student, the privacy concerns were enhanced by the plaintiff's status as a minor. In *T.V. v. Union Township Board of Education*, the plaintiff sued the school, alleging that its failure to supervise contributed to the attack, resulting in severe emotional distress for the young victim. The defense attorney sought the contents of T.V.'s privacy-protected MySpace and Facebook profiles (both via subpoena to the sites and through discovery directed toward the plaintiff herself), arguing that such information was highly relevant on emotional distress issues since it would "shed light on the plaintiff's credibility by finding out what she wrote on social networking sites in unguarded moments." The defense also argued that the plaintiff had waived privacy rights on issues that could lead to evidence of her mental state, and that its request was akin to seeking e-mails and other discoverable communications. The plaintiff's attorney argued in favor of a broad prohibition against the discoverability of social networking evidence in such cases, particularly where minors were concerned. He said, "In our society, minors now communicate by computer far more often than they do by telephone, and the minor plaintiff has relied on the ability to communicate confidentially with her friends, via the

Internet, just as she would have by telephone prior to the advent of the Internet." The court declined to allow the discovery, and issued a protective order against releasing the social media evidence, saying "it seemed like a big step" to order the turnover of the plaintiff's private communications. A key issue for the judge was that the defense hadn't yet conducted more traditional discovery before showing that the information couldn't be obtained through other means, such as finding out who the plaintiff's testifying witnesses would be and then interviewing or deposing them.

Courts, however, are not always so deferential of a teenager's privacy. In *Bass v. Miss Porter's School*, South Carolina teenager Tatum Bass sued Miss Porter's School of Farmington, Connecticut, alleging that the exclusive private academy had failed to adequately protect her from bullying by a group of girls at the school and had expelled her for absences brought on by the resulting emotional distress. Although the minor plaintiff acknowledged that part of her claim rested on Facebook postings and e-mail correspondence during her time at the school, she hesitated on privacy grounds to provide the defense with the requested social media evidence. Facebook itself, in response to a subpoena, provided 750 pages of documents to Ms. Bass, but Ms. Bass in turn only gave one hundred pages of that to the defense. Rejecting the plaintiff's privacy arguments, the court ordered her to produce all the documents, and pointed out that "Facebook usage depicts a snapshot of the user's relationships and state of mind at the time of the content's posting. Therefore, relevance of the content of plaintiff's Facebook usage as to both liability and damages in this case is more in the eye of the beholder than subject to strict legal demarcations, and production should not be limited to plaintiff's own determination of what may be 'reasonably' calculated to lead to the discovery of admissible evidence." *Bass ex rel. Bass v. Miss Porter's School*, 3:08-CV-1807 (JBA), 2009 WL 3724968 (D. Conn. Oct. 27, 2009).

A further consideration regarding discovery of social networking content is whether the requested disclosure might violate the privacy interests of third parties, such as the plaintiff's Facebook "friends." In many jurisdictions, courts have discretion to take such privacy interests into account when weighing whether to allow such discovery. Unless there is a sufficient showing that the need for the disclosure being sought outweighs third-party privacy interests, a court may not allow the discovery. Although they don't deal with social media, court decisions like that in *Matter of New York County DES Litigation* are instructive here. *Matter of New York County DES Litig.*, 168 A.D.2d 44 (N.Y.A.D. 1991). In that case, the court held that the privacy interests of the non-party relatives of the DES plaintiff were deserving of protection.

One judge in a personal injury case found an interesting solution to this privacy argument. In *Barnes*, the plaintiff was a patron of the well-known establishment who was—in typical Coyote Ugly fashion—encouraged to climb onto the bar and dance. *Barnes v. CUS Nashville LLC d/b/a Coyote Ugly Saloon*, No. 3:09-cv-00764, 2010 WL 2265668 (M.D. Tenn., June 3, 2010). The plaintiff slipped and fell, striking the back of her head. The defendant subpoenaed Facebook for the plaintiff's Facebook information, including photos of Ms. Barnes and her friends dancing on the bar. The court quashed the subpoena; the defendant then issued subpoenas to the plaintiff's friends. The magistrate judge found that these subpoenas (issued out of Colorado and Kentucky, where the witnesses lived) couldn't be enforced by the district court in Nashville. Magistrate Judge Brown crafted a novel solution to the discovery dilemma. He offered to create his own Facebook account "for the sole purpose of reviewing photographs and related comments in camera…and disseminat[ing] any relevant information to the parties." The court would then close the Facebook account.

As is discussed in other chapters, juggling privacy interests with a party's need for discovery of evidence is a recurring theme in other areas of law in which social media evidence can be pivotal, such as employment law. In the personal injury realm in particular, however, attorneys should keep in mind the availability of information from social media resources other than an individual's personal (and possibly privacy-restricted) MySpace or Facebook page. Consider, for example, support group-type social networking presences. A colleague of mine defending a medical malpractice case first told me about CaringBridge.org., a social networking site where ill or injured people (many of whom, on my review, seem to be cancer patients) share their stories and journal about their experiences. Some users link to other social networking profiles, such as their Facebook pages. This lawyer accessed a plaintiff's page on CaringBridge and found a journal roughly one hundred pages long discussing the subject matter of the case.

In addition, supporters and family members of those who have suffered from nursing home abuse and neglect have turned to social networking as well, forming virtual support groups like Illinois-based Families Against Nursing Home Abuse (which has Facebook, MySpace, and Twitter pages, blogs, and even YouTube videos). Content on sites like these can point a resourceful attorney to new fact witnesses or even contradictory information. Accordingly, one should look beyond just the social networking site of a named plaintiff or defendant.

Personal injury attorneys should send written discovery requests seeking the party's user ID and password for a social networking site. If you're not sure the responding party is being completely forthcoming, or is denying the existence of a social networking profile, consider using a resource like Spokeo (ww.spokeo.com). Spokeo is a kind of "friend tracker," or profile aggregator that gathers information from other social networking sites (including information on one's contacts), using an e-mail address (or addresses) and password, if available. Within a flash, at your fingertips are everything from Amazon.com items, MySpace posts, LinkedIn information, Flickr photos, and Pandora playlists. Spokeo's privacy page "finds only publicly available information by default. In other words, everything on Spokeo could have been seen by you and others all these times." The composite formed by seeing all this information in one spot can be revealing—which is all the more reason to caution clients, witnesses, experts, and others not to share anything on a social media site that he or she would not want to be confronted with in court. Whether it's a personal injury plaintiff posting photos from a vacation or athletic competition that belie his alleged physical limitations, a defendant driver confiding online that he really was at fault in that car accident, or a company's engineer sharing information on a work group forum about design flaws that haven't yet come to light, attorneys would be well advised to warn the people connected with their case to stay offline. Some, in all likelihood, won't listen for a variety of reasons. For example, the plaintiffs in a case about the North Carolina Identity Theft Act decided to go online with their allegations against a union that allegedly retaliated against them by posting their Social Security numbers, and thus exposing them to the risk of identity theft. *Fisher v. Communications Workers of America*, 2008 NCBC 18 (N.C. Super. Ct. Oct. 30, 2008). The plaintiffs, aided by the National Right to

Work Legal Defense Foundation, uploaded a video to YouTube in which they discuss their claims and the lawsuit.

I certainly wouldn't advise creating such deposition fodder for opposing counsel, or running the risk of having my clients potentially breach privilege. In today's wired world, however, you need to not only keep tabs on the opposing party's online activities, but you need to make sure your own house is in order. For example, consider the cautionary tale of "Flea," a Boston-area pediatric specialist who was sued for medical malpractice. Unbeknownst to his defense attorney, the doctor was a frequent blogger going by the screen name "Flea." The doctor used his blog to rail against not only medical malpractice suits in general, but to opine about his case in particular. As the trial approached, the doctor discussed defense strategy, concerns over how he would come off, and even shared advice he had received from a jury consultant about how to act while testifying. During the trial itself, his online alter ego continued speaking out, saying unflattering things about the plaintiffs, the plaintiffs' counsel, and even members of the jury. Unfortunately for him, however, opposing counsel had been following the good doctor's unvarnished views of lawyers, jurors, and the trial process online. In a Perry Mason moment for the Internet age, the plaintiff's counsel confronted the defendant about his blog and his screen name. Before the jury could hear the innermost thoughts of the doctor, the case was temporarily adjourned and the case quickly settled.

8

Social Media and Employment Law

As with so many other areas of law, social networking is affecting employment law, primarily because its effects are being felt in the workplace itself. According to a September 2008 survey by Jackson Lewis LLP, of the more than one hundred large employers in the New York metropolitan area that were surveyed, nearly a third regarded visits to sites like MySpace and Facebook as a drain on productivity. Of the employers that responded, 38 percent blocked access to such sites entirely while 56 percent acknowledged monitoring employees' Internet use to determine whether they were accessing social networking sites. Less than a third of the survey's participants had adopted a formal policy that restricted or prohibited use of such sites during work hours. That percentage is likely to change as the rapidly increasing popularity of social networking and concerns over liability force employers to develop and implement policies that delineate the permissible use of sites like Facebook.

Other studies indicate a deep chasm between management and employees when it comes to social networking sites. An April 2009 survey by Deloitte about social media in the workplace indicated that 60 percent of the respondents with managerial job titles agreed that businesses have a right to know how employees portray themselves and their companies on sites like Facebook. However, 53 percent of the employees said their social networking profiles are none of their bosses' business. Sixty-one percent even said they wouldn't alter their online activities even if their employer was monitoring them.

With attitudes as divergent as this, it's hardly surprising that an even bigger concern for employers than the potential drain on productivity that social networking represents is the content of employees' online comments. What winds up being posted on an employee's MySpace or Facebook page, and the employer's subsequent discovery of it, can have serious consequences. Consider the following examples:

- Thirteen Virgin Atlantic Airlines cabin crew members were fired after sharing their candid impression of their employer, Virgin's planes, and even passengers in a Facebook group. According to a Virgin Atlantic representative, "There is a time and place for Facebook. But there is no justification for it to be used as a sounding board for staff of any company to criticize the very passengers who ultimately pay their salaries."

- In June 2006, Marion County, Florida, Sheriff's Deputy Brian Quinn was fired for "conduct unbecoming an officer" after discovery of information on Quinn's MySpace page. Among other things, Quinn had posted a picture of himself in uniform, along with comments about women's breasts, binge drinking, and nude swimming.

- On October 31, 2007, Kevin Colvin told his employer at Boston's Anglo Irish Bank that he had to miss a day of work due to an emergency at home in New York. The next day, Colvin's manager happened to check the employee's Facebook page, where Colvin had thoughtfully posted a photograph from a Halloween party he had attended the previous night, featuring him in a sparkly green fairy costume (complete with wand) and holding a can of beer. Colvin's manager responded to an e-mail from his soon-to-be-ex-employee, attaching the photo of Colvin in costume (and blind copying the entire office), and stating, "Thanks for letting us know—hope everything is okay in New York (cool wand)." Colvin was terminated for lying.

- In April 2009, a Swiss woman lost her job after employers spotted her using Facebook after claiming to be too ill to use a computer at work due to migraines. The employer, National Suisse, maintains that a co-worker had noticed her online presence on Facebook after she had called in sick. The woman claims that the company was using a "ghost" or fictitious Facebook persona to become "friends" with her and thus monitor her online activities; she also maintains that she was merely using her iPhone while in bed.

- Also in April 2009, Kimberly Swann of Clacton, England, was fired from her job at Ivell Marketing & Logistics after describing her office job as "boring" on her Facebook page. According to employer Steve Ivell, the company is a small, close-knit group and "it is important that all the staff work together in harmony. Had Miss Swann put up a poster on the staff notice board making the same comments and invited other staff to read it, there would have been the same result."

- Waitress Ashley Johnson was working at Brixx Pizza in Charlotte, North Carolina, in May 2010 when she had a couple who stayed late (an hour past Johnson's quitting time) and left what she considered to be a measly tip. Johnson then proceeded to post on Facebook, "Thanks for eating at Brixx, you cheap piece of s--- camper." A couple of days later, Johnson was fired by managers who had read her Facebook status, for making disparaging remarks about customers and casting the restaurant in a negative light.

- In Dallas, Texas, radio producer Mike Bacsik was fired in April 2010 for remarks he made through his personal Twitter account. While "drunk at a bar" (Bacsik's description) watching the San Antonio Spurs defeat the Dallas Mavericks in the NBA playoffs, Bacsik tweeted ethnic slurs about San Antonio fans.

- Politicians aren't immune either. Scotland's Labour Party sacked one of its candidates, Stuart MacLennan, following his posting of dozens of offensive comments on his Twitter page making profane rants about other politicians and referring to the elderly as "coffin-dodgers."

- East Stroudsburg University professor Gloria Gadsden posted what she thought were funny Facebook updates after tough days at school. One comment in January 2010 read, "Does anyone know where I can find a very discrete (sic) hit man? Yes, it's been that kind of day." Another status update in February said, "Had a good day today. DIDN'T want to kill even one student. Now Friday was a different story." In an era replete with incidents of shootings on American college campuses, the Pennsylvania university suspended Professor Gadsden. Gadsden, who insists she was just venting on what she thought was a private page, planned to appeal the disciplinary action.

Screening Employees

One potential minefield for employers is the use of social networking sites for screening potential employees. According to a 2010 study by Microsoft, 70 percent of U.S. employers surveyed acknowledged that they had rejected potential employees because of information found out about them online. In addition, 89 percent of recruiters and human resources professionals surveyed believed it appropriate to consider online data when evaluating a candidate. Yet, strikingly, fewer than 15 percent of people believe their online information will matter in getting hired. The numbers have gone up over the last several years, as more employers have found out what a digital treasure trove social networking sites can be.

According to a 2007 survey by privacy think-tank Ponemon Institute, 23 percent of the hiring managers look up job candidates on social networking sites, and 35 percent reported using Google to conduct online background checks. In the same survey, respondents indicated that about one-third of these Internet searches resulted in rejections. Executive job search agency ExecuNet conducted its own study, which concluded that 75 percent of recruiters use web searches as part of their applicant-screening process. In this same survey, 35 percent of the recruiters reported eliminating job candidates based on revelations discovered online.

And while a CareerBuilder.com study concluded that just one in ten employers has used social networking sites in the selection process, the value of the information discovered is clearly significant: 63 percent of the employers surveyed said they declined to hire applicants based on what they found on social networking sites. The discoveries made about prospective employees went beyond embarrassing photos and included lies about their qualifications, links to criminal behavior, and expressing negative and questionable comments about their previous company or co-workers.

To be fair, information found online won't always negatively affect a company's search. The same CareerBuilder.com survey also found that the web could yield positive information. Hiring managers responding said that in 64 percent of the cases, the background information learned supported the applicant's professional qualifications, while 40 percent reported that searches revealed the candidate to be well rounded with wide-ranging interests. Though some companies, including Enterprise Rent-a-Car and Ernst & Young, say they do not use the Internet to check out job applicants, others such as Microsoft acknowledge that research on social networking sites has become typical. Warrant Ashton, group marketing manager for the Washington state software giant, says, "It's becoming very much a common tool. For the first time ever, you suddenly have very public information about almost any candidate."

That very public information can expose more than just personal foibles like sexual escapades, binge drinking, or those embarrassing spring break photos. The *New York Times* related the story of UCLA student Tien Nguyen, who found little luck getting call-back interviews until he Googled himself and found a link to a tongue-in-cheek essay he'd written about how to cheat the system to make employers have a better impression of you: its title was "Lying Your Way to the Top." After requesting that the essay be taken down, Nguyen experienced an easier time getting interviews and, later, job offers. Other companies have discovered discrepancies between a prospective employee's academic credentials and online sources. Given the increasing importance of social networking sites to prospective employers, it's hardly surprising that 47 percent of college graduate job-seekers in a 2007 survey had either changed or planned to change the content of their MySpace or Facebook sites. Yet while some critics point to the privacy concerns as a reason not to research a job candidate's social networking presence, many such candidates remain oblivious to what is or is not open to the public about their online services. In a 2006 Carnegie Mellon University study, nearly half of Facebook users surveyed gave incorrect answers when asked who could view their profiles on the site.

Not all employers are embracing the digital treasure trove of information that job applicants' social networking profiles can represent. Amegy Bank of Texas, an eighty-seven-branch, Houston-based bank, was recently profiled for its decision *not* to incorporate social networking research as part of its candidate evaluation process. Amegy's management and counsel pointed to concerns that, due to the impossibility of filtering the tape of information visible on any individual's site, they could get information they're not legally entitled to, and they might one day be called to task to prove that such information wasn't used in the hiring process. Amegy's outside counsel, Cristela Portela Solomon, offered this hypothetical by way of illustration. A woman applies for a bank teller position, and a human resources representative researches the candidate online, finding her Facebook page. On the site are postings about the candidate's upcoming baby shower. Based on this, the human resources representative makes the decision not to hire her—a violation of the Pregnancy Discrimination Act. "If you hired her and you didn't know [about the pregnancy] and then she has attendance issues, you could fire her—it's a legal reason. But the fact you didn't bring them on board to begin with, that would be hard for the employer, once they'd been exposed to illegal information, to be able to demonstrate that it wasn't the fact that she was pregnant, it was something else," says Solomon. Amegy acknowledges that its "off limits" approach to social networking sites (the company's Internet systems block access for all employees, not just the human resources department) is not based on any case law, but rather its low threshold for risk.

Meanwhile, at the other end of the spectrum lies Bozeman City, Montana. Applicants for jobs with the municipality are required to list "any and all current personal or business websites, web pages or memberships on any Internet-based chat rooms, social clubs or forums, to include, but not limited to: Facebook, Google, Yahoo, YouTube.com, MySpace, etc." There are then three lines where applicants must list the websites, their user names, log-in information, and their passwords. City representatives justify the intrusiveness by rationalizing that in seeking employees for everything from law enforcement to city hall positions, it is important "to make sure the people that we hire have the highest moral character and are a good fit for the City." Observers have criticized the policy, pointing out not only individual privacy concerns for applicants, but also nothing that such information gives the city access to pages belonging to an applicant's online "friends."

Monitoring Employees/Privacy Concerns

Screening candidates isn't the only potential trouble area for employers. Monitoring employees can be as well, even though it is necessary for a variety of reasons to be aware of what employees are saying on sites like Facebook, MySpace, or Twitter. The primary reason is to protect the company. Intellectual property, such as a company's trade secrets or confidential information, is at risk of being disclosed by employees blogging, Tweeting, or otherwise discussing a new product, service, or other developments that an employer would prefer to keep under wraps. In addition, employees who make disparaging or libelous comments about a competitor could expose the company to liability. Finally, securities violations may also be triggered by employees' online activities. Material misstatements made through a company-sponsored blog, Facebook page, or Twitter account could expose a publicly traded company to securities fraud. On August 1, 2008, the Securities and Exchange Commission issued Release No. 34-58288, which addressed potential liabilities arising out of the use of "interactive communications forums." That release made it clear that a company employee "speaking" in a company-sponsored interactive forum may never be deemed to be acting in an individual capacity. Consequently, the employer will likely be held liable for all employee statements made in that context.

Similarly, disclosure of material non-public information through a publicly traded company's blog, Facebook page, or Twitter account could be deemed a prohibited selective disclosure under federal securities regulations. Tweets or blogging that hype the company as jumping the gun and making a prohibited offer of a publicly traded company's securities. And if a company's blog, Facebook page, or Twitter account feature any forward-looking statements, they should include the appropriate cautionary language.

In addition, the company could face liability for "cyber harassment" by its employees, even if such harassment took place outside of the workplace. In *Blakey*, the New Jersey Supreme Court held that derogatory and harassing remarks posted by male co-workers about a female pilot on an online computer bulletin board outside of the workplace could give rise to employer liability and a duty to stop the harassment. *Blakey v. Continental Airlines*, 751 A.2d 538 (N.J. 2000).

But monitoring is not without its risks for employers. The 2009 federal court case of *Pietrylo v. Hillstone Restaurant Group*, No. 06-5754, 2009 WL 3128420 (D.N.J 2009) serves as a cautionary tale. Two employees at a Houston's Restaurant in Hackensack created a forum about their workplace on MySpace in 2006. Bartender Brian Pietrylo and waitress Doreen Marion e-mailed invitations to co-workers, who then would log in using a personal e-mail address and a password. On the forum, the two made fun of Houston's décor and its customers, made sexual references, and posted negative comments about supervisors. Hostess Karen St. Jean was allegedly coerced by supervisors into providing them with her e-mail and password information for her MySpace. After the comments made their way up the chain of command to management, Pietrylo and Marino were fired for violating company policies about professionalism and positive attitude. The former employees filed suit against Hillstone Restaurant Group (owners of Houston's), alleging that the managers violated not only their privacy rights under New Jersey law, but also federal wiretapping statutes by accessing the discussion group forum. In the summer of 2009, the plaintiffs recovered a verdict against their former employer.

To minimize the risks associated with employee monitoring, attorneys should advise their clients regarding formulating, implementing, and of course following certain policies on obtaining information from online sources like social networking sites.

First, make sure company personnel who research the social networking site or blog of a potential or existing employee comply with the appropriate third-party terms of use agreements. In virtually all cases, the individual will have already agreed to a terms of use statement mandated by the social networking provider. Company personnel, in using what they discover, should adhere to the terms of use as well. Moreover, a company's policy should set appropriate limits on the use of such information. For example, if the information pertains to work and/or affects the employee's job-related duties, it should be fair game, while other information should remain private. By way of illustration, revelations about an individual's DWIs or prior motor vehicle accidents could properly be taken into consideration when making a hire whose responsibilities include driving on company time.

Second, update the company's employee manual or handbook to disclose that certain information obtained from social networking research may properly be used (such as the driving-related information discussed above), while other information will not be. This includes data concerning race, age, gender, sexual orientation, or religion. Third, be sure to update appropriate disclosure forms and/or background search permission acknowledgments for employees and prospective employees. Evidence of consent can help negate many causes of action.

If your client doesn't already have a "social media policy," "electronic communications policy," "online activities policy," or whatever it cares to call it, it should. Such a policy, together with the employee's signed acknowledgement of receiving it and being bound by its terms, is usually the first—and best—line of defense to employee privacy claims.

Beware of potential challenges to social media policies by union representatives; employers should certainly keep in mind labor concerns when implementing such a policy. In December 2009, the National Labor Relations Board considered whether the social media policy promulgated by Sears Holding Corp. violated §8(a)(1) of the National Labor Relations Act. The primary complaint was with Sears' prohibition in the policy against disparagement of the company's "executive leadership, employees [or] strategy." The Board opined that, read in context among many prohibited activities, a reasonable employee would not consider that provision to be an improper limit on his/her conduct, and so it dismissed the charge.

Litigation Uses for Social Networking

The value of mining social networking sites is by no means limited to the applicant screening process, or to monitoring employee online activities. It can also come in handy in a variety of litigation contexts.

One Dallas litigator uncovered the details of a former employee's plans to circumvent her non-compete agreement by establishing a competing company when he looked at the Facebook page of her spouse (who went by a different surname). After the scheme was uncovered, the litigation ended quickly and favorably. In addition to discovering an employee's violation of employment agreements or a company's intellectual property rights, employers can also mine social networking sites for help in defending sexual harassment allegations. In defending a chief executive officer from sexual harassment and sexual assault allegations, one Houston attorney found a very different plaintiff than the demure, innocent "wannabe nun" who presented herself as the victim. Her MySpace page looked like outtakes from a "Girls Gone Wild" video, complete with photos of the plaintiff in scanty attire and engaged in provocative horseplay with friends. Although she later took down the photos, the damage was already done and the defense attorney had printed off what he needed.

In *Mackelprang v. Fidelity National Title Agency Inc.*, 2007 WL 119149 (D. Nev. 2007) defense attorneys wanted to discover whether the plaintiff in a sexual harassment suit had engaged online in the sort of sexually charged banter that her pleadings described happening in her allegedly hostile work environment. The court displayed some sensitivity to the personal nature of the information being sought, and excluded "private email messages between plaintiff and third persons regarding allegedly sexually explicit or promiscuous emails not related to plaintiff's employment." However, the court did permit discovery of what online accounts the plaintiff maintained, any online statement the plaintiff might have made about her lawsuit, any online activity around the time of two alleged suicide attempts the plaintiff made and attributed to the defendants' treatment of her, and any site information relevant to the plaintiff's emotional distress claims. In the case, Ms. Mackelprang had supposedly engaged in sexually explicit e-mails and MySpace private messages around the same time that she claimed to have been subjected to unwelcome and offensive sexual advances in her workplace. In addition, Mackelprang's claim of severe emotional distress brought on by the alleged harassment was attacked using evidence from her son's MySpace page, which discussed other possible causes for her distress, such as an ongoing, bitter child custody battle.

But perhaps the most interesting information sought by the defendants and allowed by the court were Ms. Mackelprang's own MySpace pages. That's right, pages. Ms. Mackelprang had two MySpace pages. In one (created shortly before her lawsuit was filed in 2006), she identifies herself as a thirty-nine-year-old married woman with six children, and she states that she loves being a mother. But another MySpace page, created closer in time to the alleged sexual harassment, identifies Mackelprang as a single female who indicates, "I don't want kids." Defense attorneys contended that they should be allowed to rebut Mackelprang's claims and impeach her credibility by showing that she was "voluntarily pursuing, encouraging or even engaging in extra-marital relationships on or through MySpace." The court agreed.

The *Mackelprang* decision is an important one, not just for its analysis of the use to which social networking evidence can be put in employment litigation. It also provides helpful discussion of how to go about obtaining such information and tailoring the requests for the content of a social networking page to that material that is relevant to the claims at hand. 2007 WL 119149 (D.Nev. 2007).

A more recent sexual harassment case also dealt with discoverability issues. In *EEOC v. Simply Storage Mgmt. LLC*, No. 09-1223 (S.D. Ind. May 11, 2010), the Equal Employment Opportunity Commission brought an action on behalf of two female employees of a self-storage firm. The employees, a property manager and an assistant manager, alleged that they and other female employees had been subject to groping, sexual assault, sexual commentary, and other harassment by a male manager, resulting in extreme emotional distress. Counsel for the self-storage company defendants sought discovery from the plaintiffs that included information from their MySpace and Facebook accounts, including profiles, status updates, photos, wall posts, and so on that "reveal, refer, or relate to any emotion, feeling, or mental state, as well as communications that reveal, refer, or relate to events that could reasonably be expected to produce a significant emotion, feeling, or mental state."

The Equal Employment Opportunity Commission objected, claiming that the requests were harassing, would embarrass the plaintiffs, and would improperly infringe on their privacy. Magistrate Judge Lynch, however, overruled these objections and ordered the production sought. In doing so, he reminded the claimants that just because social networking profiles are private or "locked" doesn't shield them from discovery. And while the social networking context sought would have to be relevant to a claim or defense in the case, the plaintiff's allegations of depression and stress disorders were likely to be discussed extensively within the social networking content sought. Everything from when stress purportedly occurred, to what degree, and what factors contributed to or caused it was likely to be among the topics covered by the plaintiffs online. As to the plaintiffs' privacy concerns, Judge Lynch disposed of that argument by pointing out that "the production here would be of information that the claimants have already shared with at least one other person through private messages or a larger number of people through postings." *EEOC*, No. 09-1223 (S.D. Ind. May 11, 2010).

The moral of the story: if your client feels the information was good enough to share with his or her Facebook friends, it is good enough to produce in discovery to the other side.

Another recent case demonstrates the importance of social media in employment litigation. In a suit filed in federal court in Minnesota in March 2010, Hanover, Maryland-based TEKsystems Inc. accused several former employees of its Edina, Minnesota, office of breaching their non-compete and non-solicitation agreements. In a digital twist on the typical non-compete case, however, TEKsystems says it has electronic proof of the alleged wrongful conduct by its former technical recruiter Brelyn Hammernik: Hammernik's LinkedIn page. Among other allegations, TEKsystems claims Hammernik used the social networking site to contact at least sixteen TEKsystems employees. The company claims that she messaged an invitation, through LinkedIn, to a TEKsystems employee to visit her new workplace at Horizontal Integration Inc. (also a defendant). One of the LinkedIn conversations, according to the plaintiff, stated (on December 8, 2009), "Tom—Hey! Let me know if you are still looking for opportunities! I would love to have you come visit my new office and hear about some of the stuff we are working on! Let me know your thoughts! Brelyn." The defendants have denied the allegations, and have filed a counterclaim. Among other contentions, they maintain that the plaintiff gave the employees permission to leave, and they argue that TEKsystems didn't have policies and procedures in place that would prohibit former employees from using social media in this manner.

Legal analysts agree that this may be the first time someone's LinkedIn activity has been used as the basis for a lawsuit, but it's not likely to be the last. Courts could be faced with the task of deciding whom the online connections an employee makes belong to—the employer or the employee? In addition, will social networking activity join the list of items and conduct that will be addressed specifically in non-compete and non-solicitation agreements in the future, just like customer lists? And, like customer lists, will social networking contacts be susceptible to being viewed as a trade secret? As social media continues to make its influence felt in areas like employment law, the answer to questions like these will gradually take shape.

If you do regard things like client lists as trade secrets, then take the necessary steps to protect them as such – even on social networking sites. Sasqua Group, Inc. an executive search consulting firm for financial services professionals, found this out the hard way. After one of its consultants, Lori Courtney, left and started her own consulting firm, Artemis Consultants. Before long, three former Sasqua consultants were working there with her. Sasqua didn't have a non-compete or non-solicitation agreement with Courtney, but it did file a lawsuit against her, claiming that her "client contacts" were trade secrets. Courtney responded that the information was known outside the business, or readily ascertainable through LinkedIn, Facebook, and Google—therefore, it wasn't protectable as a trade secret.

The court agreed with Courtney, noting her testimony about the availability of contact information and professional details on the Internet in an age where "everyone . . . puts it out there for the world to see because people want to be connected now." *Sasqua Group Inc. v. Courtney*, 2010 WL 2613855 (E.D.N.Y. Aug. 2, 2010).

9

Libel by Twitter: The Collision of Social Media and Defamation Law

One of the most rapidly expanding areas of the law affected by the advent of social media is defamation law. As any specialist in this area of law will acknowledge, what we say and how we say it can have consequences. Accordingly, should it matter whether the defamatory statement is made in a book or magazine article as opposed to a MySpace page for all the world to see? Is an unflattering portrayal of someone less actionable because it was embodied in a YouTube video and not a television program or motion picture? Can what is communicated in 140 characters or less via Twitter still constitute a "statement" as that term is understood for defamation purposes? And does the fact that a libelous statement appeared via Facebook or as a "tweet" to a very limited audience of "friends" or "followers" make it less of a "publication" when calculating liability or damages?

We have already seen in the family law context that a communication as fleeting as a friend request or a poke on Facebook can be considered enough of a statement to violate a protective order's prohibition against contact. Paul Chambers of the United Kingdom is one person who probably wishes that such fleeting messages weren't viewed as actual statements. On January 6, 2010, the twenty-six-year-old finance supervisor was frustrated when he learned that snowfall threatened to delay his travel plans to Ireland on January 15. So he sent an angry tweet to his 600 followers on Twitter expressing his frustration, saying that Doncaster's "Robin Hood Airport is closed" and that unless airport personnel remedied the situation in time for him to travel, "I'm blowing the airport sky high!!"

He also sent a separate tweet to the lady friend he was going to meet in Ireland stating that if airport closings interfered with his plans, "I've decided that I'm going to resort to terrorism."

Chambers later said that he was just "venting his frustration," and that it never crossed his mind that "Robin Hood would ever look at Twitter or take it seriously because it was innocuous hyperbole." But an off-duty manager doing a Twitter search several days after the messages were posted alerted airport security, who passed it on to police even though they considered it to be non-credible. Police arrested Chambers at his workplace on January 13, 2010. Although Chambers' lawyer argued that the message might have been "immature" or "tactless" but not criminal, District Judge Jonathan Bennett disagreed. He found that the tweet "was of a menacing nature in the context of the times in which we live," and found Chambers guilty of violating the Communications Act of 2003 by sending a message by means of a public electronic medium that was grossly offensive or of an indecent, obscene, or menacing character. Chambers was ordered to pay £400 in fines and £600 in court costs.

Paul Chambers is believed to have been the first person arrested in Great Britain for comments on Twitter. Making legal history, however, was probably the furthest thing from his mind when the self-described "most mild-mannered guy you could imagine" was arrested, had his laptop, iPhone, and home computer seized, and saw his Twitter post deleted by law enforcement authorities. Clearly, at least one judge believes that what you say—even if you say it in 140 characters or less—has repercussions.

Social media and the Internet demonstrate that what can be a positive force cannot only serve negative purposes, but can serve them with frightening speed and efficiency. In an era in which political opinion can be shaped by social media, and in which consumer loyalties (and consequently sales) can rise and fall based upon comments and self-published product ratings on social networking sites, individuals and companies alike can be disparaged at the speed of a search engine, reaching an audience of millions. When Gregg Hartley of Cassidy & Associates took exception with a critical *New York Times* story on one of his firm's largest clients, the oil-rich nation of Equatorial Guinea, he could have voiced his concerns with the newspaper's editorial staff or reporter Ian Urbina, or taken other, less direct approaches.

Instead, Hartley chose to fight media fire with social media fire, posting on his personal feed that the venerable newspaper had a conflict of interest, in light of the fact that Urbina's father was a federal judge who had presided over a high-profile case involving Equatorial Guinea. Asked why he made Twitter his chosen media, Hartley said that one thing about social media was that "you don't have to always be right."

Indeed, social media and the Internet have become equalizers in clashes between businesses and unhappy consumers. A dissatisfied customer can make devastating comments about a company on a social networking site, including ones that specialize in consumer ratings and feedback like Yelp. By the same token, however, businesses haven't exactly been shy about fighting back with defamation lawsuits. For example, restaurant owner Travis Redmon of Tennessee spoke out on Facebook and Twitter about his unhappiness with the marketing firm of Low & Tritt. Calling the firm's management "crooks," he made comments like "Do not ever use Low & Tritt marketing firm" to his 310 followers on Twitter and his 279 Facebook fans. Low & Tritt responded with a $2 million libel suit against Redmon in October 2009.

Thom Alascio of Florida was not happy, to say the least, with the service he got from Vero Beach auto dealer Route 60 Hyundai in 2008 and 2009. By October 2009, Alascio had escalated a running war of words to the world of social networking, and began the first of what would be thirteen tweets on Twitter and seventeen status updates on Facebook referring to the dealership. His comments covered the spectrum from little jabs to more pointed remarks like the one referring to Route 60 Hyundai as "crooks," and the post that read, "There is not a worse dealership on the planet." The comments went to Alascio's 342 Facebook friends and 160 Twitter followers, but they also attracted the attention of the dealership's lawyer, who sent a cease-and-desist letter threatening a defamation lawsuit and demanding that the comments be removed from the popular social networking sites. Alascio had to get a lawyer of his own to get the dealership to back down.

Of course, some businesses who venture down this road wind up learning a costly lesson about the power of the Internet. In January 2010, T&J Towing of Kalamazoo, Michigan, removed a car belonging to Western Michigan

University student Justin Kurtz from Kurtz's apartment complex parking lot. The towing company claims the car lacked the necessary parking permit, while Kurtz insists he had a permit and the towing crew scraped it off. To retrieve his car, Kurtz reluctantly paid a $118 fee. But then he started the Facebook page "Kalamazoo Residents Against T&J Towing." Since February, the page's membership has grown to over 11,000, many of whom have similar criticism of the towing company's methods. Since the incident, T&J has lost half of its commercial towing accounts (including Kurtz's apartment complex) and the Better Business Bureau assigned T&J an "F" rating because of the pattern of complaints against the company. These complaints range from towing vehicles in error even if they had the required parking pass to accepting only cash payments and refusing to provide change if the vehicle owner doesn't have the exact amount owed.

Instead of apologizing to Kurtz and asking him to remove his Facebook page, T&J Towing filed a $750,000 libel suit against the student in April. Kurtz promptly countersued for violating both his rights to free speech as well as Michigan consumer protection laws. And the bad publicity has continued for T&J Towing, to the point where Kurtz's attorneys are going through the dissatisfied consumers on the Facebook page to possibly convert Kurtz' counterclaim into a class action suit. One expert feels this is an example not of libel, but of how social media is empowering consumers. "Social networking has put the little guy and the big guy on the same footing and has made everyone accountable," says Professor Mike Bernacchi of the University of Detroit (Mercy).

While for some companies, filing a defamation suit over comments made via a social networking site is an ill-fated decision, for others it is seen as a tactical necessity. In the spring of 2008, Brain Research Labs was sued over claims that its dietary supplement, Procera AVH, didn't live up to its claims of improving memory. The California litigation became a class action lawsuit, and if that wasn't enough to put Brain Research Labs on the defense, the lead plaintiffs' lawyer, Thomas Clarke Jr., uploaded a nine-minute YouTube video about the case. In it, Clarke allegedly referred to Brain Lab's personnel as "scam artists" and thieves, and allegedly implied that the product was killing people. Brain Research Labs, contending that Clarke had crossed the line, promptly sued the lawyer and his firm, arguing that their comments were defamatory. Lawyers for Clarke and his firm characterized the defamation lawsuit as a SLAPP (strategic lawsuit against public participation), and maintained that Clarke was within his rights under the law to reach out to potential witnesses and litigants. The fact that Clarke reached out using a social networking site was beside the point, his lawyer James Wagstaffe, said. "The law doesn't change simply because there's a new communication technique used," he pointed out.

However, Judge Harold Kahn disagreed, holding that the YouTube video was commercial speech that was not entitled to protection under California's anti-SLAPP law. He ruled that releasing a YouTube video was not simply an attempt to communicate with potential class members, but indeed was more of an effort to try the case in the court of public opinion. Kahn wrote that "by invoking the 'new media' of the Internet and its capacity to display videos, Clarke chose, in a twenty-first century way, to 'litigate in the press.'"

Depending on what country you live in, posting allegedly defamatory content can result in more than simply a civil suit. In South Africa, Duane Brady posted demeaning comments on Facebook about his former boss. But instead of just losing his job, Brady found himself under arrest when his online comments were reported to police. He was charged with "crimen injuria," a criminal offense in South Africa committed when one person deliberately injures another's dignity. Like the unfortunate Briton Paul Chambers, Duane Brady made legal history, becoming the first South African charged with such a crime for posting unflattering messages on Facebook.

Businesses in particular would do well to remember that disparagement of their brand via social media might not always come from irate consumers. Sometimes, the disparaging comments come from within; a recent study by Proofpoint Inc. revealed that 17 percent of U.S. companies reported "exposure incidents" by employees on sites like Facebook and LinkedIn, and that 15 percent had disciplined employees over violations of a social media/online activities policy—such as badmouthing the company online. An equally significant concern for companies, however, is the potential business disparagement by competitors making use of social media. In August 2010, Ocean Spray Cranberries Inc. filed a lawsuit in federal court in Boston against rival Decas Cranberry Inc. According to Ocean Spray's

Complaint, Decas hired a media firm to develop a "false and misleading social media campaign" (including the creation of a fictitious Facebook identity to publish a smear campaign under the guise of consumer advocacy), accusing Ocean Spray of harming the cranberry industry by using fewer berries to make a particular product. Ocean Spray claims this "Scamberry" campaign has hurt its business relationships, while Decas considers the lawsuit a "totally frivolous" bullying tactic.

Libel by Twitter

From the Queen of England to P. Diddy, from Ashton Kutcher to Oprah Winfrey, it seems everybody is tweeting. Not surprisingly, not everything said on Twitter is nice. Just ask Austin, Texas, fashion designer Dawn "Boudoir Queen" Simorangkir. Rocker Courtney Love discovered Simorangkir's designs online, and started buying from her in 2008. On January 29, 2009, the clothing designer and her husband met Love in Los Angeles, and Love allegedly gave Simorangkir various remnants and other items, and commissioned the designer to create a number of custom pieces for her. Sometime thereafter, there was a dispute over payment. According to Simorangkir, after she suspended work for the rocker due to non-payment, Love went on a series of online rants on MySpace and particularly Twitter, making what Simorangkir described as "delusional accusations and lies" as well as "threats of harm." Among other statements, Love allegedly referred to the designer as a "thief and burglar," a drug addict, a prostitute, a felon, an embezzler, a cocaine dealer, and an unfit mother who had "lost all custody of her child." On March 26, 2009, Simorangkir filed a lawsuit in Los Angeles Superior Court alleging libel, invasion of privacy, breach of contract, intentional infliction of emotional distress, and intentional interference with a prospective economic advantage. In August 2009, Love filed a motion to strike the lawsuit under California's anti-SLAPP statute, only to have the motion denied in October 2009; the court felt that Simorangkir had demonstrated a high probability of prevailing in her defamation lawsuit. It should be noted that at the time, Courtney Love had 40,339 followers on Twitter. The suit was expected to go to trial in the summer of 2010.

Courtney Love isn't the only celebrity attracting the wrong kind of attention for her tweets. On December 28, 2009, Dr. Sanford Siegal filed a defamation suit against reality television personality Kim Kardashian in Florida state court. According to the lawsuit, Dr. Siegal—creator of "Dr. Siegal's Cookie Diet"—read some flattering comments that Kardashian had made about his weight loss cookies and shakes, and had a supply delivered to her in the spring of 2009. Dr. Siegal later posted a link on his website to an article describing how Kardashian had lost weight, thanks to his diet. But on October 29, 2009, Siegel alleges that Kim Kardashian sent the following and supposedly defamatory tweets from her Twitter account: "Dr. Siegal's Cookie Diet is falsely promoting that I'm on this diet. NOT TRUE! I would never do this unhealthy diet! I do Quick Trim!" and "If this Dr. Siegal is lying about me being on this diet, what else are they lying about? Not cool!!"

Siegal's lawsuit goes on to claim that these tweets were false, defamatory, and made with a commercial motive in mind (Kardashian has a deal with rival diet company Quick Trim). But will Kardashian's tweets be interpreted as merely her own opinion (and therefore harmless enough), or as false statements of fact? Generally, mere opinion does not rise to the level of defamation; the speaker/writer must be making a statement of fact that's false, and must do so with actual malice.

Perhaps the most critical test to date of how social media is blurring the boundaries of existing defamation law came in January 2010, with a court considering for the first time whether a tweet could be libelous. On May 12, 2009, with sixteen words that would lead to the first judicial ruling on "libel by Twitter," Amanda Bonnen—a tenant at a Chicago apartment complex managed by Horizon Realty Group—sent the following tweet: "@JessB123 You should just come anyway. Who said sleeping in a moldy apartment was bad for you? Horizon Realty thinks it's ok." Bonnen only had twenty followers on Twitter at the time, and Horizon Realty (which manages fifteen Chicago buildings) didn't learn of the Twitter message right away. In fact, Bonnen actually filed a housing class action lawsuit against Horizon on June 24, 2009, alleging that the landlord violated Chicago's tenant-friendly housing ordinance by failing to pay interest on her $250 security deposit and by failing to include mandatory "porch safety language" in her rental agreement. She moved out of her apartment on June 30, 2009.

That same day, having learned of Bonnen's Twitter post, Horizon poured gasoline on the smoldering embers of a minor landlord-tenant dispute by filing a $50,000 libel suit against Bonnen over her simple Tweet. The lawsuit attracted national publicity, and Horizon fanned the flames with some early statements that it was a "sue first, ask questions later" type of organization. Even before the litigation reached the inside of a courtroom, Horizon was losing the public relations battle by claiming to have suffered "a great injury" as the result of a simple tweet to only twenty followers. Nevertheless, Horizon maintained that the statement was false, defamatory, and constituted libel per se since it damaged Horizon's business reputation.

Bonnen came back with some legal firepower of her own. Represented by lawyers from John Marshall Law School's Center for Information Technology and Privacy Law, Bonnen filed a motion to dismiss the case in November 2009, arguing that the tweet didn't meet the legal definition of libel. Under Illinois law, she argued, the defendant must have made a false statement regarding the plaintiff, published to a third party, and which damaged the plaintiff. But above all, it has to be a statement of fact, and not something that would be construed as opinion. As support for this, Bonnen's defense attorney pointed to many of the other tweets Bonnen had written around the same time that were clearly opinions or exaggerations, arguing, "When one considers Ms. Bonnen's allegedly defamatory Tweet in the social context and setting in which the statement was published, it's nature as rhetorical hyperbole is readily apparent." The defense team also cited a 2009 study of Twitter that concluded that more than 40 percent of tweets were nothing more than "pointless babble."

Horizon's lawyers countered that Twitter wasn't mere babble, but rather a "legitimate medium used by reporters to report up-to-the-minute updates on legal actions, by rabbis, by people to support specific causes or engage in a certain activity, and as a marketing tool." The plaintiff argued that tweets should be treated no differently than other forms of communication. Ultimately, Cook County Circuit Judge Dianne Larsen agreed with the defendant, and on January 20, 2010, granted Bonnen's motion to dismiss with prejudice. Even in victory, however, Bonnen's lawyers were cautious, pointing out that just because this case was dismissed doesn't mean tweeting can't be defamatory. Richard Balough, one of the defense attorneys, warned, "Just because you are doing something in 140 characters doesn't mean there can't be libel or defamation. People always need to exercise caution, regardless of whether they are tweeting, talking, or writing an e-mail."

The Bonnen case illustrates many of the thorny legal issues yet to be sorted out as social media affects different areas of law, and the age-old struggle of the law trying to keep pace with technology continues. Bonnen's tweet may have been merely opinion and therefore not defamatory, but what if it had constituted of factual statement instead? Since defamation law requires publication to one or more third parties in order to be actionable, the number of Twitter followers may not matter (except in calculating damages), but what about the use of "re-tweet" an integral feature on Twitter allowing friends and followers to share information? If others re-tweeted a defamatory message, would they be exposing themselves to libel lawsuits of their own? Generally, a person who repeats someone else's defamatory statement can be liable for defamation themselves if they knew or had reason to know of its defamatory nature. Internet service providers and hosting companies have their own safe harbor in Section 230 of the Communications Decency Act, which provides: "No provider or user of an interactive computer service shall be treated as the publisher or speaker of any information provided by another information content provider." Consequently, sites like MySpace, Facebook, and Twitter themselves have no civil liability for content posted by others on their sites. However, it remains to be seen whether this would protect a blogger or re-tweeter.

Another problem that arises concerns who actually made the statements. A number of famous figures, from billionaire Bill Gates to baseball manager Tony La Russa to former Secretary of State Condoleezza Rice, have been the victims of "Twitterjacking," a form of identity theft in which someone "tweets" pretending to be someone else. Who bears the responsibility for statements made under the guise of someone else? Certainly the person falsely using that identity, but what about Twitter itself for not taking adequate measures to verify a user's identity? An emerging body of law is forming regarding the creation of false and defamatory social networking profiles of teachers and/or school administrators by vengeful students, but because such cases have primarily been examined in the context of free speech, they are separately discussed in the chapter on social networking and First Amendment issues.

From its admittedly limited treatment so far, it appears that statements made via social networking sites will be examined under the prism of existing defamation law. Beginning with consideration of whether it is actually a statement of fact and not an expression of opinion, and continuing on to issues of publication and damages, what is uttered is apparently more important to legal determination than where it was uttered (i.e., a Twitter post as opposed to a billboard or newspaper article).

The Question of Anonymity

While an entire book could probably be written on the subject of Internet defamation itself and not simply social media's impact on defamation law (and, as such, is beyond the scope of this chapter), it is worth pointing out that this arena is still evolving. One particularly difficult issue that is more common with blogs than with social networking sites is the anonymity of the author of the allegedly defamatory comments. To pursue a case of defamation, one has to be able to identify the responsible individuals—a task that's not always easy.

Typically, courts require a party to satisfy an evidentiary burden before they will allow discovery of an anonymous author on the Internet in a case of online defamation. However, just how high the bar will be set depends on the court itself. One of the leading cases setting forth a standard for identifying an anonymous defendant is a case out of New Jersey, *Dendrite Int'l v. Doe*, 775 A.2d 756 (N.J. Super. Ct. App. Div. 2001). In *Dendrite*, a corporation was trying to assert defamation and related causes of action against the John Doe defendants who had allegedly posted defamatory messages on an electronic bulletin board that drove down the value of the company's stock. The New Jersey appellate court affirmed the trial court's denial of a motion compelling the defendants' Internet service provider to reveal their identities and, in so doing, adopted a multi-pronged test that would weigh the anonymous defendants' free speech rights against the merits of the plaintiff's case and the legal necessity for disclosure. The *Dendrite* court said courts should examine the following factors in determining if a plaintiff was entitled to identification of an anonymous blogger: (1) whether any attempt had been made to notify the anonymous parties about the legal proceedings and give them a chance to respond; (2) what was the exact nature of the online statements; and (3) could the plaintiff state a *prima facie* cause of action and make a showing supporting the requisite elements of its case? Several years later, the Delaware Supreme Court elaborated on the *Dendrite* test, and added that the plaintiff must show that its cause of action would survive a motion for summary judgment. *Doe v. Cahill*, 884 A.2d 451 (Del. Super. Ct. 2005). Courts in a number of states have tended to follow these models as they walked the legal tightrope of safeguarding anonymous free speech while providing an avenue for those claiming defamation. An excellent resource for tracking the developing law in this area is the website maintained by the Citizens' Media Law Project.

For lawyers faced with whether to pursue an anonymous blogger for defamation, there are important practical considerations. Can your client withstand the level of judicial scrutiny required to obtain the necessary identifying information? You should have each of the anonymous postings carefully laid out, along with an explanation of how each statement relates to your causes of action. You should also explore whether the information could be obtained from either sources, without the need for judicial intervention. And since a number of states have anti-SLAPP statutes, you need to be prepared to show that your efforts are a legitimate attempt at redress for your clients, and not singly an attempt to quash public discussion of a matter. Finally, consider whether the harm to your client truly justifies the legal action that it is contemplating. In today's world of search engine optimization strategies, a company with an established online identity may be able to "drive down" one unfavorable blog posting or entry with articles, company blogs, and other web content of its own. As a result, the negative impact of a single, arguably defamatory posting could be significantly lessened without risking the public relations backlash, cost, and uncertainty of a lawsuit.

10

You Are What You Post: Discoverability and Evidentiary Issues and Social Networking

Introduction

Given the prevalence of social media, the lawyer who overlooks evidence to be mined from social networking sites like Facebook, MySpace, and Twitter may be committing malpractice. Nearly 60 percent of adult Internet users in the United States have a profile on a social networking site. According to a September 2009 Nielsen survey, Internet users spend 17 percent of their online time on social networking sites; social media usage is growing at a rate of three times that of overall Internet usage. MySpace, founded in 2003, has more than 250 million users. Facebook, founded in 2004, boasts more than 500 million users, and they are loyal: roughly half of Facebook users visit the site on at least a daily basis. "Facebook Nation" enabled Facebook to surpass Google in March of this year as the most-visited website in the world. And if it were indeed a nation, Facebook would be the third most populous on Earth.

Twitter, founded in 2006, is a social networking/micro-blogging site. Posts, or "tweets," cannot exceed 140 characters. Twitterers "tweet" news as it happens directly from their cell phones to followers that can number in the thousands, or even millions in the case of celebrities like Oprah Winfrey or Ashton Kutcher. Such tweets may share observations or news, with links to more in-depth articles or blogs. Twitterers may also "re-Tweet" to their follower's tweets that they find informative or interesting. There are roughly

77 million Twitter users. To put the meteoric growth of social sites such as Twitter in perspective, consider that three years ago, Twitter handled 5,000 tweets a day. Currently, the site handles 600 tweets every second—a staggering 50 million per day.

With such an abundance of statements, photos, videos, and other potential evidence appearing on social networking sites every day, it's no wonder that lawyers from all areas of practice are digging in this digital goldmine. A February 2010 study by the American Academy of Matrimonial Lawyers revealed that 81 percent of the attorneys responding reported they found and used evidence from social networking sites. The most popular source for such evidence was Facebook; 66 percent of the respondents indicated they used the site for information. From prosecutors and criminal defense attorneys to personal injury litigators and employment lawyers, attorneys around the country are making use of evidence from social networking sites. For example, a chemical exposure/manganese poisoning case brought in federal court in Cleveland, Ohio, against several welding equipment companies was recently dismissed due to what defense lawyers discovered on social networking sites. Welder Ernest Ray had claimed serious personal injuries, including permanent neurological damage, because of manganese exposure. But defense attorneys introduced evidence from Ray's Facebook page, including photos of the supposedly disabled plaintiff competing in high-speed boat races and other rigorous physical activities.

This chapter will examine discoverability and evidentiary issues associated with social networking evidence, including authentication.

The Importance of Being Creative

Scholars of Native American history often point out that the Lakota Sioux used virtually all of the buffalo after a hunt: meat for sustenance, hide for clothing and shelter, bone and sinew for tools, etc. Lawyers consideing options for using evidence from social networking sites would be well advised to take a similar approach. While photos, video, or statements posted on a social networking site are most frequently used for their evidentiary value, don't overlook other features associated with social networking sites.

Mood Indicator

Sites like MySpace and Facebook have a feature where the user can share what kind of mood he or she happens to be in that day. Such information was put to good use by a public defender in New York in 2009.

Gary Walters, a paroled burglar, faced charges of carrying a loaded weapon following an altercation with New York police officer Vaughn Ettienne. Officer Ettienne claimed that when he arrested Walters in 2006, the defendant had been carrying a loaded 9mm pistol. But Walter's attorney, Adrian Lesher, sought to convince the jury that the gun had been planted on his client as an excuse for breaking Walter's ribs during the arrest. Lesher wanted to portray officer Ettienne, a bodybuilder who'd been disciplined in 2007 after testing positive for steroids, as a cop filled with "roid rage," trying to emulate Denzel Washington's corrupt narcotics officer character in the movie "Training Day."

Lesher had some help, courtesy of Ettienne's own social networking profile. On the day before the arrest, Ettienne's mood on the page was set to "devious," complete with an angry red emoticon being licked by flames. And in the days leading up to the trial, the hulking policeman had even set his status to read, "Vaughn is watching 'Training Day' to brush up on proper police procedure." Lesher's digital sleuthing also turned up incriminating comments Ettienne had made on the Useless Junk video sharing site, under his screen name "Blakryno." These included comments supportive of police who had beaten a handcuffed suspect (and then videotaped doing it), saying, "If you were going to hit a cuffed suspect, at least get your money's worth 'cause now he's going to get disciplined for a...love tap."

In the end, the defense worked, and Waters was acquitted of the more serious charges and his conviction was downgraded to resisting arrest, all because the jury was convinced by the evidence of Ettienne's social networking activities. Ettienne himself, while denying that his Internet self reflected his true character as a police officer, recognized the permanence of online miscues. "You have your Internet persona, and you have what you actually do on the street...what you say on the Internet is all bravado talk, like what you say in a locker room. I'm not going to say it was the best of things to do in retrospect...stupidity on the Internet is there for everyone to see for all times in perpetuity. That's the case for me."

Status Updates

The Missouri Court of Appeals recently affirmed a case in which the trial judge properly excluded evidence of a sexual assault victim's Facebook status update in a criminal case. *State v. Corwin*, 295 S.W.3d 572 (Mo. Ct. App. 2009). In this alleged date rape case, the defendant maintained that he and the complainant had been out for drinks before returning to his dorm room (where the alleged assault took place), and the defendant's main argument was that the victim's recollection of events that night were unreliable. His counsel tried to introduce status updates from the Facebook page describing her lifestyle, purportedly describing nights of binge drinking followed by mornings where she couldn't remember what happened the night before. At least one update referenced being out on one occasion (after the alleged assault) and not realizing how she had gotten several bruises.

The trial court, over the defense's objections, excluded this evidence—none of which related to the night in question. The appellate court affirmed, nothing that "the complaining witness in a sex offense case may be impeached by evidence that her general reputation for truth and veracity is bad but ordinarily by proof of specific acts of misconduct." The status updates in question, the court noted, included references to "partying, sex, drinking, schoolwork, and at least one sexually suggestive photograph," but "went beyond any evidence even tangentially related to events of the night in question." Accordingly, the court held that the status updates were irrelevant and were properly excluded.

Recently, New York Facebook status updates were used as alibi evidence for the first time. In October 2009, nineteen-year-old Rodney Bradford of Brooklyn was arrested in connection with a robbery. On paper, he might have made a plausible suspect, given the fact that he was already facing charges in connection with another robbery. But Bradford had an unusual alibi for his whereabouts at 11:49 a.m. on October 17, 2009, and it was one that could be verified. Bradford was on Facebook at the time, updating his status to read "on the phone with this fat chick...wherer my i hop [sic]" (a reference to talking with his pregnant girlfriend and a trip to get some pancakes).

Proving the alibi wasn't simply a matter of taking Rodney Bradford's word for it, thanks to the electronic trail he'd left. Although eyewitnesses identified him in a lineup, Bradford's father and stepmother confirmed the fact that the youth was at his father's Manhattan apartment using the computer. Corroborating his story further was evidence from Facebook itself. A Brooklyn district attorney subpoenaed Facebook's records and verified that the server log-on/log-off records matched Bradford's time on the social networking site, and that the status update was posted from an Internet protocol address that matched the one registered to Bradford's father. The district attorney dropped the charges.

Robert Reuland, Bradford's defense attorney, says that Facebook verification "made the day." "What we had in hand was irrefutable proof," he said. "And that's really where it turned the trick." Legal observers hailed this as the first known instance in which social networking evidence—often used to impeach or help convict a criminal defendant—has been used as alibi evidence. Some of those commenting on the case were more skeptical, however. Joseph Pollini, who teaches at John Jay College of Criminal Justice in New York, maintains, "With a user name and password, anyone can input data in a Facebook page."

What Mr. Pollini and other skeptics overlook, however, is the fact that there was more than just a Facebook update operating in Rodney Bradford's favor. Besides the testimony from corroborating witnesses like Bradford's father and stepmother who were with him at the same residence, the matching Internet protocol address and Facebook server records would be difficult for even an accomplished hacker to fake. Although one can update a Facebook page with someone's user name and password from a remote location, the use of proxy servers, a public terminal, or any number of other techniques to hide the sender's physical location would still leave a trail more likely to *disprove* an alibi, not create one. As defense counsel, Reuland was quick to point out, "This is a nineteen-year-old kid. He's not a criminal genius setting up an elaborate alibi for himself."

Ultimately, no one was more relieved than Rodney Bradford and his family. "If it weren't for Facebook, I'd still be on Riker's Island," says the teenager. Ernestine Bradford, Rodney's stepmother, agreed. "Facebook saved my son... Normally, we yell at our kids. 'Oh, you're on the computer.' It's completely different. If it weren't for Facebook, my son wouldn't be here." A Facebook representative said the social networking giant was "pleased" to be "able to serve as a constructive part of the judicial process."

With the prevalence of social networking, and an apparent willingness of people to reveal more of themselves online, there is a greater cyber trail to follow than ever before. For many, those digital footprints have led to criminal convictions. For Rodney Bradford, they led to exoneration. Bradford's case may have been the first "Facebook alibi," but it isn't likely to be the last.

Log-On/Log-Off Records

Sometimes, the amount of time spent on a social networking site can become an evidentiary focal point. In a Canadian case, a British Columbia court found that a plaintiff's late-night computer usage on Facebook—as demonstrated by the server log-on/log-off records—was evidence relevant to his personal injury claim against his employer. *Bishop v. Minichiello*, B.C.J. No. 692 (S. C.J.) (2009).

"Random Things about Me"

Social networking sites like MySpace often have a section for the user to share "random facts" about him or herself, including likes and dislikes, career goals, etc. In a vehicular homicide case in a jurisdiction that allowed "victim statements" or "impact statements" from a crime victim or her family, the prosecutor chose (in lieu of submitting letters from family members) to read something the victim had written prior to her death; in this instance, an excerpt from her MySpace page under "Random Facts about Me." During the penalty phase, to help the court in deciding on sentencing, the prosecutor read about such "random facts" as the victim's love of chocolate milkshakes, visiting Disneyland, and goals that would remain unfulfilled, like learning to play the piano.

The overall point? Don't think that photos or statements are the only evidentiary nuggets to be gleaned from a social networking site.

The Federal Rules and Authentication of Electronic Communications

To be admissible, online digital information such as a MySpace or Facebook profile (or statements contained in such a profile) must be relevant, authentic, and not excluded as hearsay. The relevancy issue is one that will vary according to the facts of the case. For example, in the *Mackelprang* sexual harassment case, the court ruled that the defendant was entitled to discovery information from the plaintiff's MySpace pages and instant messages relevant to her sexual harassment allegations, alleged emotional distress, and mental state. However, to the extent that the defendant sought to learn about Mackelprang's private sexual conduct on the theory that she was voluntarily pursuing or engaging in extramarital relationships through MySpace, the court was less tolerant. Questioning the relevance of such non-work-related sexual conduct since "what a person views as acceptable or welcomed sexual activity or solicitation in his or her private life may not be acceptable or welcomed from a fellow employee or a supervisor," the court concluded that the defendant failed to demonstrate a relevant basis for obtaining production of that MySpace information. *Mackelprang v. Fidelity National Title Agency of Nevada Inc.*, 2007 WL 119149 (D. Nev. 2007).

With regard to the authenticity requirement, courts have been reluctant to come up with unique rules for authenticating electronic data. In dispensing with an appellant's argument that e-mails and text messages are "inherently unreliable" and would have to be the subject of a "whole new body of law," one court noted that electronic communications could be properly authenticated within the existing legal framework, since "the same uncertainties exist with traditional documents. A signature can be forged, a letter can be typed on another's typewriter; distinct letterhead stationery can be copied or stolen." *In re F.P.*, 878 A. 2d 91, 95 (Pa. Super. Ct. 2005).

Once a court determines that information is relevant and can be heard by the jury, the attorney presenting such evidence has to make a *prima facie* showing of genuineness. Fed. R. Evid. 901. It will be the jury's responsibility to decide authenticity. For example, in a commercial litigation/defamation case involving two providers of satellite television programming, the plaintiff challenged archived pages of its own website as not properly authenticated and coming from an unreliable source. The court rejects that argument, noting that F.R.E. 901 requires only a *prima facie* showing of genuineness. It further concluded that while the plaintiff was free to raise its reliability concerns with the jury, the fact that an affidavit attested to the fact that these were copies of the website as it appeared on the dates in question, and that the plaintiff failed to deny or challenge the archived pages' veracity, were sufficient to meet the authentication threshold. *Telewizja Polska USA Inc. v. Echostar Satellite*, No. 02-C-3293, 2004 WL 2367740 (N.D. Ill., Oct. 15, 2004).

Authentication of digital information can be accomplished by direct proof, circumstantial evidence, or a combination of both. In the *F.P.* case, for example, the instant messages that were at issue were authenticated by direct proof—the person in question acknowledged his screen name, admitted authorship, and admitted to printing the instant messages from his computer. In a case involving printouts of chat room logs, they were authenticated by not only the appellant and other witnesses confirming his screen name, but also by the fact that when a meeting was arranged with that screen name user, the appellant showed up. *United States v. Tank*, 200 F.3d 627 (9th Cir. 2000).

Of course, sometimes that proof isn't so convincing. In a recent shareholder class action case against a drug manufacturer, for example, the plaintiffs tried to bolster their claims of fraud by showing that the pharmaceutical company was warned internally that the cholesterol drug in question had various shortcomings. *In re Pfizer Inc. Securities Litigation*, 538 F.Supp.2d 621 (S.D.N.Y. 2008). The basis for this contention came from an anonymous blog posting by someone known only by the screen name RADmanZulu, who the plaintiffs asserted was "a former Pfizer vice president...who also acted as medical director of Pfizer's Cardiovascular Risk Factors Group." However, the court observed that the post contained neither any information about RADmanZulu's identity nor was the allegation claimed to be based on personal knowledge. In fact, the posting didn't even describe "when, how, on what basis, by whom, or to whom the alleged warning was communicated." Accordingly, the court ruled that the source of the purported statement was not sufficient, and granted a motion to dismiss the case.

To authenticate a web page, you should obtain testimony from the person who obtained the copy of the web page. In addition to having the person who performed the Internet research describe when and how the page was found, the declaration should also sate that the copy accurately reflects what was viewed on the web. The web page itself should be printed out, with the URL listed, and it would be advisable to print any page on the site reflecting the ownership of the site. In the case of a MySpace or Facebook profile, the homepage itself should be sufficient; for other types of website evidence, this can usually be found on the "About Us" page. Be aware that searching domain registries to verify ownership won't necessarily divulge the true owner of the website, since domain registries don't guarantee that real names are used.

In addition, be prepared to offer evidence that the author of the web page actually wrote it. This can consist of an admission by the author, a stipulation entered into by the parties, the testimony of a witness who assisted in or observed the creation of the web page, or content on the web page itself that connects it to the author. You could also use evidence of similarities between the web page at issue and an already authenticated web page as circumstantial evidence of authorship. MySpace and Facebook profiles usually feature photos of the author, background information about him or her (such as hobbies or preferences), as well as commentary by the author. If such circumstantial evidence supports the person identified with the page as being the true author, a reasonable argument exists under Fed. R. Evid. 901(b)(4) that the distinctive characteristics are enough for a jury to find that the purported author is indeed the one responsible for the web page's content.

To make the process of proving authorship as simple and direct as possible, consider asking the witness about his or her online social networking during a deposition. Bring a laptop with Internet access to the deposition, and have the deponent log into his or her space on the web, and have him or her navigate through the site and its features. Other than the difference in media, this is no different from having a deponent produce and go through a written diary.

The most common objections to printouts from a web page are hearsay objections. Typically, however, courts follow the reasoning that such printouts are not "statements" at all, but rather merely images and text found on the websites. *Perfect 10 Inc. v. Cybernet Ventures Inc.*, 213 F. Supp. 2d 1146, 1155 (C.D. Cal. 2002). *Telewizja Polska USA Inc. v. Echostar Satellite*, 2004 WL 2367740 (N.D. Ill., Oct. 15, 2004). In addition, printouts should be admissible pursuant to the best evidence rule, and/or as admissions of a party opponent. Id. In the *Perfect 10* case, the court noted that the pictures and web pages printed off the Internet had sufficient circumstantial indicia of authenticity, such as dates and web addresses, to support a reasonable juror in the belief that the documents were as they purported to be. Id. at 1154; Fed. R. Evid. 901(a).

While statements on websites that were made by a party opponent would be admissible under Fed. R. of Evid. 801(d)(2), be wary of postings made by third parties. Such postings would be considered out-of-court statements, and if offered for the truth of the matter asserted, they are hearsay. Online pictures and video can be authenticated in the same manner as any other picture or video—through witness testimony that it is a fair and accurate representation of an event. However, beware of the "Photoshopping" allegation if a photo looks enhanced. Also, in light of the fact that MySpace and Facebook profiles can be created by third parties, be careful to elicit testimony or introduce other evidence of authorship. For example, there are a number of reported cases of "cyber-bullying" where individuals have maintained that a fake social networking site profile was created to make fun of, harass, or humiliate a person. This is becoming more prevalent in the case of Internet-savvy students creating fake MySpace profiles of teachers or school administrators. See, for example, *A.B. v. State*, 863 N.E.2d 1212 (Ind. Ct. App. 2007), and *Lasyschock v. Hermitage School District*, 412 F.Supp.2d 502 (W.D. Pa. 2006).

Those seeking a useful primer on the admissibility of online information (including social networking sites) should familiarize themselves with *Lorraine v. Markel American Insurance Company*, 241 F.R.D. 534 (D. Md. 2007). Although this case revolved around the enforcement of an arbitration award and didn't deal specifically with social networking sites, it contains a very useful discussion of the admissibility of electronically stored information, which the court notes came in "multiple evidentiary 'flavors' including email, website ESI, Internet postings, digital photographs, and computer-generated documents and data files." Id. at 538. The opinion not only analyzes authentication issues and hearsay concerns, but also examines particular types of digital evidence, including e-mail, website postings, test messages, and chat room content.

Other States and Admission of Social Networking Evidence

Sometimes, in criminal cases, a defendant's own statements make it easy for the prosecution. Consider, for example, bank robber Joseph Northington of Roanoke, Virginia. After robbing a bank in North Augusta, South Carolina, Northington rather helpfully changed his status update to read "Wanted" and posted the statement "On the run for robbin a bank. Love all of y'all." His online confession was used against him.

The following is a sampling of the kind of cases and uses for social networking evidence.

In *People v. Liceaga*, a 2009 Michigan murder case, the prosecutor sought to admit photos from the defendant's MySpace page (which showed the defendant holding the gun allegedly used in the crime, and in which he was displaying a gang sign) as evidence of intent and planning. Michigan Rule of Evidence 404(b)(1) allows evidence for the limited purpose of proving intent and showing a characteristic plan or scheme in committing the offense. The appellate court upheld the admission, finding that its probative value exceeded any danger of unfair prejudice. 2009 Mich. App. LEXIS 160 (Mich. Ct. App. January 27, 2009).

In the North Carolina case of *In the Matter of K.W.*, the trial court admitted into evidence an alleged child abuse victim's MySpace page as impeachment evidence. The court held that the victim's positing of suggestive photographs along with provocative language could be used to impeach inconsistent statements made to the police about her sexual history.

Similarly, in *Ohio v. Gaskins*, a statutory rape case, the trial court permitted the defendant to introduce evidence that the victim had listed herself on her MySpace page as an eighteen-year-old. Photos of the girl that she had posted were admitted, along with witness testimony about their authenticity. *State of Ohio v Gaskins*, 2007 WL 2296454 (Ohio Ct. App. 2007).

In October 2007, the Indiana Supreme Court upheld the use of statements made by a murder defendant on his MySpace page. Ian Clark was convicted of beating his girlfriend's two-year-old daughter to death in 2007. He argued that the prosecutor shouldn't have been allowed to introduce the social networking evidence. Clark had taken the stand himself and testified about his character as a reckless drunk in an attempt to show that reckless homicide, a lesser charge, would be more appropriate. But according to the Indiana Supreme Court, this opened the door for the prosecution "to confront Clark with his own seemingly prideful declarations that rebutted his defense," noting that "Clark's MySpace declarations shared much with his boast to the police after he killed Samantha: 'It's only a C Felony. I can beat this.'"

Social networking content has also been held to be admissible evidence of Social Security fraud. When the defendant claimed that he was not operating a business out of his home, federal agents refuted his claim with printouts of his MySpace profile, showing the defendant operating a tattoo parlor from his house. *United States v. Morales*, 2009 U.S. Dist. LEXIS 122110 (S.D. Ga. Dec. 17, 2009).

Courts are taking note not just of the admissibility of social networking evidence, but the very nature of it that renders it valuable. In considering a case involving the taunting and cyber-bullying of a private school student, one court observed that "Facebook usage depicts a snapshot of the user's relationships and state of mind at the time of the content's posting. Therefore, relevance of the content of the plaintiff's Facebook usage as to both liability and damages in this case is more in the eye of the beholder than subject to strict legal demarcations." *Bass ex rel Bass v. Miss Porter's School*, 2009 WL 3724968 (Conn. App. Ct. 2009).

How closely are courts paying attention to social media evidence? Consider the recently issued "Findings of Fact and Conclusions of Law" in *Sedie v. United States*, No. C-08-04417, 2010 WL 1644252 (N.D. Cal. April 21, 2010). In this bench trial of a 2006 car accident brought under the Federal Tort Claims Act, U.S. Magistrate Judge Elizabeth LaPorte found for the plaintiff, but noted how social media evidence undermined the extent of the plaintiff's damages claims:

> For example, plaintiff's online writings show that his hip was not constantly "hell on earth" as he claimed. Plaintiff maintained his pages on MySpace and Facebook since the accident, and as of January 12, 2010, his MySpace page listed various activities and hobbies, and friends of plaintiff. Plaintiff wrote entries on his MySpace page, including one on June 3, 2007, in which he described painting as a frustrating activity when his arm hairs would get caught in paint. Yet painting was on the list of activities that plaintiff claims were adversely affected by the accident. Plaintiff also testified that he had not done any painting since the accident, but the MySpace entry was written in the present tense at a time just prior to his microdiscectomy. Plaintiff testified that the MySpace entry was a joke, but the court did not find the testimony credible. (citations omitted)

However, some judges view social media evidence in certain contexts with a more jaundiced eye. Unlike the courts in *Liceanaga* and *Munoz*, the Eleventh Circuit recently disapproved of the admission of certain MySpace evidence at trial, although the appellate court ruled it constituted harmless and allowed the conviction to stand. *U.S. v. Phaknikone*, 605 F.3d 1099 (11th Cir. 2010). Souksakhone Phaknikone (who called himself "Trigga Fully Loaded" on his MySpace page) was convicted in federal court in Georgia of fifteen armed robberies and sentenced to 167 years in prison. Over objection, the trial court allowed prosecutors to admit Phaknikone's MySpace profile (listing his name as "Trigga") as well as various photographs from the defendant's MySpace page depicting him brandishing a gun and bearing gang tattoos. The court had problems with the prosecution's earlier efforts to admit this evidence to show that the defendant "behaves like a gangster" and robbed the banks "gangster style," but ultimately allowed the evidence with a limiting instruction that it could be considered to prove only intent or absence of mistake or accident. The Eleventh Circuit disagreed, holding that the photographs were inadmissible character evidence offered for no purpose other than "to show action in conformity therewith," under Fed. R. Evid. 404(b).

Discoverability Issues

Certain recent decisions have raised interesting questions about the discoverability of social media evidence. In *Moreno v. Hartford Sentinel Inc.*, a MySpace user who posted an article on the social networking site later claimed invasion of privacy when a newspaper subsequently published it. 91 Cal. Rptr. 3d 858 (Cal. Ct. App. 2009). The appellate court observed that the facts contained in the article, once posted on MySpace, were not private at all. In contrast, a court in Puerto Rico considering First Amendment implications in an alleged witness tampering case (where the defendant sent a Facebook message to the prosecution's witness in a related case) noted that messages sent to a user's Facebook inbox were not publicly viewable. Therefore, they were not considered to be in the public domain where First Amendment rights might attach. *Maldonado v. Municipality of Barceloneta*, No. 07-1992 (JAG) (JA), 2009 WL 636016 (D.P.R. March 11, 2009).

Courts have not been shy about rejecting a party's claim of privacy as it pertains to a social networking site. Besides the *EEOC v. Simply Storage Management* case and the *Romano v. Steelcase* case discussed elsewhere in this book, multiple courts have addressed this issue. The Sixth Circuit, for example, held that users of social networking sites "logically lack a legitimate expectation of privacy in the materials intend3ed for publication or public posting." *Guest v. Leis*, 255 F.3d 325, 332 (6th Cir. 2001). The Maryland Supreme Court observed that "The act of posting information on a social networking site, without the poster limiting access to that information, makes whatever is posted available to the world at large." *Independent Newspapers Inc. v. Brodie*, 966 A. 2d 432 (Md. 2009). And in 2009, a Minnesota appellate court held that information that was posted on social networking sites was deemed to be public information. Yath *v. Fairview Clinics*, 767 N.W. 2d 34, 43-44 (Minn. Ct. App. 2009).

In fact, one court has even directed a personal injury plaintiff to turn over not just the content of his profile, but the passwords themselves to his MySpace and Facebook pages. In *McMillen v. Hummingbird Speedway, Inc., et al.*, the plaintiff was rear-ended while taking a "cool down lap" after a stockcar race at the defendant's track. Case No. 113-2010 CD (Pa. Ct. of Common Pleas, Sept. 9, 2010). After the injury and ensuing lawsuit, the plaintiff posted material about engaging in such pastimes as fishing and attending the Daytona 500 race. Instead of relying on the plaintiff to turn over the relevant content of his social networking accounts, the defense counsel sought the login names and passwords for each of the claimant's accounts. The judge rejected plaintiff's claims of a "social networking privilege," holding that "Confidentiality is not essential to maintain the relationships between and among social network users, either. The relationships to be fostered through those media are basic friendships, not attorney-client, physician-patient, or psychologist-patient types of relationships, and while one may expect that his or her friend will hold certain information in confidence, the maintenance of one's friendships typically does not depend on confidentiality."

Meanwhile, other courts have considered the discoverability of private social networking messages. In *Barnes,* the plaintiff was a patron of the well-known establishment who was—in typical Coyote Ugly fashion—encouraged to climb onto the bar and dance. *Barnes v. CUS Nashville LLC d/b/a Coyote Ugly Saloon,* No. 3:09-cv-00764, 2010 WL 2265668 (U.S. D. Ct. – M.D. Tenn., June 3, 2010). The plaintiff slipped and fell, striking the back of her head. The defendant subpoenaed Facebook for the plaintiff's Facebook information, including photos of Ms. Barnes and her friends dancing on the bar. The court quashed the subpoena; the defendant issued subpoenas to the plaintiff's friends. The magistrate judge found that these subpoenas (issued out of Colorado and Kentucky, where the witness lived) couldn't be enforced by the district court in Nashville. Magistrate Judge Brown crafted a novel solution to the discovery dilemma. He offered to create his own Facebook account "for the sole purpose of reviewing photographs and related comments in camera…and disseminat[ing] any relevant information to the parties." The court would then close the Facebook account.

In *Crispin v. Audigier,* 2010 WL 2293238 (C.D.Cal., May 26, 2010), the subpoena of someone's Facebook page in a civil lawsuit (this time a copyright infringement case) was also at issue, but for the first time a court considered the implications of the federal Stored Communications Act. Audigier, a garment manufacturer sued over alleged use of Crispin's copyrighted work, subpoenaed third-party businesses—including Facebook and MySpace—seeking communications referencing Audigier between Crispin and a tattoo artist. Crispin moved to quash the subpoenas. The magistrate denied the motion, stating that the Stored Communications Act didn't apply. The district judge largely reversed that ruling, finding that since there were actual messages and wall posts involved on Facebook and MySpace, the Stored Communications Act would apply since the social networking sites could properly be considered providers of electronic communications services. The court also found that since "a Facebook wall positing or a MySpace comment is not protectable as a form of temporary, intimidate storage," the social media sites would also fall under the Stored Communications Act under that standard as well. In short, the court quashed those portions of the subpoenas that sought "private messaging," and remanded for an evidentiary hearing on the allegedly private nature of the wall postings and comments.

Texas Rules and Texas Case Law

Getting social networking evidence is often fairly simple, especially when a party or witness hasn't restricted access to his or her social networking page through use of privacy controls. Even if he or she has, however, there are other ways of obtaining such information, including written discovery requests and asking him or her about the profile in deposition. If you believe that such evidence may have been removed or altered, consider making a request to inspect his or her computer. A party may request access to an opposing party's hard drive or other electronic storage device. *In re Honza*, 242 S.W.3d 578, 581-82 (Tex. App. 2008, orig. proceeding). Such access will normally be granted if that party' conduct suggests that it may be withholding, concealing, or destroying discoverable electronic information. *In re Weekley Homes*, 295 S.W.3d 309 (Tex. 2009). You may also subpoena a Facebook account's records directly from Facebook itself. While they have generally been cooperative in the past with criminal subpoenas, Facebook is likely to resist on privacy grounds without a subpoena.

Authenticating social networking evidence is the main hurdle. Texas Rule of Evidence 1001 includes electronic communications in its definition of "writings and recordings." Evidence needs to be relevant, authentic, and not subject to exclusion under hearsay or best evidence rules.

Proving that pictures can indeed be worth a thousand words, Texas courts have been increasingly open to admitting evidence—particularly photographic evidence—from social networking sites. For example, in *Munoz v. State*, the defendant appealed his conviction of aggravated assault and engaging in deadly conduct, arguing that the evidence was insufficient to show he was a member of a gang. The court affirmed the conviction, pointing to the proper admission of photos of Munoz posted on his own MySpace page, which depicted him throwing gang signs, wearing gang colors, and associating with known gang members. *Munoz v. State*, 2009 WL 695462 (Tex. App. 2009, no pet. h.)

In *Hall v. State*, the prosecutor introduced statements from Hall's Facebook page in convicting her of taking part in a murder. One such incriminating statement was "I should really be more of a horrific person. Its [sic] in the works." The court of appeals affirmed admission of such statements, as well as her screen name, her favorite quote, and a list of her favorite films (all of which were notable for their violence), as proper evidence of motive. *Hall v. State*, 283 S.W.3d 137 (Tex. App. 2009, pet. denied).

A frequent issue is the "How do you know I posted that?" question. After all, handwriting experts are useless for electronic statements. Some courts have required as little as what a victim reportedly read on a defendant's MySpace page—without any personal knowledge that the defendant himself or herself had typed that admission. See, for example, *In re J.W.*, 2009 WL 5155784 at 1-4 (Tex. App. Dec. 30, 2009). Others require additional testimony from third parties as authentication. In *Mann v. Dept. of Family and Protective Services*, the appellate court upheld the trial court's admission of several photos and their captions from the appellant mother's MySpace page as proof of her underage drinking in violation of a court order to refrain from such activity for the welfare of the child. 2009 WL 2961396 (Tex. App. September 17, 2009.)

Is a "Tweet" or a "Poke" a Statement or Communication At All?

Courts have recognized that communications made via social networking sites are statements, no less than a written letter.

In October 2009, Shannon Jackson was charged with violating a Summer County (Tennessee) General Sessions Court protective order to refrain from "telephoning, contacting, or otherwise communicating" with the petitioner when she "poked" the woman on Facebook (a "poke" is a quick message sent by one Facebook user to another). In July 2009, a Providence, Rhode Island, judge imposed a gag order ordering Michelle Langlois not to post comments about a bitter child custody case involving her brother and his ex-wife (the complaint that prompted the order was later dismissed after the American Civil Liberties Union contested it on free speech grounds).

And in a case of first impression, a Staten Island (New York) family court judge ruled that a MySpace "friend request" can constitute a violation of a temporary order of protection. Judge Matthew Sciarrino Jr. noted, "While it is true that the person who received the 'friend request' could simply deny the request to become 'friends,' that request was still a contact," and that using MySpace as a "conduit for communication" was prohibited by the court's mandate that the "Respondent shall have 'no contact' with Sandra Delgrosso." *People v. Fernino*, 851 N.Y.S. 2d 339 (N.Y. Crim. Ct. 2008).

Contrast this with the *Bonner* case from Illinois. In May 2009, Amanda Bonner was a tenant of Horizon Realty Group's apartments in Chicago. Bonner tweeted "Who said sleeping in a moldy apartment was bad for you? Horizon realty thinks it's ok." The tweet went to her (then) twenty followers. In July, Horizon Realty sued Bonner for libel, arguing that the allegedly defamatory statement hurt its reputation as a landlord. A motion to dismiss was filed in November, arguing that the statement was made in a context in which the average reader would understand that it was merely opinion and not an objectively verifiable fact. Furthermore, Bonner's attorneys argued that it was rhetorical hyperbole and akin to the findings of a 2009 study that concluded 40 percent of tweets are "pointless babble."

Horizon Realty, on the other hand, argued that Twitter is a "legitimate medium used by reporters to report up-to-the-minute updates on legal actions, by rabbis, by people to support specific causes or engage in a certain activity, and as a marketing tool." Ultimately, the court ruled on the side of babble, and granted Bonner's motion to dismiss on January 20, 2010.

11

Digging in the Digital Dirt: Some Practical Pointers on Discovery

It's been said that a new legal trend or development hasn't truly hit the big time until you've seen it worked into the plot of a hit television legal drama like *Law & Order*. Well, the use of social networking evidence in litigation has already been enshrined in popular culture, thanks to the CBS legal drama *The Good Wife*. During one first-season episode, the intrepid lawyers at the fictional firm Stern Lockhart & Gardner were zealously representing a client in need of an emergency medical procedure against the health insurance company that was denying coverage for the operation since it was an "experimental" surgery. The insurance company's lawyer confronted the patient's husband on cross-examination about whether he'd lied on the health insurance application. Of course not, he replied. She them impeached him with his signed application, where he indicated that he was a non-smoker, contrasted with photos from his social networking profile showing him smoking with his buddies on a camping trip. Bam! Coverage gone, with the speed of a search engine.

You Snooze, You Lose

If you're eager to find that "smoking gun" piece of evidence amidst the social networking profile of your adverse party or witness, be prepared to invest a little time, and be ready to act quickly. When you find a site or link with potentially helpful information, be sure to download and print off the web page, screen shots—anything you intend to use. At any time, the person with the page could take it down, delete comments posted, remove photos, or set the formerly public profile to "private."

Take the Path of Least Resistance First

Ideally, your subject will have his or her profile and its contents publically available, with few if any privacy restrictions. Get as much information as you can from such informal discovery, but be sure to document how and when it was obtained (and by whom) so it can be authenticated later.

Don't Simply Focus on the Obvious

Everyone thinks of social networking evidence as incriminating photos, statements, or wall postings. Be sure not to overlook less obvious pieces of information—status updates, mood indicators, and the like have all been used to great effect in cases. If you're disappointed in the lack of photos or statements, explore your subject's friends and other potential links. Perhaps he or she wrote on someone else's wall, or perhaps he or she is in a useful photo that someone else "tagged" on their site, or the site of a group to which he or she belongs.

Be Creative

Assuming you are unsuccessful in your initial efforts to discover a subject's social networking profile informally, expand your efforts with a search using Google or other search engines for that person. You might uncover other useful information (I've found articles that experts didn't list on their bios and wished they'd forgotten) or leads that will take you in other directions. If you have a subject's e-mail address, try using a site like www.spokeo.com to reveal other digital trails they've left on the Internet. And never underestimate how many people will respond automatically to a friend request; just be sure you do not misrepresent who you are (see the chapter on "Social Media and Legal Ethics"). Also, don't limit yourself to just Facebook, MySpace, and Twitter. Check out other sharing sites, such as the www.caringbridge.org site discussed in the chapter on personal injury law.

Be Specific

Assuming you haven't found what you're looking for informally, you now have to send formal discovery requests like interrogatories or requests for production (if you're really being stonewalled, you can seek to compel a forensic inspection of the adverse party's hard drive). But rather than sending a global request for "all contents of any and all social media profiles of Jane Doe," try to be more specific. Judges are more likely to overrule the other side's objections if you can demonstrate how narrowly tailored they are to address the claims or defenses in the case. For some useful discussion of casting too wide a net in discovery, read the opinion in the *Mackelprang* case discussed in the employment law chapter. In that sexual harassment case, the court wasn't inclined to give the defense access to any and all messages referencing the plaintiff's sex life, but it was willing to give it those that were relevant to the case.

I ask for "all online profiles, postings, messages (including, but not limited to, tweets, replies, re-tweets, direct messages, status updates, wall comments, groups joined, activity streams, and blog entries), photographs, videos, and online communications" that refer or relate to the adverse party; refer or relate to the allegations or claims asserted in the plaintiff's petition/complaint; refer or relate to any of the defenses asserted in the defendant's answer; or refer or relate to [insert names of specific witnesses]." When there are allegations of mental anguish or emotional distress, I seek online information that would "reveal, refer, or relate to any emotion, mental state, or feeling," or which would "reveal, refer, or relate to events that could reasonably be expected to produce a significant emotion, mental state, or feeling." If the facts of the case enable you to use more specific date/time restrictions, by all means do so.

Get Consent

If you're not sure that the information you're seeking is going to be produced, or produced in its entirety, by the adverse party, you can try to obtain it directly from a site like Facebook using their consent. This is much like obtaining a medical records authorization or employment records authorization from a personal injury plaintiff (along with a list of their healthcare providers and previous employers), as opposed to a request directed to the plaintiff for "all records or medical treatment from 2005 to the present." The Stored Communications Act, 18 U.S.C. § 2703(b)(3) (West 2009) allows a holder of electronic communications like Facebook to provide the user or subscriber's records with "the lawful consent of the originator or an addressee or intended recipient of such communication, or the subscriber in the case of remote computing service."

What should be in the consent? I'd recommend the full name of the account holder or user (be careful to include the account holder, especially where a non-party spouse may actually have the account in his or her name). You should also include a "user ID," "group ID," or screen name if known, along with the person's date of birth and address. If you have an e-mail address, especially if you're seeking e-mail, include that. In addition, be sure to include a detailed description of what you're seeking; simply asking for "all online content" is likely to be viewed as overly broad or vague. Finally, get the notarized signature of the person giving consent. If there is more than one person involved, or a different account holder, get all the signatures needed—the more the merrier.

If the plaintiff/user or account holder refuses to sign your consent, file a motion to compel and seek a court order. As many of the decisions cited in multiple chapters demonstrate, "private" isn't so private anymore when you communicate it to one or more friends on a social networking site (even with privacy settings), and especially not when you decide to file a lawsuit. There is case authority to indicate that a party may be compelled to sign this consent. See, for example, *Flagg v. City of Detroit*, 2008 WL 787061 (E.D. Mich. 2008) (where a party was compelled to produce text messages within its control, including those held by an Internet service provider); *O'Grady v. Superior Court*, 44 Cal. Rptr. 3d 72 (Cal. App. Ct. 2006).

The site, after receiving consent, will turn the records over to the account holder or the attorney, from whom you can have the documents produced.

Subpoenas: The Last Resort

If all else fails, you can try to subpoena records of social media content directly from a site like Facebook. However, be forewarned that you're in for a fight. The state of Virginia found that out. Facebook's general counsel, Mark Howitson, has even been quoted as saying, "We're itching for that fight. We don't want to have to deal with these requests" (referring to clarifying Facebook's legal responsibilities with respect to protecting a user's privacy).

According to Facebook itself, "If you are or represent a party to a civil case and believe basic subscriber information is indispensable and is not within the possession of a party, you must personally serve a valid California or federal subpoena on Facebook. Out-of-state civil subpoenas must be domesticated in California." Caveat: "basic subscriber information" may not equal "content." Be prepared for disappointment. The subpoena should be served on:

> Custodian of Records
> Facebook Inc.
> c/o Corporation Services Company
> 2730 Gateway Oaks Drive, Suite 100
> Sacramento, California 95833

In addition, get out your checkbook. "Facebook charges a mandatory, non-refundable processing fee of $500 per user account." And if you want a notarized declaration from the records custodian, tack on another $100.

It's not surprising, then, that Facebook tries to warn you about potential futility:

> Facebook urges parties to civil litigation to resolve their discovery issues without involving Facebook. Almost without exception, the information sought by parties to civil litigation is the possession of, and readily accessible to, a party to the litigation. Requests for account information are therefore better obtained through party discovery.

> Federal law and Facebook policies prohibit the disclosure of user information. Specifically, the Stored Communications Act, 18 U.S.C. § 2701 et seq., prohibits Facebook from disclosing the contents of a user's Facebook account to any non-governmental entity even pursuant to a valid subpoena or court order. The most Facebook can provide is the basic subscriber information for a particular account.

> If a Facebook user deletes content from their account, Facebook will not be able to provide that content. Effectively, Facebook and the applicable Facebook user have access to the same content. To the extent a user claims it does not have access to content (e.g., the user terminated their account), Facebook will restore access to allow that user to collect and produce the information to the extent possible.

MySpace requires personal service of subpoenas on its registered agent at: 2121 Avenue of the Stars, Suite 700, Los Angeles, California 90067. MySpace, like Facebook, will only accept subpoenas from out-of-state civil litigants that have been domesticated by a California court. MySpace also requires more information to go on—information you may not have—including the "user's unique friend ID number or URL," "the password associated with the account," the user's zip code, and "the birth date provided to MySpace" (and we know no one *ever* lies about their age online).

Google, by the way, takes the position (likely untenable from a procedural standpoint) that it will only accept subpoenas issued from the Santa Clara Superior Court. To subpoena Google, it must be served on the Google records custodian, 1600 Amphitheater Parkway, Mountain View, California 94043.

After a few experiences attempting to get information from these providers, you may understand why a satisfied smile crept across my face watching the scenes of California crumbling into the sea during the apocalyptic movie "2012."

In conclusion, you can find a wealth of social media evidence. Some is easier to locate and acquire than others. But generally, you should be able to obtain information that a party has made public through a social network, such as writing on his or her wall or someone's else, information a party has not made available to the general public through use of privacy settings (but that may be discoverable anyway), and private messages passed between users of social networks, where a site like Facebook is merely a conduit (while not likely to be obtained via subpoena thanks to the Stored Communications Act, these may be discoverable anyway from a party whose production can be compelled by a court). Happy digging!

12

Facebook, Eh?
Social Networking and Canadian Law

American lawyers may wonder, "Why is he devoting a chapter of this book to discussing social media's treatment under Canadian law?" The simple truth is that our professional counterparts in the Great White North have been at the forefront of dealing with social media issues in their legal system. In a relatively short time, a growing body of law has emerged in Canada, particularly with regard to the discovery and admissibility of social networking evidence. In fact, one recent U.S. federal court decision permitting broad discovery of a litigant's social networking sites relied heavily on Canadian legal authority in reasoning that a plaintiff's privacy concerns were trumped by the fact that such information had been shared online for all to see. *EEOC v. Simply Storage Mgmt. LLC*, No. 09-1223 (S.D. Ind. May 11, 2010),

One of the most recent cases is also the one that has received the most media notoriety. Natalie Blanchard of Bromont, Quebec, was a twenty-nine-year-old IBM employee in the fall of 2009. For well over a year, she had been on sick leave for severe depression, and had been receiving monthly benefits from IBM's insurance carrier, Manulife. But then the payments stopped. When Blanchard phoned Manulife to find out why, an insurance representative told her that she wasn't sick—at least, not according to her pictures on Facebook. It seems the company had "reevaluated" her after viewing her Facebook profile, on which Blanchard looked anything but depressed—frolicking on the beach, enjoying a birthday party, mountain climbing, and attending a Chippendales show surrounded by male strippers.

For her part, Blanchard claims she only went on several short trips, after consulting with her psychiatrist, as a way to temporarily forget her problems. She denies that her depression is cured. Manulife's spokesman maintains that the company "would not deny or terminate a valid claim solely based on information published on Web sites such as Facebook." Unable to pay her monthly bills or mortgage without her benefits, Blanchard and her lawyer, Thomas Lavin, filed suit against Manulife and IBM. Lavin insists that his client was never even notified about the termination of benefits—they simply stopped coming. Of bringing a lawsuit because of the carrier's reliance on social media evidence, Lavin says, "Because there are no precedents, it's a free-for-all right now, and probably there are no rules or boundaries."

In fact, social media evidence is becoming increasingly significant as an investigative tool in cases involving disability and workers compensation payments. In Canada in April 2009, the British Columbia Supreme Court ruled that defense attorneys were entitled to examine the computer hard drive of a claimant seeking disability payments. Brendon Bishop claimed that, following a July 2005 car accident, he was too fatigued to work, and so he sued the provincial insurance agency as well as the other driver for permanent disability payments. Over fierce opposition, the court held that the defense could analyze his online activities to find out how much time Bishop was spending on social media networking sites like Facebook. Supreme Court Judge Thomas Melnick ruled that the computer information in question "may have significant probative value in relation to the plaintiff's past and future wage loss," and that privacy concerns are not an issue "because the order sought is so narrow that it does not have the potential to unnecessarily delve into private aspects of the plaintiff's life." *Bishop v. Minichiello*, B.C.J. No. 692 (S.C.J.) (2009).

Here in the United States, disability and workers compensation carriers have found that social networking sites are a rich source of information that can expose insurance cheats. "It's the new video camera," says Pierre Khoury of Pennsylvania-based insurer Harleysville Group Inc. More cost-effective than traditional surveillance, insurance investigators have found a mother lode of incriminating information online. For example, claimants who post the dates, results, and sometimes even video of athletic events in which they're competing frequently find that the joy of that perfect bowling game or softball win is short-lived once the workers compensation carrier finds out. One claimant was confronted with a video of him riding a bucking bronco at a rodeo, at a time when he supposedly couldn't get out of bed. One carrier was tipped off to a fraudulent workers compensation claim when it saw Facebook postings promoting the "injured" worker's new business selling jerky at flea markets.

Not all social media is easily obtained, however. A Virginia employer and the state's Worker's Compensation Commission tried to subpoena "all documents, electronic or otherwise, related directly or indirectly, to all activities, writings, photos, comments, e-mails, and/or postings" related to an employee's Facebook postings about a recent vacation. The employer felt the evidence would show that its employee was not as injured as she claimed. When Facebook refused, the commonwealth of Virginia threatened fines of $200 a day. But when Facebook invoked the Electronic Communications Privacy Act, Virginia backed down.

Getting back to Canadian law, courts north of our border have shown little hesitation to permit discovery into a party's social networking activities, and have been quick to consider such online evidence as potentially devastating to a litigant's personal injury claim. In April 2009, Dennis Terry of Newfoundland recovered only $40,000—far short of the over $1.3 million he was seeking—thanks to Facebook evidence. Terry claimed whiplash from two accidents in 2001 and 2003, but the shakiest part of his claims had to do with the accidents' impact on his enjoyment of life. Terry maintained that after the injuries, his social life became nonexistent when friends stopped calling him because he had turned down repeated invitations; in fact, he testified, he couldn't engage in one of his favorite pastimes, playing pool, because he was unable to bend over the table to make shots.

But the defense attorneys confronted Terry with evidence from his Facebook page, including photos of him shooting pool. Supreme Court Justice James Adams was not amused at Terry's exaggeration of his injuries. Judge Adams noted that the plaintiff "went to and hosted parties, attended weekend outings at summer cabins, drank alcohol frequently, smoked marijuana daily, and appeared to have a number of friends with whom he communicated and socialized on a regular basis. I find it incredible that Mr.

Terry's social life miraculously improved in the few months he was communicating on Facebook and that for the remainder of the time from 2001 to 2007 he essentially had no or little social life. Without this evidence, I would have been left with a very different impression of Mr. Terry's social life."

Similarly, in *Bagasbas v. Atwal* in April 2009, a plaintiff seeking $40,000 for soft tissue injuries sustained in a 2006 car accident in British Columbia got a rude awakening. Justice Satanove of the British Columbia Supreme Court awarded only $3,500 in pain and suffering. While the plaintiff had testified that she could no longer kayak, hike, or bicycle, defense attorneys produced photos from her Facebook page, showing her engaged in all of these activities and more. In particular, the court noted that the "photographs of the plaintiff dancing illustrate arm, neck, and back movements, executed in approximately two-inch heels, that contradict any claims of restricted range of motion or significant pain in these areas."

In *Kourtesis v. Joris*, the plaintiff claimed that following a car accident, she was unable to engage in one of her favorite activities, Greek dancing. On cross-examination, she was impeached with photos from her Facebook page depicting her dancing. While the court acknowledged that such photos could be taken out of context, it nevertheless regarded them as "highly relevant" to the issues of damages. The judge also discarded the plaintiff's objections based on surprise and prejudice, pointing out the claimant's awareness of the photos' existence, since she had posted them on her own Facebook page.

Other Canadian cases have attempted to set boundaries on the discoverability of social networking evidence, as opposed to its admissibility for impeachment purposes. In the 2007 Ontario case of *Weber v. Dyck*, for example, the parties in a car accident case were at a fairly late stage (post-discovery cut-off, pre-trial) in the proceedings when the defense sought leave to take additional discovery from the plaintiff. The reason, they said, was that they had recently discovered photos on the plaintiff's MySpace page showing her on trips, playing piano, and graduating from college and relocating. This change in the claimant's career and employment status, the defense attorneys argued, entitled them to conduct further discovery. Furthermore, they wanted "all photographs and video recordings from trips." While the court was amenable to ordering production of employment-related documents that showed the change in the plaintiff's circumstances since they would be relevant to the question of damages, it declined to compel production of the photos and video. The judge reasoned that the defense could have sought such evidence at an earlier stage (but didn't), and that such photographic evidence was hardly relevant since the plaintiff was not claiming that the injury altered her ability to travel. In another case, *Knight v. Barrett*, the court ordered a party who had obtained Facebook information about its adversary to include it on its list of documents to be used at trial, and to allow cross-examination into how the social networking evidence had been obtained. This, the court reasoned, would allow both parties to be prepared for trial and would prevent the Facebook profile from being used in a trial by ambush.

Much of the developing Canadian jurisprudence on social networking evidence has centered on privacy concerns. For example, in December 2009, a New Brunswick court overruled a plaintiff's privacy arguments and ordered her to turn over her Internet records and specifically to disclose her Facebook activities. Rosemary Carter sued Herbert Connors following a 2004 car accident claiming that since the accident, she hadn't been able to return to her full-time employment as an administrative clerk at Miramichi Hospital—a job that necessarily involved a good deal of computer work. Court of Queen's Bench Justice Fred Ferguson ruled that the information sought was likely to be relevant since it could possibly provide "a window into what physical capacity the plaintiff has to keyboard, access the Internet, and communicate with family, friends, and associates on Facebook and thus what capacity she may have to work." In that sense, Justice Ferguson stated that the request for the Facebook disclosure was reasonably calculated to lead to the discovery of admissible evidence. He went on to note that plaintiffs necessarily have to expect some loss of privacy by virtue of filing suit. Ferguson said, "It must not be forgotten that this legal action was commenced by the Plaintiff and in launching it she thus implicitly accepted certain intrusions into what otherwise might be private information, the disclosure of which would ordinarily be left to her own personal judgment."

The first Canadian case to balance privacy concerns with the party's right to full and open discovery involved not publicly viewable information, but a limited-access Facebook profile. In *Murphy v. Perger*, plaintiff Jill Murphy sued the defendant following a car accident that allegedly left her suffering from a chronic pain disorder. As a result, she sought damages for (among other things) loss of enjoyment of life and an inability to participate in social pastimes. The defense attorney found a publicly viewable Facebook profile called "The Jill Murphy Fan Club," which features post-accident photos of Murphy at a party. That led the attorney to Murphy's restricted-access profile on the social network site; however, due to the privacy settings, he could only view the Plaintiff's name and list of her 366 Facebook friends. He sought production of the restricted Facebook profile, to which Murphy's attorney objected, characterizing it as a "fishing expedition" premised on just the mere possibility of relevant information.

Justice Rady of the Ontario Superior Court of Justice ordered the production of the private Facebook profile, noting that since the plaintiff herself had already put pre-accident photos of herself into evidence, post-accident pictures would also be relevant. He also concluded that where there was a public Facebook profile with relevant information, one could reasonably infer the likely existence of relevant information from a private profile. In addition, Justice Rady swept aside all concerns over privacy. He stated, "Having considered these competing interests, I have concluded that any invasion of privacy is minimal and outweighed by the defendant's need to have the photographs in order to assess the case. The Plaintiff could not have a serious expectation of privacy given that 366 people have been granted access to the private site. *Murphy v. Perger* (2007) O.J. No. 5511 (S.C.J.) (Ontario Superior Court of Justice).

Perhaps the leading Canadian case to examine such privacy concerns took the *Murphy* reasoning a step further, holding that one could infer that relevant information exists on a private Facebook profile, simply because of the existence of the site. In *Leduc v. Roman*, plaintiff John Leduc sued following a February 2004 car accident. Among other causes of action, he claimed that the defendant's negligence had lessened his enjoyment of life and limited his physical activities. Defense counsel didn't argue about Leduc's social networking presence, but it came to light during an examination by a defense expert psychiatrist, in which he idly mentioned having a lot of Facebook friends. The defendant's lawyers then sought production of Leduc's private Facebook profile as well as an order directing Leduc to preserve all Facebook profile information.

Although the trial court rejected the defendant's request on the basis that the mere existence of the plaintiff's Facebook profile was not reason to believe it contained relevant evidence, Justice Brown of the Ontario Superior Court of Justice overruled it. In doing so, Justice Brown stated, "With respect, I do not regard the Defendant's request as a fishing expedition. Mr. Leduc exercised control over a social networking and information site to which he allowed designated 'friends' access. It is reasonable to infer that his social networking site likely contains some content relevant to the issue of how Mr. Leduc has been able to lead his life since the accident…a court can infer, from the nature of the Facebook service, the likely existence of relevant documents on a limited-access Facebook profile."

But Justice Brown went even further, and his holding in *Leduc* actually outlines a new duty for parties and their counsel as far as social media is concerned. The court observed, "Given the pervasive use of Facebook and the large volume of photographs typically posted on Facebook sites, it is now incumbent on a party's counsel to explain to the client, in appropriate cases, that documents posted on the party's Facebook profile may be relevant to allegations made in the pleadings." *Leduc v. Roman*, 2009 Can L II 6838 (ON S.C.).

Later on, however, another Ontario court would disagree with Justice Brown's analysis. *Schuster v. Royal & Sun Alliance Insurance Co. of Canada* was another car accident case in which the plaintiff sued her insurance carrier for her injuries and claimed that the crash had affected her ability to work and socialize. The defense learned that Schuster had a private Facebook profile, viewable only by her sixty-seven friends. It sought an order to prevent her from deleting the content on that profile, based on the rational in *Leduc*. The court, however, disagreed with the automatic presumption of Justice Brown, and denied the defense motion on the basis that there was no proof that the plaintiff's Facebook profile contained relevant evidence.

So what is the status of Canadian law on the discoverability of social networking evidence? While Canadian legal observers may disagree about whether *Leduc* or *Schuster* is the last word on the subject, certain points appear clear. Canadian law goes beyond its American counterpart to not only impose a duty to preserve social networking evidence, but also to obligate counsel and their clients to affirmatively disclose the existence of such information that could be relevant to the issues in a lawsuit. Also, Canadian courts have had little difficulty in allowing impeaching social media evidence to affect a party's recovery. Finally, Canadian courts have cast a similarly jaundiced eye on the relative importance of privacy when it comes to allowing discovery of social media evidence. Like a number of American courts, they remind plaintiffs that they sacrifice a certain amount of privacy when they file a lawsuit, and the courts admonish litigants that the very nature of social media communications renders them discoverable. To paraphrase one judge, individuals don't go on Facebook to have monologues with themselves.

13

Intellectual Property Concerns in the Age of Social Networking

The brave new world that is social media is still being explored by lawyers in all practice areas. One group that cannot afford to ignore social networking sites is the community of intellectual property attorneys, and the companies and individuals they represent. Sheer numbers alone demand that intellectual property specialists pay attention to social networking. Fifteen years ago, the Internet had just a few thousand websites; today there are hundreds of millions of sites, and billions of web pages. Five years ago, Facebook was a small network used by college students, and Twitter didn't even exist. Yet today, the growth of social media means that owners of intellectual property have to police their brands across an ever-widening virtual landscape.

It's not just the intellectual property holders who need to keep up with social media. Those accused of violating intellectual property rights have also discovered the benefits of social media. In 2009, Rock Art, a tiny Vermont brewer of a barley-based wine called "Vermonster," received a cease-and-desist letter from Hansen Beverage, maker of the popular Monster energy drink. Hansen claimed that Vermonster was infringing on its trademark and creating confusion between its alcoholic brew and Hansen's own energy drink. When Vermonster's owner, Matt Nadeau, sought legal advice, attorney after attorney told him he'd probably win, but that the legal costs of slugging it out with a big company like Hansen would make it a Pyrrhic victory. So Nadeau waged a guerrilla campaign online, posting about the threat on Facebook, YouTube, and other social media sites, and garnering considerable media coverage. As word spread, stores across the northeastern United States were pulling the energy drink from their shelves. It was a public relations disaster for Monster's owners, as even one of Vermont's U.S. senators, Bernie Sanders, weighed in on the controversy. Senator Sanders found the notion of consumer confusion ridiculous, saying, "Any person who would get confused by the two different products and names should probably slow down a bit, and lay off energy drinks." He went on to observe that "the American people are getting tired of the greed and recklessness of large corporations, which use their size and power to push individuals and small businesses around." Ultimately, Monster and Vermonster resolved the dispute, with the Vermont brewer continuing to make its drink and agreeing that it would never get into the energy beverage market. Matt Nadeau attributed the "new power of traditional media, combined with social media" for getting Hansen Beverage to stand down.

Intellectual property owners need to be acutely aware of the potential for a backlash when they come across as heavy-handed, especially given the speed with which negative publicity can go viral. But that doesn't mean holders of intellectual property rights should keep their heads in the sand either. Besides being aware of the constantly evolving technologies and platforms on which something trademarked or copyrighted may appear, intellectual property owners and/or their counsel should have a plan for monitoring key sites. Not only is this important from the standpoint of policing possible infringement, but it also gives the owner insight into the degree to which particular sites may be popular with a company's target demographic of consumers.

Intellectual property owners need to begin their monitoring efforts at home, by developing online activities/electronic communications policies for employees. Such policies (discussed in greater detail in the "Social Media in the Workplace" section) should address limits on an employee's discussion of or incorporation of a company's activities and intellectual property on a social networking site or blog. No company wants its trade secrets being divulged by an employee in any form, and no one wants his or her company's trademarks being used in an inappropriate context. Addressing social media use ahead of time can also eliminate confusion over who is authorized to speak on the company's behalf.

Outside of its own employees' use of social media, a company will need to carefully consider the investment in both financial and human capital demanded by monitoring social networking sites. Third parties that use, incorporate, or mention trademarks in product or online service reviews, message board posts, or blogs are likely to be a lower priority, especially if the marks are correctly identified by the owner. A greater concern to intellectual property owners are social media sites that engage in actual trademark infringement, that promote the sale of counterfeit goods or services, that impersonate the actual mark owner or otherwise mislead the public, and that refer to the company or its intellectual property in a disparaging or derogatory way. One key component of any company's efforts to protect its intellectual property online is awareness of a site's trademark use policies (most "terms of use" agreements prohibit a social networking site's users from posting infringing materials), as well as the site's complaint procedures.

Intellectual property owners need to be prepared to take swift action. In 2009, Facebook announced a new policy allowing users to create customized usernames for their profiles, along with personalized URLs. The development was announced mere days before it was scheduled to go into effect. To prevent potential third-party registration that incorporated their trademarks, intellectual property owners had to spring into action. For those companies who were unaware of the new policy or simply unfamiliar with Facebook, it was a situation of "you snooze, you lose."

To illustrate the importance of monitoring social networking sites to protect intellectual property, consider the case of Oklahoma-based natural gas distributor Oneok. In 2009, Oneok filed a trademark infringement lawsuit in Tulsa federal court against Twitter. According to Oneok, Twitter had wrongfully permitted an anonymous user to include the company's logo, as well as certain information about Oneok, on a profile named "Oneok_i." Oneok already had its own authorized Twitter account. Twitter quickly responded by disabling the "Oneok_i" account, and Oneok voluntarily dismissed the lawsuit one day after it was filed. Oneok maintained that it had asked Twitter both to reveal the identity of the holder of the imposter account, as well as to turn over the account to Oneok; however, Twitter did not comply, resulting in the lawsuit. The plaintiff's complaint explained the reasoning behind the filing, noting that "if this situation is allowed to persist, the unknown Oneok Twitter account holder can use the Twitter system to damage Oneok's reputation in the investor community and energy industry."

The Oneok case underscores the opportunity for online imposters to engage in everything from trademark infringement to unfair competition to consumer fraud. Twitter, for example, doesn't require identity authentication to set up an account. After a rash of "celebrity imposter" accounts were set up (including one impersonating professional baseball manager Tony La Russa of the St. Louis Cardinals, who sued upon learning that someone was posting comments posing as him), Twitter instituted a verified account option. Under it, Twitter will contact the person the account purports to represent to ensure the user is not an imposter. Unfortunately, that option was not initially made available for businesses.

Twitter does feature terms of service that provide a mechanism through which individuals or companies can act if their intellectual property rights are threatened. According to the company's policy, "Twitter respects the intellectual property rights of others and expects users of the Services to do the same." Furthermore, accounts exhibiting a "clear intent" to mislead others will be suspended immediately. According to Twitter, this would conceivably apply to accounts using brand names or logos in an attempt to steer visitors toward purchasing counterfeit merchandise. Like most social networking sites, Twitter also provides a procedure for law enforcement personnel seeking information about its users. Twitter also has a protocol for consideration of copyright complaints.

Speaking of copyright law and Twitter, one issue that has been debated by legal analysts is whether "tweets" on Twitter are worthy of copyright protection. Dallas Mavericks owner Mark Cuban pondered this after ESPN republished a tweet of his (without consent) critical of NBA officiating. Twitter's own terms and conditions of use certainly seem to regard what's posted as deserving of copyright protection. The policy advises users, "You retain your rights to any [c]ontent you submit, post, or display...what's yours is yours—your own content."

But are "tweets"—limited to 140 characters or less—too brief to come under copyright protection? Generally, shorter expression faces an uphill battle when it comes to satisfying copyright's requirement of originality. Ordinary phrases, for example, are usually not entitled to copyright protection. See, for example, *Narell v. Freeman*, 872 F.2d 907, 911 (9th Cir. 1989). Slogans and other short phrases might be able to be trademarked, but generally won't be deemed worthy of copyright protection, per 37 C.F.R. § 202.1(a). And according to the Copyright Office's Circular 34, "names, titles, and short phrases or expressions are not subject to copyright protection," even those that are "novel or distinctive." So, even though certain writings known for their brevity can be accorded copyright protection—haikus, for example—in the world of copyright law, size matters. *N.Y. Mercantile Exch. Inc. v. Intercontinental Exchange Inc.*, 389 F.Supp.2d 527 (S.D. N.Y. 2005).

As for the requirement of being an original work of authorship, tweets are often unoriginal; they may just be updates on what a person is doing, a comment about something as mundane as the weather or grocery shopping, or a brief factual statement. While a telephone directory can be copyrighted because of the original way it organizes facts, mere facts themselves are not protected by copyright. *Feist Publications Inc. v. Rural Telephone Service Co.*, 499 U.S. 340 (1991). Viewed by themselves, tweets may be barely indistinguishable from other factual expressions. However, when organized into a compilation of tweets in a manner that is original, that collection of tweets might be worthy of copyright protection. The question is one that may merit additional scrutiny, in light of authors who have discussed the possibility of releasing novels that are collections of tweets (the short, declarative sentences of some authors such as Ernest Hemingway might actually be adaptable to a Twitter format). In fact, the tweets of Garry Trudeau's fictional broadcast journalist Roland Hedley in the comic strip *Doonesbury* have been "collected" into a short, humorous book.

So, what about Mark Cuban's speculation about copyright protection for his tweets? One of the exceptions to copyright infringement provided for under the Copyright Act (outlined at 17 U.S.C. § 107) is fair use. For something to qualify as fair use, courts look at several factors, one of which is the "purpose and character of the use." Since the tweets wound up in a news story as opposed to being used in a commercial, they would likely fall into the fair use category. Courts also examine the nature of the work. At least one court has noted that a significant percentage of Twitter's content is "mindless babble." In light of Twitter's growing community (55 million users and counting) and the social purpose underlying use of the site, one could certainly argue that Twitter users *intend* to disseminate their tweets to the widest audience possible, accumulating as many followers as possible. Yet another factor that courts consider in determining if something was fair use is the effect that use had on the potentially infringed work's value or potential market. For the most part, a single tweet has limited if any market value; the only exception that comes to mind are the testimonial tweets by celebrities like Kim Kardashian and others, some of whom claim to realize as much as $10,000 for a single tweet. The final factor studied by courts in deciding whether a fair use defense applies is the amount and substantiality of the portion used in relation to the copyrighted work as a whole. In a scenario where one tweet is taken from an entire collection, this factor would in all likelihood not mean much.

Copyright and Other Social Media

Written works of original authorship aren't the only forms of expression on social networking sites. Everyday, millions of people upload photos or video on social networking sites like Facebook, YouTube, and Flickr. Under copyright law, such photographs and video could be considered "original works." But what if someone else copies a photo or video and uses it without the owner's permission?

Such was the case with Alison Chang and Justin Ho-Wee Wong. Wong took a photo of Chang (a minor) and uploaded it to Flickr, attaching a Creative Commons Attribution 2.0 license to it. Virgin Mobile wound up using Chang's picture in an Australian advertising campaign, a fact she discovered by accident. Chang and Wong sued Virgin Mobile in federal court in Texas (where Chang resided), alleging misappropriation of Chang's right of publicity and other tort claims. However, the Texas court ruled that it has no personal jurisdiction over the Australian-based Virgin Mobile Pty. Ltd. As a result, the court didn't get to the substantive issues of rights to someone's likeness taken off a social networking site. *Chang v. Virgin Mobile USA LLC*, 2009 WL 111570 (N.D. Tex. Jan. 16, 2009).

Generally, once an original mark of authorship is fixed in a tangible medium (on paper, in electronic form, or even carved in stone), its creator enjoys copyright protection. However, to be able to recover certain remedies and enforce such rights, the mark must be registered by filling the appropriate Copyright Office form. To recover statutory damages for a published work under 17 U.S.C. § 412, it needs to be registered with the Copyright Office before the infringement occurs, or within three months of the work's first publication. Whether "publication" has taken place is another issue courts must tackle.

For creators of original works, like photographers, filmmakers, and other artists, social media can offer entrée to an incredibly wide audience. Moreover, people from all walks of life can share photos and videos with an ever-increasing global audience through social networking sites like YouTube, Facebook, and Twitter. A recent survey by Ruder Finn showed that nearly 38 percent of all cell phone users go online to post photographs or video. But what, if any, copyright protection exists for such photos or videos, which copyright law considers original works?

Most of those who venture online aren't aware of the potential copyright implications of posting their work on the Internet, where it becomes available to all. Although copyright protection exists from the moment a work is created— "fixed" in a tangible medium—legal remedies will depend on whether a work is registered with the Copyright Office (and when), and whether it has been "published." Whether something can be considered published by virtue of appearing online or on a social networking site is a murky area. The Copyright Office itself acknowledges this; in its Circular FL-107, the office states, "The definition of publication in the U.S. copyright law does not specifically address online transmission. The Copyright Office therefore asks applicants, who know the facts surrounding the distribution of their works, to determine whether works are published." Mere public display will not be sufficient to deem a work published. Instead, copies of a work must be distributed (or offered for distribution) to the public by sale or lease.

Why is it significant to be viewed as published? Copyright law permits statutory damages (which are often more than actual damages) and attorneys' fees to be recovered for published works if the work was registered before the alleged infringement or within three months of the first publication. If a work is considered unpublished, such remedies are only available if the work was registered prior to the infringement. In one case, *Getaped.com Inc. v. Cangemi*, a New York federal court held that a web page is considered distributed and published when it goes live on the Internet. Getaped had filed suit against Cangemi for infringement, claiming portions of its scooter business website had been copied. Cangemi responded that merely making a website available to the public wasn't a publication, but rather more like a public display. The trial court disagreed, noting, "merely by accessing a webpage, an Internet user acquires the ability to make a copy of that webpage, a copy that is, in fact, indistinguishable in every part from the original. Consequently, when a website goes live, the creator loses the ability to control either duplication or further distribution of his or her work. A webpage in this respect is indistinguishable from photographs, music files, or software posted on the web—all can be freely copied."

So is a work posted on Facebook protected under copyright law? If access is limited to a select group of people, one might argue that the work is more like a public display, and not being put up for distribution. If the work is viewable by all, who are capable of copying and disseminating it, then that argument won't apply. Also, consider the fact that Facebook's own intellectual property rights policy purports to give Facebook a non-exclusive free worldwide license to use any works a user might post. Applying the view of the *Getaped* court, such a license might be enough to change each instance of posted content from mere public display to publication.

Once again, issues of copyright protection in the age of social media serve as another illustration of how the law has not kept pace with technological innovation. The definition of "publication" may have to be adapted to take social networking into account. Until then, concerns like whether every work posted on a social networking site should be registered, or whether the frequency of posting images on a given site translates to costly registrations, will remain in one of the law's many gray areas. Pending resolution of issues like these, creators of original works should register whatever they consider important or commercially viable, and they should mark what is being posted—indicating the source and whether it can be reproduced without the artist's permission.

14

Disclosure and the Twitter Nation: Social Media and Securities Law

According to an April 27, 2009, *Wall Street Journal* article, eighty-one Fortune 500 companies sponsor public blogs, and twenty-three of these link to corporate Twitter accounts. Twitter, meanwhile, has gone from processing 5,000 tweets a day in 2006 to more than 50 million per day currently. Given the popularity of Twitter for providing information, as well as the limitations inherent in the 140-character restriction on Twitter messages, what ramifications might there be for using social networking sites when it comes to securities laws?

The potential for a serious problem is easily illustrated by the example of one corporate blogger who, during a single earnings call, sent out dozens of tweets to Twitter followers that purport to be direct quotes of executive statements made during that call. None of the tweets were accompanied by any standard securities disclaimers, and for a logical reason: it would take at least a half-dozen tweets (many of which include hyperlinks to additional cautionary statements) to issue such disclaimers.

The Securities and Exchange Commission tried to address the implications that Web 2.0 would have for disclosure laws when it launched the Twenty-First Century Disclosure Initiative in 2008. This initiative hoped to address disclosure in light of updated technology and the new ways shareholders receive stock information. Part of the initiative deals with compliance with public disclosure requirements, and the circumstances under which information posted on a corporate website is considered "public." The initiative also examines the liability for information presented by a corporation online. Under existing federal securities laws, companies are liable for statements made online in the same way they are responsible for statements made in any other medium on a company's behalf. Because of this, and because of the potential for a single employee to blog, tweet, or post on Facebook information that could be considered a "forward-looking statement," publicly traded companies need to actively identify, classify, and control all forms of communication with shareholders and investors.

The rules regarding formal corporate disclosures have been updated, just as there has been a significant rise in using social media—Twitter, Facebook, LinkedIn, corporate blogs, personal blogs, etc.—to communicate about everything from question-and-answer sessions with investors to inside looks at company events. Whether these communications are formally part of a company's corporate communications or investor-relations practice is irrelevant, especially when that tweet or post can be perceived by the public and investors as having been made on behalf of the company itself. Because of this, companies using social networking tools to deliver complex financial information should make sure to have two things: an electronic communications policy for employees that makes it clear what the restrictions are for posting corporate information online, and a good understanding of the Securities and Exchange Commission's website guidance and the resulting compliance policies and standards that must be in place.

Social networking may have provided companies with new opportunities for exchanging information, but it has also opened the door to new risks involving both formal and informal disclosure of potentially sensitive information. Social networking issues are cropping up in other aspects of securities law as well. For example, in one 2009 case, a corporation attempted to use social networking evidence to support its claim that certain shareholders were trying to gain control of the company by making materially false statements in proxy materials. *Quigley Corp. v. Karkus, et al.*, 2009 WL 1383280 (E.D. Pa. May 15, 2009). Plaintiff Quigley Corp. alleged that some of these shareholders maintained extensive personal and professional connections, such that the court should find that they were acting in agreement to solicit proxies and note shares. If the group was seen has having acquired a sufficient degree of "beneficial ownership," it would trigger statutory disclosure requirements under Section 13(d) of the

Exchange Act. However, the court rejected the plaintiff's arguments, assigning "no significance" to the fact that certain numbers of the purported group were Facebook "friends." As the court noted, "electronically connected 'friends' are not among the litany of relationships targeted by the Exchange Act on the regulations issued pursuant to the statute. Indeed, 'friendships' on Facebook may be as fleeting as the flick of a delete button."

The financial industry, perhaps out of necessity, has been at the forefront of businesses adapting to the social media tidal wave. As far back as 1999, the Financial Industry Regulatory Authority (FINRA) was providing guidance to securities brokers, dealers, and other professionals in the application of communication rules to interactive websites. In March 1999, for example, the FINRA stated that a registered representative's participation in an Internet chat room would be subject to the same requirements as if he or she were making a presentation in person to a group of investors. This interpretation was later codified in 2003, when the term "public appearance" in the National Association of Securities Dealers (NASD) rules was defined to include participation in an interactive electronic forum.

In September 2009, the FINRA organized a Social Networking Task Force to look at how firms and their registered representatives could use social media sites for business purposes in a manner that would ensure investor protection from false or misleading claims or representations. After studying the issue, the FINRA came out with Regulatory Notice 10-06 in January 2010, a guide on applying the existing communications rules to social media. Among other observations and conclusions, this notice set forth the following guidelines:

- Firms that communicate through social media sites must retain records of those communications under the Securities and Exchange Act of 1934 and NASD rules.
- Even when communicating a "recommendation" through avenues as widely available as social networking sites, broker-dealers must still adhere to NASD Rule 2310 and make sure the recommendation is suitable for every investor to whom it's made.

- Blog posts that advertise a particular product must receive prior approval, while posts intended to raise awareness of industry issues or engage readers in a discussion do not require such approval.

- Social networking sites have both static content (such as profiles) and active content (such as status updates). While static content must be pre-approved, there is no such requirement for real-time communications.

- In general, the FINRA does not count third-party postings on social media sites to be attributable to the firm, but if a firm is involved in any way (such as by providing content), it may be exposed to liability.

Social media is already being used to perpetrate alleged securities fraud, according to the Manhattan U.S. attorney's office. In October 2010, federal prosecutors filed charges in a classic "pump and dump" scheme of approximately $7 million in touting penny stocks. According to investigators, the individuals charged used more than fifteen websites, Facebook pages, and Twitter feeds to "defraud the investing public into purchasing stocks that were being manipulated by participants in the conspiracy." USA v. Susser, et al., U.S. Dist. Ct. for the Southern District of New York.

As with virtually every other area of law being affected by social networking, the full measure of how securities law is being influenced remains to be seen.

15

Ethical Issues and Social Networking

In a 2009 American Bar Association survey, 43 percent of the responding lawyers indicated that they were members of at least one social networking site (the figure had risen dramatically from the previous year, when only 15 percent of the lawyers surveyed had an online social networking presence). Besides the reality of social media's tremendous impact on society as a whole, it's no wonder that the legal profession is embracing it as well. After all, being familiar with this technology can aid lawyers in obtaining valuable information for their cases. In addition, the social media-savvy lawyer often finds that exchanging practice tips and referrals with other attorneys can be accomplished with just a few mouse clicks. Similarly, forming attorney-client relationships and providing advice can also happen with lightening speed thanks to Web 2.0. Yet while technological advances have helped lawyers do their work and market their practices, they have also opened the door to a host of potential ethical pitfalls. To date, court rulings, state ethics rules, and ethics advisory opinions have provided little guidance for attorneys trying to navigate the murky waters of online legal ethics.

Not surprisingly, the spread of social media and the uncertainty over applying ethics rules adopted long before there was an Internet or sites like Facebook has led to more lawyers getting in hot water for their online conduct. Consider the following examples:

When the late NFL star Sean Taylor was charged with aggravated assault in Florida in 2006, one of the members of the prosecutor's team was Miami-Dade Assistant State Attorney Richard Grieco. Grieco, who moonlighted as a DJ in the South Beach nightclub scene, had a MySpace page promoting his sideline business, complete with risqué photos. On the page, he also bragged about his role in the Taylor matter, and discussed the prosecution's case. Taylor's attorney, prominent Miami criminal defense attorney Richard Sharpstein, filed a dismissal motion based on Grieco's "inappropriate and unethical" conduct, characterizing it as "a misuse of public office for private gain." Grieco withdrew from the case, and later resigned; a different prosecutor later offered the football player a plea bargain to a misdemeanor charge. Sharpstein says the social media evidence "turned the case around for me."

In February 2010, a Somali man convicted of attempted murder in Minneapolis filed a motion for a new trial, citing the prosecutor's comments about the case on Facebook. According to the motion on behalf of Ahlmed Ali, Assistant Hennepin County Attorney Gretchen Gray-Larson engaged in prosecutorial misconduct by posting allegedly derogatory statements about people from Somalia on Facebook during the trial. In addition, the defense claimed that the prosecutor made statements on Facebook about feeling "comfortable" about her case because of a juror's college affiliation.

In April 2010, a prosecutor in a Florida felony gun case allegedly posted a poem on Facebook about what his co-counsel called the "trial from hell." The ditty was intended to be sung to the tune of the "Gilligan's Island" theme song, and included the lines "Just sit right back and you'll hear a tale/A tale of fateful trial/That started from this court in St. Lucie County… Six jurors were ready for trial that day for a four-hour trial, a four-hour trial/The trial started easy enough/But then became rough/The judge and jury confused/If not for the courage of the fearless prosecutors/The trial would be lost, the trial would be lost." Although the judge granted a mistrial, the Facebook parody song wasn't cited as a basis (it was posted after deliberations had ended). Nevertheless, Chief Assistant State Attorney Tom Bakkedahl acknowledged that the Facebook posting, which included references to the "gang banger defendant" and "the weasel face" defense attorney, was "immature" behavior that his office did not encourage. He said what prosecutors should and shouldn't say on social media sites would be a subject for discussion. Bakkedahl stated, "Now they're putting it down in an electronic medium where it's saved forever… So we're in a learning curve and we're going to address that."

In early 2009, the San Francisco public defender's office was rocked by allegations of juror racial bias that surfaced from the MySpace blog postings of a former intern. The intern, a Golden Gate University law student named Carrie Wipplinger, posted about a case in which her bosses gave the following advice on jury selection: "[D]on't pick any Asian jurors, because (and I quote): 'Asians don't drink, they love Jesus, and they're creeped out by everything.'" Although the attorneys who worked with the intern denied making such comments, the superior court and public defender Jeff Adachi launched an investigation into the alleged bias. Adachi called Wipplinger's MySpace postings "highly inappropriate" and said he was "dismayed" that an intern would "apparently write a public blog about her experiences here, including supposedly confidential discussions that she was privy to."

In May 2010, a former Illinois assistant public defender received a sixty-day suspension for disclosing a little too much information on her blog. Kristine Ann Peshek, an assistant public defender in Winnebago County, maintained a blog called "The Bardd Before the Bar—Irreverant (sic) Adventures in Life, Law, and Indigent Defense." According to the Illinois Attorney Registration and Disciplinary Commission, Peshek revealed protected client information on the blog, and made false statements to a tribunal about a client's drug use. Although she referred to clients by their jail identification numbers or their first names, it was still possible to identify them. Of one client, she wrote, "This stupid kid is taking the rap for his drug-dealing dirt bag of an older brother because 'he's no snitch'... My client is in college. Just goes to show you that higher education does not imply that you have any sense." Regarding another client, "Dennis the diabetic," Peshek wrote that not only did he test positive for cocaine, but also that "He was standing there in court stoned, right in front of the judge, probation officer, prosecutor, and defense attorney, swearing he was clean and claiming ignorance as to why his blood sugar wasn't being managed well." According to the complaint, Peshek was no more discreet when it came to judges, referring to one judge as "a total asshole" and to another as "Judge Clueless." She also failed to correctly inform the court about another client's methadone use after that defendant misinformed the judge about her drug usage. The blog entries in question took place between June 2007 and April 2008; after Peshek's supervisor found out about the blog that April, she was terminated.

Florida criminal defense attorney Sean Conway also blogged about his cases. Among other bouts of venting on the subject of judges supposedly giving defense lawyers inadequate time to prepare for trial, he singled out Broward County Circuit Judge Cheryl Aleman. Conway referred to her as an "evil, unfair witch" who was "seemingly mentally ill" and had an "ugly, condescending attitude." Although Conway contended that his speech was protected by the First Amendment, the Florida Bar disagreed. It reprimanded him in April 2009 for violating several ethics rules, including impugning a judge's qualifications or integrity. The Florida Supreme Court declined to hear Conway's constitutional challenge, in effect upholding the reprimand.

Not only should lawyers be careful about online comments about the judge, but they should remember that the judge might be online too. Galveston, Texas District Court Judge Susan Criss has caught more than one lawyer venting, making inappropriate comments, or just plain lying on social media sites. In 2009, a lawyer requested and got a weeklong continuance from Judge Criss in order to attend a funeral. However, the jurist kept tabs on the lawyer through her Facebook postings, which showed her out drinking, riding motorcycles, and other activities that didn't exactly shout "grieving." When the attorney returned, and another lawyer with that office requested an additional continuance, Judge Criss denied the request and called out the lawyer on her rather unconventional "mourning period." And Judge Criss is hardly the only judge monitoring Facebook. One judge denied a defense attorney's motion for continuance, citing the attorney's frequent status updates with comments like "should be working but watching Real Housewives of Atlanta instead...again."

In December 2005, temporary San Francisco prosecutor Jay Kuo was handling a misdemeanor case that he made the subject of online discussions, blogging on livejournal.com. His commentary included, at various points, calling his opposing counsel "chicken" when she requested a continuance, alluding to her with posting titles containing obscenities, and mentioning a prior conviction that had not yet been deemed admissible at trial. After hearing about the online comments, Superior Court Judge Curtis Karnow was not amused. Although he denied a defense motion to dismiss the entire case, Karnow referred to Kuo's conduct as "juvenile, obnoxious, and unprofessional," as well as reckless, stating that he should have known the posts might be "uncontrollably distributed." He sent a copy of his ruling to the State Bar, and Kuo resigned from the prosecutor's office and eventually left the private firm he was with to pursue interests outside the law.

Lawyers need to be careful about their online selves, even when they're not acting as lawyers. Attorney Frank Wilson served as the foreman of a jury hearing burglary charges against Donald McNeely in California. Wilson (who had identified himself during jury selection as a "project manager" for his company because it sounded "[m]ore neutral than lawyer") blogged extensively about the case while it was going on. He commented on McNeely, the charges, as well as about his fellow jurors and their discussions—particularly about one juror who was "threatening to torpedo two of the counts in his quest for tyrannical jurisprudence." In June 2007, a California appellate court reversed McNeely's burglary conviction after Wilson's blogging came to light, ruling that the defendant had been deprived of a fair trial by juror misconduct that included discussing the deliberations online. Wilson lost his job, and later received a forty-five-day suspension from the California Bar.

Attorneys can find themselves in ethical trouble even when using social networking sites for reasons unrelated to working on cases or advertising their services. The Supreme Court of Oregon found that a lawyer had engaged in unethical conduct when he hid his identity and posed as a high school teacher. *In re Carpenter*, 95 P.3d 203 (Or. 2004). The attorney in question went on classmates.com, adopting the identity of a local teacher (purportedly a former high school classmate of the lawyer), and posted a message suggesting that the teacher had sex with students. Although he claimed it was just a prank and did not involve professional misconduct of any kind, the Oregon Supreme Court disagreed and publically reprimanded the lawyer. The court held that Carpenter had violated Oregon Code of Professional Responsibility Disciplinary Rule 1-102(a)(3), which prohibited dishonesty, fraud, deceit, and misrepresentation.

The ambiguousness of social media and its utility for lawyers has resulted in increasing concern about where the ethical boundary lines are drawn as the profession strains to keep episodes like those detailed above to a minimum. Continuing legal education seminars are starting to pop up with titles like

"Social Networks: Friends or Foes? Confronting Online Legal and Ethical Issues in the Age of Social Networking." Questions abound, from whether lawyers can go "undercover" online and friend a witness who might have helpful information, to whether tweeting about one's cases breaches confidentiality. Looming above all other questions seems to be this one: does the legal profession need new ethics rules in the age of Twitter and Facebook? Even the American Bar Association's Commission on Ethics 20/20 has targeted—among other twenty-first century ethics concerns—whether existing ethics rules are adequate to address the foibles of social media use by attorneys. Does new technology, and consequently new ethical missteps, require new ethics rules?

My modest proposal is this: the existing ethics standards are, by and large, perfectly fine for governing the online ethical lapses by attorneys. Law is never going to keep pace with technology. Adopt a specialized rule now addressing a particular medium, and both the medium and the rule will be obsolete before you know it. Lawyers engaged in the same sort of misconduct before social media, whether it was criticizing judges, revealing client confidences, or engaging in improper forms of advertising. The difference with making these ethical lapses online is that how there's a digital trail to follow. Perhaps it seems like such behavior is happening more frequently because lawyers, like virtually everyone else, are lulled into a false sense of security and anonymity by the Internet. Or perhaps a generational shift, in which younger people who are accustomed to living their lives online share far more about themselves than earlier generations did, has begun affecting lawyers just like other segments of society.

If the latter is the case, law students need to take care to monitor their social networking profiles. In July 2009, the Florida Bar's Board of Bar Examiners decided to adopt a policy of investigating the social networking profiles of bar applicants on a case-by-case basis. Although the board considered adding a question to the Florida Bar application that would require applicants to list their sites and grant access to the profiles, it decided "if applicants are required to provide access to their social websites, they are likely to delete any derogatory material before staff has the opportunity to review it." Nevertheless, as part of the board's character and fitness investigation, it will investigate the sites of certain categories of candidates. These include applicants with a history of substance abuse or dependence, "so as to ascertain whether they discussed or posted, photographs of any recent substance abuse"; applicants with "significant candor concerns," such as lying on employment applications or inflating their résumés; applicants who have a history of unauthorized practice of law allegations; applicants who have previously been required to establish rehabilitation (to determine from online comments whether they "displayed any malice or ill will" toward those associated with the proceeding where rehabilitation was ordered, like former clients); and applicants who disclosed on their application "involvement in an organization advocating the overthrow of a government in the United States," to discover if the candidate is still involved with such terrorist activities.

While Florida is the first state to formally announce a policy of checking on the social media activities of its bar candidates, it is not likely to be the last. Law students and others seeking licensure in other states would be well advised to take a cold, hard look at their online selves, given the fact that bar examiners may soon use social networking site content when assessing a candidate's character and fitness to practice law. For example, the State Bar of Texas's character review has as its express purpose the exclusion from practicing law of those with character traits "that are likely to result in an injury to future clients, in the obstruction of the administration of justice, or in a violation of the Texas Disciplinary Rules of Professional Conduct." Law students with Facebook photos and postings about wild parties, binge drinking, and drug use could be inviting uncomfortable questions from the board of bar examiners about their fitness to practice and their ability to live up to duties to both clients and the profession itself. It's also worth remembering that one also has to be concerned with what other social networking site users or "friends" might post, and not just what an individual memorializes on his or her own site. If "friends" tagged a photo of an applicant or posting that reflected him or her engaging in inappropriate behavior, such content might be viewed by bar examiners as well.

So what are the biggest areas of ethical concern for lawyers regarding social media, and how do existing rules of professional conduct address them? The first—and perhaps the most closely examined and debated by legal analysts—involves the gathering of information about a party or witness. As we explore more extensively in other chapters, evidence from an individual's Facebook or MySpace page can yield all sorts of incriminating and impeaching evidence. Where such areas are unrestricted and everyone can view the person's profile, there appear to be no ethical issues involved in attorneys viewing this conduct. While no case law has yet specifically addressed this scenario, a good analogy can be found in authority like *State ex rel. State Farm Fire & Cas. Co. v. Madden*, in which the Supreme Court of West Virginia held that lawfully observing a represented party's activities that occur in full view of the general public does not violate any ethical rule. 451 S.E. 2d 721, 730 (W. Va. 1994).

However, it gets a little trickier with social networking profiles of those who have restricted access to part or all of their page, allowing only designated "friends" to view such non-public material. Can an attorney, or someone working for that attorney, try to become someone's "friend" in order to gain access to this content? If the person is a represented party, such as the plaintiff in a personal injury suit, the answer is clearly no. Under Rule 4.2 of the Rules of Professional Conduct, a lawyer shall not communicate or cause another person to communicate with a person represented by counsel without the prior consent of the party's attorney.

Even if the individual concerned is not a represented party (such as a fact witness), one must still tread very carefully. Misrepresenting who you are, albeit in an online communication, could be considered a violation of Rule 4.1 of the Rules of Professional Conduct, regarding truthfulness in statements to others. It states that a lawyer, in the course of representing a client, shall not knowingly make a false statement of material fact or law to a third person. In the first bar association ethics advisory opinion to date to specifically address such a social networking issue, the Philadelphia Bar Association's Professional Guidance Committee held that this contact ran the risk of violating several ethics rules, including Pennsylvania's equivalent of Rule 4.1.

In this March 2009 Philadelphia example, an attorney inquired about the propriety of asking a third party to "friend" a witness in order to access information in her Facebook and MySpace pages. The lawyer had deposed the witness, learned of her social media profiles, and concluded that her testimony would be helpful to the adverse party. Although he didn't ask her to reveal the contents of her pages or ask the witness for access, he discovered through subsequent visits to the sites that access was restricted to the witness's "friends." The attorney asked if it would be ethically permissible to have a third party contact this individual and "friend" her, but while not revealing that the third party is affiliated with the lawyer or seeking access in order to gain information that might be used against the witness.

The Philadelphia Bar Association's Professional Guidance Committee found that such conduct would be unethical. Using a non-lawyer assistant to procure the information doesn't relieve the attorney of his responsibilities of the conduct of such assistants under Rule 8.4 of the Rules of Professional Conduct, the committee held. It also would violate Rule F4, since it would constitute professional misconduct for the lawyer to "engage in conduct involving dishonestly, fraud, deceit, or misrepresentation." Not telling the witness of the third party's affiliation with the lawyer, the committee reasoned, "omits a highly material fact, namely, that the third party who asks to be allowed access to the witness's pages is doing so only because he or she is intent on obtaining information and sharing it with a lawyer for use in a lawsuit to impeach the testimony of the witness. The omission would purposefully conceal that fact from the witness for the purpose of inducing the witness to allow access, when she [might] not do so if she knew the third person was associated with the inquirer and the true purpose of the access was to obtain information for the purpose of impeaching her testimony."

In September 2010, the New York City Bar Association's Committee on Professional Ethics issued the second opinion to address this issue. Like its Philadelphia counterpart, it also considered the question of whether an attorney could resort to trickery or misrepresentation in "friending" a witness to gain access to an otherwise private social networking page. And just as with Philadelphia, the New York City Bar's ethics committee held that such conduct was barred by the Rules of Professional Conduct. In particular, the New York authorities pointed to Rule 4.1's prohibition against knowingly making a false statement of fact to a third person, and to Rule 8.4's ban on conduct involving dishonesty, fraud, deception, or misrepresentation, in saying that such friending under false pretenses violates ethical rules. Significantly, this opinion took note of the increasing use of social media sites by lawyers, and specifically mentioned possible ruses like creating a false Facebook profile or contacting a YouTube account holder seeking access to his "channel" in order to view his digital postings. In particular, the Committee reasoned that deception was even easier in the virtual world than in person, with strangers much more likely to gain unfettered access to all kinds of personal information. However, the Committee also pointed out that there were no ethical restrictions against lawyers accessing the publicly viewable pages of another party's social networking profile.

The committee also rejected the idea that the proposed access to the social media pages was no different than conducting video surveillance of a plaintiff in a personal injury case to demonstrate that he or she is capable of performing physical acts he or she claims are impossible due to the injury. The committee concluded, "In the video situation, the videographer simply follows the subject and films him as he presents himself to the public. The videographer does not have to ask to enter a private area to make the video."

Clearly, this type of "pre-texting" behavior in seeking social media information about a party or witness would run afoul of multiple ethical prohibitions. More importantly, in response to the question of whether special ethics rules governing social media are needed, just pause for a moment and consider whether the lawyer's proposed course of action would have been any more proper had the activities been conducted offline. Misrepresentation and deceit are what they are, regardless of the forum in which they occur.

One caveat is worth considering however, especially in light of the growing role social media is playing in the realm of law enforcement. Many jurisdictions, while silent about the use of deception by defense counsel, permit undercover criminal investigations by government lawyers and prosecutors. In fact, one observer has noted, "The recent trend has been to permit lawyers to supervise, and thereby indirectly participate in, undercover investigations in three substantive areas of the law: criminal, civil rights, and intellectual property." "Deception in Undercover Investigations: Conduct-Based vs. Status-Based Ethical Analysis," 32 *Seattle Univ. L. Rev.* 123 (2008). For example, a 2007 ethics opinion from Alabama appears to give the green light to pre-texting in copyright, patent, and trademark infringement cases. It states, "During pre-litigation investigation of suspected infringers of intellectual property rights, a lawyer may employ private investigators to pose as customers under the pretext of seeking services of the suspected infringers on the same basis or in the same manner as a member of the general public." Alabama State Bar Office of the General Counsel: Opinion 2007-05.

Besides pre-texting (or "opposition research," as some might refer to it) there are other major areas of ethical concern for lawyers that arise out of the use of social media sites, several of which are illustrated by the anecdotes previously discussed.

<u>Communications and Maintaining Confidentiality</u>

The very purpose of social networking sites is to facilitate communications, and lawyers have been quick to exploit social media to exchange practice tips with other counsel and to update clients. Tweeting about a new piece of legislation or a recent decision that affects a client's business is an excellent and inexpensive form of marketing. Yet the ease of use of social media, and the casual, informal nature of communicating via Facebook or Twitter, can result in attorneys letting their guards down and breaching confidentiality or inadvertently creating expectations of an attorney-client relationship.

For example, a lawyer sending out a tweet about a key ruling he just received, or griping about a client who misled him about the facts of the case, runs the risk of revealing his strategy or even privileged information to a whole host of third parties—not just "followers" on Twitter, but potentially strangers who receive this information via "re-tweets." Similarly, in cases of dual representation, one disgruntled client could point to social media communications between the other client and the attorney as evidence of a conflict, including a closer relationship in which the Facebook "friend" is favored more than the client. A jury may not grasp that a friend on Facebook might be no more than an acquaintance. Even having one's contact list or "friends" list publicly viewable on a social networking site poses the risk of disclosing a confidential relationship. Just as with e-mail that is not secure, lawyers should take care to police not only their own communications using social media, but they should advise their clients about potential threats to the confidentiality of their communications, including those done via a social networking medium lacking in privacy.

<u>The Attorney-Client Relationship</u>

Under the Rules of Professional Conduct and a substantial body of case law, an attorney-client relationship can arise without the formalities of an engagement agreement; it may be implied from the conduct of the parties. Accordingly, lawyers should avoid the digital equivalent of the old "giving advice at the cocktail party" hypothetical, especially in light of the casual, spontaneous nature of communicating through social media. Take care to understand the distinction between providing general legal information and actually rendering legal advice. Giving fact-specific advice on how a person might proceed runs the risk of creating at least the expectation of an attorney-client relationship, one that could put a lawyer in a troubling conflict of interest or malpractice situation down the road. Because of this, it's best to maintain formalities and sufficiently qualify one's responses when having legal discussions online with individuals who might later claim that they regarded themselves as clients.

For such reasons, a good law firm website and social networking profile will have clear and conspicuous disclaimers of attorney-client relationships to avoid such misunderstandings. Some even feature a "click-wrap" disclaimer, in which a visitor has to confirm his or her acknowledgment that the online communication doesn't create an attorney-client relationship by clicking "accept" before he or she can further navigate the contents of the profile. A number of firms have online activities policies or electronic communications policies, pursuant to which an individual lawyer's social networking presence may be monitored or restricted. This can minimize the risks of not only the unwitting creation of attorney-client relationships, but also an individual lawyer's postings that could negatively affect the firm's profile. Attorneys should also avoid the acceptance of confidential information from online visitors to a website or Facebook page. A Ninth Circuit case held that even with user acknowledgment that there was no request for legal advice made and no attorney-client relationship formed, an online questionnaire that gathered information from potential members of a class action lawsuit was nevertheless a sign of an attorney-client relationship. *Barton v. U.S. District Court*, 410 F.3d 1104, 1107 (9th Cir. 2005).

Just as they should with advertising regulations, lawyers should check the ethics rules of their particular jurisdictions. For example, the State Bar of Arizona has issued an ethics opinion addressing legal advice provided over the Internet, cautioning that "lawyers should not answer specific legal questions from lay people through the Internet unless the question presented is of a general nature and the advice given is not fact-specific." State Bar of Arizona Formal Ethics Op. 97-04 (1997). Similarly, the New York City Bar advises that online a lawyer "should carefully refrain from giving…a general solution applicable to all apparently similar individual problems since slight changes in fact situations may require a material variance in the applicable advice." Ass'n of the Bar of the City of New York, Comm. On Prof'l and Judicial Ethics, Formal Op. 1998-2.

Advertising

Social media can be a great way of building up a network of contacts and promoting one's practice to the public, as discussed in greater detail in the chapter on marketing and social media. However, advertising online, including the use of social networking, can also pose ethical challenges for attorneys. For example, in 2008 a public relations group acting on behalf of a Seattle law firm began using Twitter as a means of finding putative class members for a possible class action suit against Verizon Wireless. Concerns about solicitation and how the lawyers would be perceived appeared in the *Wall Street Journal* and throughout the blogosphere, and the Twitter post was quickly retracted. And at least one state bar ethics opinion has concluded that an attorney's communication with a prospective fee-paying client in a mass-disaster victims' Internet chat room violated that state's Rules of Professional Conduct. California State Bar Ethics Op. 2005-166. Although many attorneys may feel that their use of social networking sites isn't intended to serve as advertising per se, there are still ethical considerations to keep in mind that can bear on a lawyer's social networking activities, particularly a state bar's ethics rules governing advertising and solicitation.

Most state bars regulate an attorney's website as they would any other form of advertising, and slowly but surely jurisdictions are beginning to address social networking. As of January 1, 2010, the Florida Bar's Standing Committee on Advertising voted that lawyers' use of social networking sites is subject to the same rules as lawyer websites. While not required to be filed for review like websites and other forms of advertising, social networking profiles must comply with other regulations—including not making statements that characterize the quality of the legal services offered, providing information regarding past results, or including testimonials. In Texas, the State Bar's Advertising Review Committee supports the use of new technology by the lawyers under its purview; however, just as it requires law firm advertising such as websites to be submitted for review, attorney or law firm videos that are uploaded to social media sites like YouTube, Facebook, and MySpace must similarly be submitted to the committee. Texas Disciplinary Rule of Professional Conduct 7.07 requires websites that go beyond just the "tombstone" sort of information (name of the attorney, contact, and biographical information) and address the qualification or the services of any lawyer or firm to be submitted for review and approval. A March 2010 interpretive comment by Texas's Advertising Review Committee explicitly imposed the same requirements for social media sites and blogs if they go beyond strictly educational, informational, or entertainment content to solicit business.

Many of the ethical concerns will depend on not only the content of the social networking profile itself, but also the advertising rules of the specific jurisdiction. For example, a number of states (including California and New York) prohibit communications that contain testimonials unless there are specific disclaimers. Yet on a site like LinkedIn, an attorney's connections can post recommendations (i.e., "John Doe is our company's go-to commercial litigator—he really knows his stuff"). Attorneys subject to such restrictions should carefully review the content of such testimonials and recommendations to avoid running afoul of ethical rules like Rule 7.02 (4), which prohibits comparisons to other lawyers' services unless substantiated by verifiable objective data. In addition, a site like LinkedIn has a field for specialties. However, a number of states, such as Texas, prohibit an attorney from holding himself or herself out as possessing special competence in an area unless they have achieved board certification. Accordingly, lawyers practicing in areas with such restrictions should avoid identifying themselves on sites such a LinkedIn as a "specialist" or "expert."

Even for those who maintain that their social media presence is not a form of advertising, but simply a constructive way to network and communicate with others, social networking can still pose ethical pitfalls. A number of state bars have already issued ethics opinions construing interactive attorney websites as communications. The American Bar Association's Model Rules of Professional Conduct Rule 7.1 requires that a lawyer must avoid false or misleading communications about the lawyer, his firm, or their services. In the rough and tumble world of social networking, in which profiles can be ripe with exaggerations and no-holds-barred commentary, attorneys with social networking profiles must take care to avoid half-truths and the dissemination of less-than-accurate information. Whether it's the immediacy of a tweet or a Facebook wall message, lawyers should avoid statements that represent anything less than the truth about themselves and their services.

Blogs that appear as part of a lawyer's social networking profile usually are not regarded as advertising, as long as they consist of commentary, educational information, or entertainment content, as opposed to advertising the firm's services or soliciting business. In addition, a number of bars have spoken out on ensuring an attorney's First Amendment rights while still balancing the critical mission of protecting the public from misleading or deceptive advertising and maintaining the integrity of the profession. Accordingly, blogs on social networking sites that are geared toward communicating information, like analysis of a recent case or statute, generally pose no ethical concerns.

In short, the safest way to avoid any ethical problems associated with social networking activities is to regard one's statements and communications made via sites like Facebook or Twitter as subject to the same ethical prohibitions as if the same words were expressed in a more traditional medium. If you wouldn't disclose a client's confidences while chatting at the neighborhood bar, you shouldn't say them on Twitter or Facebook. If you wouldn't violate your duty of candor to a court in writing a letter, you shouldn't treat your blog or Facebook wall as being any different. No matter how casual, fleeting, or spontaneous a statement might seem in the context of a social medium, once it's on the Internet it can take on a life of its own—along with its ethical consequences.

16

Why Can't We Be Friends?
Judges and Social Networking

Just as social networking can assist lawyers, it can be a terrific resource for judges as well. For example, a working knowledge of social media can help make a judge more attuned to the potential for social media "no-nos" in his or her court—including not just the "online juror" that is discussed at length in another chapter, but also the potential for abuse among his or her own courtroom staff. In April 2009, a court officer in Philadelphia was suspended after he sent a friend request to a female juror who was sitting for a case in the courtroom where he worked. The juror reported the request, leading to the officer's suspension and reassignment to another court.

Social networking can also assist a judge in keeping the lawyers and parties before him on the straight and narrow. Michigan Judge A. T. Frank uses social networking sites to monitor offenders on probation under his jurisdiction, occasionally finding photos on MySpace or Facebook pages in which the defendants are engaged in drug use or other prohibited behavior. Galveston Juvenile Court Judge Kathryn Lanan employs a similar tactic, requiring all juveniles under her jurisdiction to "friend" her on Facebook or MySpace so she can review their postings for any signs of inappropriate conduct that might warrant a return to her court. Also in Galveston, Judge Susan Criss finds her presence on Facebook helps her in keeping lawyers honest. On one occasion, a lawyer had asked for and received a continuance because of a supposed death in the family. When another lawyer from her firm asked that the continuance be extended, Criss pointed out that she had photographic evidence on Facebook that the first lawyer had been "partying that same week," and denied the request.

Indeed, a recent issue of *Case in Point*, the magazine of the National Judicial College, suggested that participating in social media provides judges with a low-cost means of staying informed while simultaneously enhancing public understanding of the judiciary. A growing number of judges, for example, have profiles on LinkedIn, including at least five U.S. Circuit Court judges, multiple federal district judges, and numerous state appellate and supreme court justices. In states where judges are elected, not appointed, to the bench, having a social media presence has simply become a matter of smart politics. As the 2008 Obama presidential campaign illustrated, a candidate's online presence helps with fundraising, keeps supporters updated on campaign developments, and exposes the judicial candidate to entirely new audiences and prospective voters. Social media and other forms of electronic communications play a vital role in getting judicial candidates' names out to voters (voter recognition and awareness can be key in judicial races, since they are usually "down ballot" races). Campaigns now regularly use contributions to buy electronic mailing lists and create websites. Press coverage of a recent race for a seat on the Texas Supreme Court, for example, featured a discussion not only of the various candidates' respective fundraising success, but also examined their respective social media activities as they kept supporters around the state updated about the campaigns and acquired more fans on Facebook and followers on Twitter. Becoming social media-savvy is now viewed as a must for judicial candidates, even if they don't always understand the nuances of newer technology. Justice Jim Moseley of Dallas's Fifth District Court of Appeals jokes, "I tell people I believe in the Holy Trinity, Facebook, and Twitter, but I can't explain any of them to you."

A study conducted by the Conference of Court Public Information Officers released in August 2010 found that while most judges agree that jurists should be familiar with social networking sites like Facebook and Twitter, less than 7 percent of the state and federal judges responding use such sites for official purposes. Roughly 40 percent of the respondents said they used social media, albeit primarily in their personal lives or for political campaign purposes or for public education. Close to half of the judges surveyed disagreed with the idea that they could use social media sites in their professional capacities without violating ethics rules.

Of course, taking advantage of new technology doesn't mean a judge is relieved of having to adhere to traditional ethics rules. Florida Circuit Judge Angela Dempsey found this out the hard way when she was formally reprimanded by the Florida Supreme Court for two mistakes that appeared in her 2008 campaign materials. One was a mailing that misrepresented Dempsey's years of legal experience, and the other was a reference to asking voters to "re-elect" her on a link for a YouTube campaign video (Judge Dempsey had been appointed, and had not been previously elected to the bench). According to the Supreme Court, this violated a judicial canon barring misrepresentations about a judge's qualifications. Chief Justice Peggy Quince stated, "This case stands as a warning to all judicial candidates. You will be held responsible and accountable for the actions of your campaign consultants including the way they choose to use new technology like the social media."

New Media, Same Ethics

Social media can get judges into ethical hot water off the campaign trail as well. Some judges forget that just as *ex parte* communications and other improper conduct are forbidden in writing, in person, and telephonically, they are just as forbidden if they occur online.

Judge B. Carlton Terry Jr. was publically reprimanded in 2009 by the North Carolina Judicial Standards Commission for friending a lawyer on Facebook during a pending case, posting and reading messages about the litigation, and accessing the website of the opposing party. After a discussion of Facebook in chambers during a child custody/child support case (in the presence of opposing counsel Jessie Conley), Judge Terry and lawyer Charles Shieck friended each other. Schieck then began posting messages referring to aspects of the case, including how long trial would last, whether one of the litigants had been guilty of an affair, and even noting, "I have a wise judge." (Apparently, lawyers can suck up in cyberspace too.) Judge Terry not only responded to these postings, but also used the Internet to independently gather information, including Googling the photography business run by Conley's client and finding various poems written by that client. After the conclusion of the trial, Judge Terry disclosed to both parties that he visited the website of Conley's client and later disqualified himself and vacated his child custody/child support order at Conley's request (a new trial was also ordered). The commission found that Judge Terry's *ex parte* communications and independent gathering of information reflected a "disregard of the principles embodied in the North Carolina Code of Judicial Conduct," and constituted conduct "prejudicial to the administration of justice that brings the judicial office into disrepute."

In December 2009, Superior Court Chief Justice Ernest "Bucky" Woods of Georgia retired after his relationship with a defendant, Tara Black, was revealed. The fifty-seven-year-old jurist had contacted Black through Facebook and initiated a relationship in which he advised her on how to respond and plead in his court. He negotiated a deferred prosecution agreement with the prosecutor and signed an order allowing her to be released on her own recognizance. Other e-mails within the thirty-three pages turned over as part of an open records request described visits the judge made to Black's apartment and the money he loaned to her. Besides helping Black "behind the scenes" in her criminal theft by deception case, he also used a photo taken off her Facebook page as a basis for issuing a revocation against a drug defendant. As it turns out, that defendant was an ex-boyfriend of Black's, and the man's family's inquiry about his case initiated the press investigation that exposed Judge Woods's relationship.

On Staten Island, a judge's Facebook activities may have gotten him transferred. Judge Matthew Sciarrino Jr. was known for updating his Facebook status even on the bench. The outspoken judge broadcasted details about his personal life, his schedule, and posted photos of his children. He even took a photo of his crowded courtroom and put it on Facebook. Following his transfer to a court in Manhattan, Judge Sciarrino's Facebook profile is now set to private.

In California, a judge's online excitement about actually being picked to serve on a jury in a murder trial may lead to trouble. Fresno County Judge James Oppliger sent four e-mails to a group of his judicial colleagues about his jury service. Among the comments was the statement "Here I am livin' the dream, jury duty with Mugridge and Jenkins!" (a reference to the two lawyers on the case). Although none of the e-mails discussed the evidence in the case, one of the judges on the receiving end of Oppliger's e-mails was Judge Adrian Harrell, the presiding judge in the case. After the defendant was convicted of second-degree murder, Judge Harrell disclosed the online communications, prompting defense attorney Mugridge to consider seeking a new trial.

Meanwhile, when accused of online improprieties, Judge Shirley Strickland Saffold of Cleveland, Ohio, evidently feels the best defense is a good offense. The Cuyahoga County Common Pleas Court judge has been linked to anonymous Internet discussions about cases in her court, resulting in her removal from the high-profile trial of an accused serial killer. More than eighty postings were made by "lawmiss" on Cleveland.com (the website of the *Cleveland Plain Dealer*), and were linked to Saffold's account. They included comments like calling a defense lawyer a "buffoon" and wishing he could "shut his Amos and Andy style mouth," and stating about the sentence in a 2008 triple homicide case, "If a black guy had massacred five people then he would've received the death penalty... A white guy does it and he gets a pat on the hand. The jury didn't care about the victims... All of them ought to be ashamed." In removing her from presiding over the trial, the Ohio Supreme Court wrote that the "nature of the comments and their widespread dissemination might well cause a reasonable and objective observer to harbor serious doubts about the judge's impartiality."

Judge Saffold was outed by the *Cleveland Plain Dealer*, which obtained public records that included the browser history of her courtroom computer. Although "lawmiss" was the judge's screen name, her daughter came forward and admitted to making some of the online comments. In spite of her insistence that she didn't write about her cases online, Judge Saffold has filed a $50 million lawsuit against the newspaper for alleged breach of contract and invasion of privacy, asserting that the *Plain Dealer* violated the terms of use of its website by disclosing her identity and that of her daughter.

Why Can't We Be Friends?

As social networking spreads, more judges are presented with the question of how to respond to the friend request. Does it create the appearance of a conflict of interest, or convey to others the idea that such "friends" carry special favor or influence with the judge? An online poll conducted by the *ABA Journal* asked if judges should be allowed to friend lawyers on social media sites. Of them, 18 percent said, "Yes, it's the way more and more people are communicating these days," while 28 percent said "Maybe." A resounding 54 percent said "No." I'm "friends" on Facebook with multiple judges and appellate justices. I don't think that gives me any enhanced status in their eyes, or that I'll receive preferential treatment in their courts. As with so many issues, however, the answer to the question of whether judges can be "friends" online with attorneys who may appear before them depends on where you are. Those of you planning a judicial career on the island nation of Malta, for example, better avoid Facebook and LinkedIn. On February 8, 2010, Malta's Commission for the Administration of Justice approved an amendment to its Code of Ethics for Members of the Judiciary. It states, "Since propriety, and the appearance of propriety, are essential to the performance of all the activities of a judge, membership of 'social networking internet sites' is incompatible with judicial office. Such membership exposes the judge to the possibility of breach of the record part of rule 12 of the Code."

Here in the United States, those few states to address the issue have taken divergent views. In a January 29, 2009, opinion, New York's Judicial Ethics Committee stated that it was perfectly appropriate for a judge to join an online social network. It pointed out that there are multiple reasons why a judge might wish to be part of a social network, including "reconnecting with law school, college, or even high school classmates; increased interaction with distant family members; staying in touch with former colleagues; or even monitoring the usage of that same social network by minor children in the judge's immediate family." The opinion reminds judges to avoid impropriety and the appearance of it, not to engage in *ex parte* communications or other prohibited conduct online, and to be mindful of the appearance that could be created by virtue of establishing an online connection with a lawyer or anyone else appearing in the judge's court.

The New York opinion on this issue is a model of common sense. It cautions judges using social networks to "employ an appropriate level of prudence, discretion, and decorum in how they make use of this technology." It also reminds judges that social networks and technology in general are subject to change, and that therefore jurists should stay abreast of new features of and changes to any social networks they use. Above all, the New York opinion emphasizes perhaps the most important ethical question for judges (and attorneys) to keep in mind about their online activities: if the same conduct occurred offline, would it violate the canons of ethics? N.Y. Op. 08-176 (Jan. 29, 2009).

Kentucky has similarly given a "qualified yes" to the question of whether judges may belong to social networking sites and be "friends" with various people who might appear before the court, such as attorneys, social workers, or law enforcement officials. In an opinion issued on January 20, 2010, the Ethics Committee of the Kentucky Judiciary pointed out many of the same cautions the New York committee did about avoiding *ex parte* communications, making public comment about a pending matter, etc. It stressed that "social networking sites are fraught with peril for judges, and that this opinion should not be construed as an explicit or implicit statement that judges may participate in such sites in the same manner as members of the general public." The opinion also warned judges that while social networking sites "may have an aura of private, one-on-one conversation, they are much more public than offline conversations, and statements once made in that medium may never go away."

However, the opinion of the committee was swayed in the end in favor of approving participation by judges in social media by one cold, hard fact: "the reality that Kentucky judges are elected and should not be isolated from the community in which they serve." The Kentucky ethics opinion, like the New York opinion, is grounded in reality, and it acknowledges that the term "friend" on Facebook (or "fan" or follower," for that matter) is a term of art used by the site, and doesn't mean "friend" in the ordinary sense of the word. As the committee pointed out, such a designation of "friend," by itself, "does not reasonably convey to others an impression that such persons are in a special position to influence the judge." Formal Judicial Ethics Opinion JE-119 (Jan. 20, 2010).

Unfortunately, not every state shares the viewpoint of New York and Kentucky. In a November 17, 2009, opinion, the Florida Judicial Ethics Advisory Committee ruled that judges may not friend lawyers who might appear before them, or permit such lawyers to friend them. The central concern for the committee was the impression that such friends might have influence over the judge. A minority on the committee, pointing out that the term "friend" in the social networking context merely conveys that a person is a contact or acquaintance rather than an actual friend, would have permitted judges to have more of a social networking presence. Florida Supreme Court Judicial Ethics Advisory Committee, Op. No. 2009-20 (Nov. 17, 2009). An October 2009 ethics opinion from South Carolina said that a judge could be a member of Facebook with court employees and law enforcement personnel as friends, provided they don't discuss anything related to the judge's work. The same opinion, however, noted that "a judge should not become isolated from the community in which the judge lives," and that allowing a judge to belong to a social networking site "allows the community to see how the judge communicates and gives the community a better understanding of the judge." Advisory Committee on Standards and Judicial Conduct, Op. No. 17-2009.

The Florida interpretation seems overly sensitive, and the split within the Florida committee may be generational. The notion of "friend" status in our increasingly wired world carries with it a completely different meaning from holding feeling of affection or personal regard for someone. The brave new world of social media offers judges new ways to stay connected with colleagues, remain up to speed on the latest developments in their field, reach out to voters, and do their jobs more effectively. As the ethical foibles discussed earlier illustrate, the same conduct—engaging in *ex parte* communications, publicly commenting on a case, etc.—would have violated judicial canons of ethics had they occurred offline. As they would in using more traditional forms of communications, judges should exercise caution in their use of social media.

17

Social Networking and Jury Selection

If you are a trial lawyer, and you are not already conducting an Internet search for background information on your prospective jurors, then one anecdote should impress upon you the potential benefits of running such searches. Florida jury consultant Amy Singer was working for the plaintiff's attorney in a product liability case involving a maintenance employee who had been severely injured while inside an industrial machine in order to clean it. The accident happened in a tight, confined space. While researching members of the panel, Singer learned that one prospective juror shared on his MySpace page that he belonged to a claustrophobics' support group. Believing this would dispose the juror to emphasize with the plaintiff, Singer advised keeping him on the panel. Not only did that juror wind up serving, but he became the foreman of the jury and the plaintiff recovered a significant verdict.

Or imagine being an attorney in a death penalty case. Wouldn't it be important to know that one of the nice people who swore to you that he could be fair and impartial and listen to all the evidence before rendering a verdict had actually written a guest editorial for a local paper on the death penalty? That actually happened.

Clearly, given the seemingly endless ways a juror or prospective juror could be sharing his or her thoughts online, it pays to ask about them, beginning with jury questionnaires (if your jurisdiction allows them) and continuing with *voir dire*. In Texas, lawyers usually get minimal information about panel members—name, age, occupation, spouse's occupation, education, religious affiliation, and whether he or she has served on a civil or criminal jury before. This information is also usually shared mere minutes before *voir dire* is to begin. Nevertheless, in a case I tried in February 2010, I had my trusty laptop there at trial and engaged in at least a basic Google search of each of the panel members. The digital goldmine that is the Internet can help select desirable jurors, weed out undesirable ones, and even assist in influencing seated jurors during a trial and closing argument. Jurors who may be hesitant to fully share their views in front of the rest of the panel during *voir dire* may be more outspoken online, enshrouded in the relative anonymity of the Internet. Information that might not come out in a courtroom may flow freely in a blog or Facebook posting, whether it happens to be a less "politically correct" attitude or perhaps personal anecdotes that might be relevant to significant issues or central themes during trial. As Richard Waites, an attorney and psychologist who heads up the Miami office of national trial consulting firm the Advocates, says, "In a courtroom, people want to say what is politically correct. They don't want to be embarrassed in front of all these people. But when they are on the computer late at night they don't feel they have to shape their answers."

Doing social media research on prospective jurors can also help avoid a mistrial or juror misconduct. In one recent murder trial, jury consultant Marshall Hennington of Beverly Hills-based Hennington & Associates was faced with a prospective juror who denied knowing a fellow panel member. Hennington discovered on the man's Facebook page that they not only knew each other, but that they were cousins. That juror wound up being dismissed. In the high-profile terrorism trial of alleged "dirty bomber" Jose Padilla in 2007, prospective jurors completed a lengthy questionnaire of more than one hundred questions. While normally that would give the lawyers on both sides a good head start, in *voir dire* it was the online research of jury consultant and lawyer Linda Moreno of Tampa, Florida, that revealed that a potential juror had lied. The woman, an unidentified government employee, had indicated on her survey that she had no experience with the criminal system. Moreno's research revealed that the prospective juror had resigned from public office and was under investigation for malfeasance. The information was brought to the judge's attention, and the juror was dismissed.

Lawyers can get real insight into the mind of a juror or prospective juror by checking their online information, or by visiting sites like www.juryexperiences.org . Subtitled "What Really Happens on Juries," this site features contributions by jurors about actual and—in some cases—ongoing trials. Subcategories on the site include "Jury Selection," "Juror Narratives," "Jury Dynamics," "Opinion," and even "Live Blogging from Jury Duty." If you were picking a jury, wouldn't you want to hear insights like the following actual quotes from this blog:

- "I have become very bitter…and feel maybe it's my chance to put someone in jail and let their families see how it feels—I know I am not going to be an [im]partial juror because of this—do I tell the judge this prior to jury duty?"

- "Yes, I am aware that the jury system is very important, particularly in criminal cases… Defense attorneys take note: I am highly likely to convict your client, whatever the facts, out of sheer spite for making me trade a week on the beach in Maui for a week in a jury box in downtown LA… Either way, your client is screwed if you pick me for your jury. Whatever, he's probably guilty anyway if he got charged."

- "The defense attorney is into a Columbo detective-style of acting stupid and asking questions in the most condescending and convoluting way that makes many completely confused and not knowing what the hell the question was…"

It can also identify the reluctant juror. During *voir dire* for a lead paint exposure/poisoning trial in Ohio, a lawyer looked up one of the potential jurors, who was actually blogging and tweeting about jury duty. Among his Twitter posts from the courtroom: "Still sitting for jury duty crap. Hating it immensely. Plz don't pick me. Plz don't pick me." Guess what—they didn't pick him. Here is just a brief sampling of what was found on Twitter recently, in response to a search for the phrase "jury duty":

- "yo i was in jury duty two weeks ago. feel asleep in court. twice. in one day. at least it was a civil case."

- "sorry I just saw your reply. Well I went to jury duty this morning and didn't get picked. It pays to show a bias ☺"

- "jury duty was cancelled. Man, and I was looking forward to being a party of the judicial system and screwing a minority. kidding."

Investigating the web presence of prospective jurors may not be that easy. Certainly, you should begin with a Google search. Many blog entries, though, are made using pseudonyms, and most Facebook and MySpace users employ screen names that may or may not incorporate part of their real names. Rather than searching sites simply for the name of a juror, it's important to get prospective jurors to provide you with the information themselves. In light of the private nature of such data, it may prove difficult to get panel members to volunteer it during *voir dire*. Massachusetts jury consultant Edward P. Schwartz, who authors "The Jury Box Blog," recommends including a couple of questions on blogs and social networking sites on a supplemental jury questionnaire, if possible. If the answers alert you to a prospective juror's online activities, you can inquire further during individual *voir dire* conducted outside the presence of the rest of the panel. There is a wealth of information online about people, from records of political contributions made to petition signatures, buying preferences, and letters to the editor. With just a few keystrokes, an enterprising lawyer or jury consultant can assemble a detailed picture of how a person votes, spends his or her money, and feels about hot-button issues.

Creative lawyers can use this information beyond the jury selection phase of trial in their opening statements or closing arguments. Let's say you've learned that a juror discusses work with a particular charity or cause on his Facebook page. You might employ analogies or references to that charity or cause in your argument, to create empathy with your client or central theme. In a personal injury case, for example, jurors whose online activity is very family-oriented (postings of family, various photos, children's sports activities, etc.) might be more receptive to a closing argument that emphasizes how the injured person won't be able to enjoy time with his or her family. One lawyer who observed from a juror's MySpace page that his favorite book was *The Seven Habits of Highly Effective People* found a way to include references to that book in his closing argument.

The prevalence of social networking is transforming the way jury consultants and lawyers do their jobs. Jeffrey T. Frederick, head of jury research for the Virginia-based National Legal Research Group, says, "If a juror has an attitude about something, I want to know what that is." He recounts one instance, while working for defense counsel in a personal injury case, where he learned that one potential juror had won the lottery. Concerned that such an experience might lead the juror to "treat the case like a lottery" or to be more open to making a large damage award, Frederick recommended using a strike on the juror. On another occasion, he discovered online references to a juror in a personal injury case being involved in an accident extremely similar to the one in which the plaintiff was injured; Frederick advised his defense attorney client to use a strike on that individual. Robert Hirschhorn of Dallas's Cathy E. Bennett & Associates has had similar finds during online investigations of prospective jurors. He's found op-ed pieces written by jurors on issues central to a case, as well as revelations about juror involvement with fringe political groups that contradicted what was disclosed on questionnaires and during *voir dire*. Hirschhorn regards those who fail to conduct online research into their prospective jurors as "bordering on malpractice."

Despite its clear importance, there are apparently still some judges resistant to the concept of technology-aided voir dire. In a 2009 medical malpractice trial in Morris County, New Jersey, plaintiff's counsel was on his laptop doing online research on members of the jury pool. The judge ordered the attorney to stop, saying "it's my courtroom and I control it." After a defense verdict, plaintiff's counsel appealed, arguing that the court erred when it prohibited him from doing online research during jury selection. The appellate court agreed, finding that banning web searches during voir dire was unreasonable. It noted,

> "There was no suggestion that counsel's use of the computer was in any way disruptive. That he had the foresight to bring his laptop computer to court, and defense counsel did not, simply cannot serve as a basis for judicial intervention in the name of 'fairness' or maintaining 'a level playing field'. The 'playing field' was, in fact, already 'level' because internet access was open to both counsel, even if only one of them chose to utilize it."

Carino v. Muenzen, 2010 WL 3448071 (N.J.Super.A.D. August 30, 2010).

The digital treasure trove of information available through online resources like social networking sites is becoming increasingly important, especially as more people have a social media presence. While many lawyers are hesitant to engage in what some may regard as invading the privacy of people engaged in doing their civic duty, remember that people with social networking sites control their own content. If they've shared it on a Facebook page for all the world to see, why shouldn't you look at it as well? If information is publically available, and can not only help you serve your client's interest but also potentially serve the cause of justice by preventing biased or unqualified jurors from sitting on a jury, why shouldn't you use it?

Besides, doing a little digital homework on jurors or prospective jurors can help prevent a mistrial or overturned verdict down the road. While the growing problem of jurors conducting Internet and social media "research" about a case and thereby threatening the integrity of the judicial process is dealt with at greater length in another chapter, a few examples of jurors' Facebook misadventures help illustrate the importance of gaining insight into the online presence of your jury panel. For instance, in the New York case of *People v. Rios*, a juror sent a trial witness (a New York City firefighter) a friend request while the jury was deliberating. *People v. Rios*, No. 1200/06, 2010 WL 625221 (N.Y. Feb. 23, 2010). The witness, Brendan Cawley, didn't respond to the request. After the verdict, the juror, Karen Krell, again sent a friend request to Cawley along with a message identifying herself as a juror. This time, Cawley accepted the friend request and responded to the message, and the two exchanged e-mails. Cawley then notified the district attorney's office about the communications. The defense filed a motion to set aside the verdict on the grounds of juror misconduct. However, the court denied it, reasoning that there was no evidence of any "feelings" by Ms. Krell toward Conley that had "necessarily tainted" the outcome of the trial.

Contrast that court decision with the Supreme Court of Appeals ruling in *State of West Virginia v. Dellinger*. No. 35273 (Va. Ct. App. June 3, 2010). In *Dellinger*, the defendant, a deputy sheriff, was accused of corruption— diverting funds intended for hiring additional DUI enforcement staff to himself for hours he hadn't worked. The deputy in question, Christopher Shane Dellinger, was convicted in early 2008 on three counts of falsifying accounts and one count of fraud. Immediately after the verdict, Dellinger's

attorney alerted the trial court to possible misconduct by juror Amber Hyre.
As an investigation revealed, Hyre sent Dellinger a message on MySpace
about a week before the trial began. It read:

> Hey, I don't know you very well. But I think you could use
> some advice. I haven't been in your shoes for a long time
> but I can tell ya that God has a plan for you and your life.
> You might not understand why you are hurting right now
> but when you look back on it, it will make perfect sense. I
> know it is hard but just remember that God is perfect and
> has the most perfect plan for your life. Talk soon!

After sending the message, the two became MySpace friends, which allowed
Dellinger to view postings on Hyre's page and vice-versa. During *voir dire*
just days later, when asked along with other prospective jurors if they had a
business or social relationship with the defendant, Hyre remained silent. As
the court's opinion details, despite the MySpace connection and other
circumstances showing some familiarity with Dellinger, "During *voir dire*,
Juror Hyre never indicated to the trial court that she knew Appellant; had
ever spoken to him 'in passing" or that they used to live in the same
apartment complex." Hyre, like other prospective jurors, was asked if she
was related by blood or marriage (or had a business or social relationship)
with any of the witnesses named by the attorneys. As it turns out, she failed
to disclose being related to one witness by marriage, or that she was "close,
personal friends" with the daughter of a witness, or that her brother-in-law
worked for another witness. During the course of the trial, Amber Hyre
posted a message about getting "home from court" and being in a "blah"
mood.

For his part, Dellinger explained alerting the court to the Amber Hyre
connection after the verdict because Hyre looked "very different" from her
website photo, and he didn't recognize her during jury selection. Hyre
testified that it was "bad judgment" that accounted for her failure to
disclose her acquaintance with the defendant, and that "I just didn't feel like
I really knew him… That's why I didn't say anything."

This didn't convince the appellate court. It noted that, "at the very least, she
believed she knew him well enough to give him advice about his divorce."

The court held that "Juror Hyre's repeated lack of candor clearly undermined the purpose of *voir dire* and, as a result, deprived Appellant of the ability to determine whether she harbored any prejudices or biases against him or in favor of the State." Accordingly, the court held that Dellinger's motion for a new trial should have been granted.

In an age in which a few clicks of a mouse can reveal an abundance of information about prospective jurors (sometimes *too much* information) and in which people are revealing more than ever about themselves online, doing social media research during *voir dire* makes more sense than ever. Not only can you avoid having a juror with a hidden agenda sitting on your panel, but you might actually prevent a mistrial or an overturned verdict on appeal.

18

Dangers of the Online Juror

I was called for jury duty recently, and as I waited for the selection process to begin, I marveled at the number of people thumbing away at their Blackberrys, iPhones, and other web-enabled wireless devices. Although most of them were probably checking in with work or sending mundane messages about having a spouse pick up the kids from soccer practice, it struck me that if any of my fellow panelists were actually picked, precious little could be done to prevent them from accessing the wealth of information lying just a few clicks away.

As it turns out, jurors engaging in such digital digging is a growing problem nationwide, and the explosive growth in popularity of social networking sites like MySpace (more than 250 million users), Facebook (which has surpassed the 500 million mark worldwide), and Twitter (at roughly 77 million users and counting, the third most widely used social network/micro-blogging tool) makes it more likely than ever that jurors will leave the privacy of the jury room for cyberspace. Consider the following recent examples:

- In November 2008, a juror on a child abduction/sexual assault trial in Lancastershire, England, was torn about how to vote. So she posted details of the case online for her Facebook "friends" and announced that she would be holding a poll. After the court was tipped off, the woman was dismissed from the jury.
- In March 2009, an eight-week-long federal drug trial involving Internet pharmacies was disrupted by the revelation that a juror had been doing research online about the case, including looking

into evidence the court had specifically excluded. When U.S. District Judge William Zloch questioned other members of the jury, he was astonished to learn that eight other jurors had been doing the same thing, including running Google searches on the lawyers and the defendants, reading online media coverage of the case, and consulting Wikipedia for definitions. After the judge declared a mistrial, defense attorney Peter Raben expressed his shock at the jurors' online activities. "We were stunned," he said. "It's the first time modern technology struck us in that fashion, and it hit us right over the head."

- In June 2007, a California appellate court reversed the burglary conviction of Donald McNeely when it was revealed that the foreman of the jury had committed misconduct and deprived the defendant of a fair trial by discussing deliberations on his blog. The foreman, a lawyer who had identified himself as a project manager for his company because it was "more neutral than lawyer," blogged about McNeely, his fellow jurors, and their discussions, particularly one juror who was "threatening to torpedo two of the counts in his quest for tyrannical jurisprudence."

- In November 2007, the Supreme Court of Appeals of West Virginia reversed the conviction of Danny Cecil for felony sexual abuse of two teenage girls. Two members of the jury had looked up the MySpace profile of one of the alleged victims, and shared its contents with other jurors. Even though it found that the online sleuthing had not necessarily revealed anything relevant, the court held that "the mere fact that members of a jury in a serious felony case conducted any extrajudicial investigation on their own is gross juror misconduct which simply cannot be permitted." As the court further noted, "Any challenge to the lack of the impartiality of a jury assaults the very heart of due process."

- In the April 2009 case of *Zarzine Wardlaw v. State of Maryland*, Maryland's Special Court of Appeals looked at the circumstances behind the conviction of a man charged with rape, child sexual abuse, and incest involving his seventeen-year-old daughter. During the trial, a therapeutic behavioral specialist had testified about working with the victim on behavioral issues such as anger management, and had opined that the girl suffered from several psychological disorders, including oppositional defiant disorder. A juror took it upon herself to research the disorder online, discovered that lying was a trait associated with the illness, and apparently shared this knowledge with the other jurors. Another member of the jury sent a note informing the judge about this development. After reading the note to counsel for both sides, the judge denied a defense motion for a mistrial and simply reminded the entire jury of his instructions not to research or investigate the case on their own "whether it's on the Internet or in any other way." The appellate court found that this was not enough, and that since the victim's credibility was a crucial issue, the juror's Internet research and reporting her findings to the rest of the jury "constituted egregious misconduct" that could have been "an undue influence on the rest of the jurors." As a result, the trial judge was reversed and a mistrial was granted.

- In October, 2010 Facebook postings by the jury foreman in a high profile Florida rape case formed the basis of the defendant's motion for a new trial. Lawyers for rapist Kendrick Morris learned that during the trial, the foreman had discussed trial testimony on her Facebook page, calling it "boring, boring, boring," and that after the verdict, a fellow juror posted a comment on tampabay.com implying that the foreman had had outside information about the case. As a result, the defense attorney subpoenaed the foreman's records from Facebook.

In some instances, the problems begin before the trial even starts. In September 2009, the South Dakota Supreme Court ruled that a judge was justified in throwing out a defense verdict and ordering a new trial in a product liability wrongful death case where a prospective juror, Shawn Flynn, had done Internet research before he even made it onto the jury.

In *Shawn Russo, et al. v. Takata Corporation* (a Japanese seatbelt manufacturer) *and TK Holdings* (its American subsidiary), the plaintiffs claimed that Takata's seatbelts were defective and had unlatched during a rollover accident. When Flynn received his jury duty summons, he did a Google search for Takata and TK Holdings, examining the web pages for the two companies that were previously unknown to him. During jury selection, Flynn was never directly asked if he'd heard of either company, and he didn't volunteer information about his online searching. He wound up serving on the jury. Several hours into deliberations, Flynn responded to another juror's question about whether Takata had notice of prior malfunctioning seatbelt claims by disclosing his earlier Google searches, and stating that his cyber-sleuthing hadn't turned up any other lawsuits. At least five other jurors either heard his comments directly or were made aware of them during the rest of the deliberations. After the jury returned a verdict in favor of Takata, the plaintiffs sought a new trial, arguing that Flynn's searches had affected the jurors' decisions about whether the seatbelt was defective and whether Takata had notice of any defects. The trial judge vacated the verdict, and the Supreme Court upheld his decision.

Controlling the flow of information into the jury room isn't the only problem. Equally troubling is the flow of information leaving the jury box. In March 2009, during the federal corruption trial of former Pennsylvania state senator Vincent Fumo, a juror posted updates about the case on Twitter and Facebook, even hinting to readers of a "big announcement" before the verdict was issued. The judge denied the defendant's motion for a mistrial, but after a guilty verdict was returned, Fumo's lawyers announced plans to use the Internet postings as a basis for appeal.

Building materials company Stoam Holdings and its owner, Russell Wright, recently sought a motion for new trial after an Arkansas jury entered a $12.6 million verdict against them on February 26, 2009. Wright was accused by two investors, Mark Deihl and William Nystrom, of defrauding them; Deihl's lawyer, Greg Brown, described the building materials venture as "nothing more than a Ponzi scheme."

Shortly after the verdict, Wright's attorneys found out that a juror, Jonathan Powell, a twenty-nine-year-old manager at a Wal-Mart photo lab, had posted eight messages, or "tweets," about the case on social networking site Twitter. (Twitter, created in 2006, is a social networking/micro-blogging service that enables users to not only send updates—text-based posts of up to 140 characters in length—but also follow updates from other users.) Although several of the Twitter messages were sent during jury selection, the ones that attracted the most attention were those actually sent shortly before the verdict was announced.

In one such "tweet," Powell wrote, "Ooh and don't buy Stoam. Its bad mojo and they'll probably cease to exist, now that their wallet is 12m lighter." In another, Powell said, "I just gave away TWELVE MILLION DOLLARS of somebody else's money." One of the lawyers for Stoam and Wright maintained that the messages demonstrated not only that this juror was not impartial and had conducted outside research about the issues in the case, but also that Powell "was predisposed toward giving a verdict that would impress his audience." The court denied Stoam's efforts to set aside the verdict, saying that Powell's actions didn't violate Arkansas law, and that the Twitter messages didn't demonstrate the juror was partial to either side before the verdict.

Texas courts haven't been immune to the epidemic of Googling jurors. The 2006 case of *Sharpless v. Sim* involved a double-fatality accident caused by a truck driver. After the jury returned a verdict in favor of the victims' family, the parties learned that one of the jurors had conducted her own independent Internet research of driver Sharpless's driving record (which, along with evidence of Sharpless's drug use, had been excluded from evidence). Lawyers for the driver and his employer sought a new trial on the grounds of jury misconduct, but the Dallas Court of Appeals ultimately denied their efforts since it wouldn't have led to a different result (the juror in question had been in the minority finding for the trucker).

In 2009, the Dallas County defamation and business torts case of *Business Results, et al. v. Dennis J. Edelman* resulted in a plaintiff's verdict, but a fairly small one. The plaintiff's attorney Michael Hurst of Dallas's Gruber, Hurst, Johansen & Hail learned that jury foreman Kim Clark had Googled one of the plaintiffs, discovering information about the value of the house he lived in and charities with which he was involved. Hurst sought a new trial, which was denied by Judge Emily Tobolowsky. Although the case later settled for a confidential sum while on appeal, Hurst remains sensitive to the potential havoc online jurors can wreak. "My sincere hope is that judges will be even more vigilant about this in the future," says the prominent Dallas litigator.

But in an era in which Americans spend 17 percent of their online time on social networking or blogging sites, and where researching a patent claim or medical disorder can be accomplished with a few keystrokes, what can judges do to adapt to the evolving legal landscape and address the problem of the wired juror? A growing number of jurisdictions are revising their current boilerplate instructions admonishing jurors not to read about or do outside research on the case they happen to be hearing, in order to specifically reference the Internet and social media. The Michigan Supreme Court changed that state's rules as of September 2009 to require judges to instruct jurors not to use any handheld device, such as iPhones or Blackberrys, while in the jury box or during deliberations. All electronic communications by jurors during trial—"tweets" on Twitter, Googling, blogging, etc.—are banned. Similar measures have been adopted or proposed in San Francisco Superior Court and in other jurisdictions.

Although Texas has yet to change its jury instructions, many Dallas County judges are already adding verbal warnings about the Internet. Criminal District Court Judge Andy Chatham told Fox News, "Every judge I've talked to instructs the jurors. We know you have your cell phones. Use them to call your work. Use them to contact your friends and family, but don't use them to research this case." Civil Judge Gena Slaughter of Dallas County's One Hundred and Ninety-First District Court concurs. Although she hasn't yet encountered any issues with jurors going online, the threat posed by such activity is "why I give a very specific instruction to jurors against researching any issues or people involved in the trial on the Internet, as well as against blogging, tweeting, etc. from the jury box. They're there for the truth as we tell it to them; things don't come in for multiple reasons, like relevance." Although Judge Slaughter, a web-savvy 1999 law school graduate, was already accustomed to Googling the experts, parties, and even lawyers involved in cases she handled as an attorney, she notes a growing realization of the importance of this issue among her older fellow jurists. "Over half of us are giving an instruction of some sort on Internet research," she says. Ultimately, she sees the potential for jurors' online misconduct as a problem that will only grow more serious. "The law, unfortunately, does not track technology. No ifs, ands, or buts: the rules need to be changed," says Judge Slaughter.

Some judges have gotten creative in combating the problem of the online juror. A judge in a high profile medical malpractice trial in Tulsa, Oklahoma took the unusual, perhaps extreme, step of taking down (for the duration of the trial) the court's entire online docket to prevent jurors from improperly accessing information about the case. Given the obvious open records concerns, I wouldn't recommend this. And when juror Hadley Jons posted on Facebook—before the verdict was in—that she was actually "excited for jury duty tomorrow" because "It's gonna be fun to tell the defendant they're GUILTY", Macomb County, Michigan Judge Diane Druzinski was not amused. She found Ms. Jons in contempt, and not only ordered her to pay a $250 fine, but also ordered her to write an essay about the Sixth Amendment.

Some observers question whether more should be done beyond revising the jury instructions. Psychologist, attorney, and jury consultant Dr. Robert Gordon of Dallas's Wilmington Institute proposes educating prospective jurors about why outside research is forbidden. "Jurors go online because they can; the anonymity of the Internet makes it possible, and more alluring. You have to explain [why Internet research is harmful], you have to actually talk to them." Dr. Gordon suggests that an educational film, similar to those viewed by potential jurors about jury duty's civic importance, may be a solution. Thomas Melsheimer, managing principal in Fish & Richardson's Dallas office, agrees that educating potential jurors about the dangers of getting information online should begin when they receive their briefing in the central jury rooms. Otherwise, he warns, "the judicial system will find itself meting out justice, not via the common sense of citizens, but via tweets, text messages, and blog postings."

Allowing jurors to consider Internet "evidence" that hasn't been subjected to scrutiny by both sides to a case, or to be influenced by the postings of Facebook "friends" or Twitter "followers," can indeed endanger constitutional guarantees of due process. And in an age in which digital intimacy is rapidly becoming the social norm and where a jury room's sanctity can be violated at the speed of a search engine, jurors venturing online will be an issue confronted by lawyers and judges for some time to come. Just don't Google it if you're called for jury duty.

19

Social Media and the First Amendment

Students are probably the most regular and extensive users of social networking sites; indeed, Facebook itself got its start as a way for Harvard students to stay in touch electronically. According to a 2010 Pew Internet Study of Social Media and Young Adults, 73 percent of wired American teens now use social networking websites; among online eighteen- to twenty-nine-year-olds, the figure is about equally high at 72 percent. And it's very much a case of "live by the sword, die by the sword." For all the utility and entertainment value of social networking among students, it can be used against them too. Law enforcement and campus police, for example, have been known to monitor social networking sites for word about parties so they can show up and investigate potential underage drinking. At Emerson College, campus police have surfed Facebook for discussion threads on student online forums that discussed not only campus parties and underage drinking, but also illicit drug use. And in Belgium, two college students thought they had successfully cheated in two courses, until university administrators confronted them with evidence obtained online. It seems the two cheaters had discussed on Facebook their method of cheating, the fact that they'd been doing it for a while, and the fact that they were pretty proud of themselves for supposedly getting away with it. The students confessed, and while they weren't happy about Facebook being used against them, the university reminded them that the online conversations in question were not restricted.

As many college sports fans know, the NCAA has a dizzying array of rules governing the recruiting of student athletes. Now, coaches and athletic directors have one more headache: navigating rules about contacting recruits via social media. Because of the NCAA's insistence that "all postings from coaches to prospective recruits on social networking sites must be made in a direct person-to-person, non-public manner," coaches can privately message a prospect on Facebook, but can't publicly post a message on his or her wall. The University of Virginia's football coach ran afoul of this rule, posting to a recruit's wall when he meant to send a private message via Facebook; Virginia's athletic department self-reported the potential violation to the NCAA in 2010.

When it comes to students speaking out against teachers or administrators on social networking sites, trying to decide where free speech ends and defamation begins is a murkier issue. Under the seminal ruling in *Tinker v. Des Moines Independent Community School District*, the U.S. Supreme Court said a "showing that the students' activities would materially and substantially disrupt the work and discipline of the school" is required to justify suppressing student expression. 393 U.S. 503 (1969). Subsequent decisions have looked at whether the speech in question occurred on or off campus in determining the potential for disruption. But what about online speech, which may be critical and downright derogatory of teachers? Is cyberspace off-campus, especially when students and teachers alike can access the comments via computer or smartphone while in the classroom?

Many courts are coming down on the side of free speech. In *Evans v. Bayer*, honor student Katherine Evans used her home computer to create a Facebook group called "Ms. Sarah Phelps is the worst teacher I've ever met," after clashing with the English teacher over assignments. After Principal Peter Bayer found out, he disciplined Evans two months later by suspending her and removing her from Advanced Placement classes. Evans sued and Bayer sought a dismissal of the suit. In February 2010, a Florida federal judge not only denied the motion to dismiss, but also held that Evans had a First Amendment right to make the Facebook comments. The court noted that the statements were published off-campus and did not cause any campus disruption. Judge Barry Garber also observed that because of the gap in time between the comments and the principal's disciplinary action, Bayer's measures were punitive rather than calculated to protect the learning environment. As a result, Evans was allowed to move forward with her suit, in which she sought her attorneys' fees and nominal damages.

In another 2010 case, the Third Circuit Court of Appeals ruled that school officials went too far when they disciplined a student for creating a false MySpace profile. In *Layshock v. Hermitage School District*, high school senior Justin Layshock was suspended for ten days after he created a phony MySpace page for his school principal, Eric Trosch, which described Trosch as "a big steroid freak" and a "big hard ass" who smoked a "big blunt." In ruling that the principal had violated Layshock's First Amendment rights, the Third Circuit said it would create a "dangerous precedent" to allow the state in the guise of school authorities to reach into a child's home and control his or her actions there to the same extent that they control the child when he or she participates in school-sponsored activities." Essentially, the mere fact that a social networking site or the Internet may be accessed at school doesn't give school officials blanket authority to censor the web.

But another 2010 Third Circuit opinion upheld a school's right to discipline students for their online conduct. In *J.S. v. Blue Mountain School District*, a fourteen-year-old female student was suspended after creating a phony MySpace page portraying her principal as a sex addict and pedophile whose hobbies included "hitting on students and their parents." This time, the court seemed to be persuaded by the vulgarity and the profile's blatant allusions to sexual misconduct, which the court believed presented not only an attempt to undermine authority, but also signaled the likelihood of future disruption. While the *Layshock* case and the *J.S.* decision—handed down the same day—would seem to contradict each other, the two are distinguishable. Unlike the fake MySpace page in *Layshock*, the one in *J.S.* was vulgar, lewd, and promoted or discussed unlawful behavior (such as sex with minors); as such, one could understand the school's belief that a disturbance on campus was imminent.

Other lawsuits pending around the country involving behavior on a social networking site include a Georgia case brought by a former school teacher who was forced to resign over profanity and pictures of her holding a glass of wine that appeared on her Facebook page. Another involves Indiana high school students who are challenging their punishment for allegedly posting sexually suggestive photos of themselves on MySpace during their summer vacation. All of them, however, deal with the tightrope educators have to walk in this digital era, balancing the need to monitor information while not infringing students' rights to free speech. Once again, the law has failed to keep pace with technology. While speech online at a social media site is still speech and thus worthy of protection, the power of social networking and the Internet allows that speech to be directed at the school community in ways we never could have anticipated decades ago.

As discussed in the chapter on family law, sometimes court "gag orders" that impact social media use by one or more parties are challenged on First Amendment grounds. For example, an Arizona appellate court struck down a trial judge's edict against estranged wife Kimberly Cockerham publishing "audiotape, videotape, or written documentation about the legal proceedings." At issue, among other things, was a YouTube recording posted by Ms. Cockerham under the title "Dr. Patrick Kelledy, yelling at his ex-wife AGAIN." The appellate court called it a classic prior restraint on speech concerning a public proceeding, and vacated the trial court's order. *Kelledy v. Cockerham*, No. 1 CA-CV 09-0093 (Court of Appeals, Arizona, Division One (Memorandum Decision, 8/12/10)).

And when directed at other students, when do attacks using social media go beyond First Amendment boundaries and become defamation or cyber-bullying? A recent defamation case in Long Island, New York, dealt with a private Facebook page that never identified the plaintiff, Denise Finkel, by name. On the page (set up by several of Finkel's classmates), Finkel was characterized as someone of dubious character who engaged in bestiality, intravenous drug use, and other offensive sexual behavior. A state supreme court judge in Nassau, though, said that while the social networking page displayed an "utter lack of taste and propriety," it didn't constitute libel. The ordinary reader, the court said, wouldn't take such accusations seriously. The court also denied the plaintiff's claim of negligent entrustment against the children's parents. As Judge Randy Sue Marber wrote, "To declare a computer a dangerous instrument in the hands of teenagers in an age of ubiquitous computer ownership would create an exception that would engulf the rule against parental liability."

One recent California decision was emphatic in its rejection of juvenile probation restrictions that encompassed social media use. Generally, courts have broad discretion in crafting conditions of probation, and juvenile court judges have even broader discretion. But in *In Re J.J.*, a California appellate court struck down probation restrictions that included no Facebook use as a violation of the youth's First Amendment rights. *In Re J.J.*, Case No. D055603, (Cal. Ct. App. Oct. 15, 2010). J.J., a 15 year-old placed on probation for the alleged theft of a motorcycle, was ordered by the court not to use a computer for any other purpose than school-related work (and then only under supervision). The judge specifically prohibited J.J. from using instant messaging services through MySpace, Facebook, and others, and in fact decreed that J.J. "shall not have a MySpace page, a Facebook page, or any other similar page and shall delete any existing page. [He] shall not use MySpace, Facebook, or any other similar program."

The appellate court observed that such restrictions bore no relationship to J.J.'s criminal history, and that the ban was so overly broad that it "forecloses access to countless benign and protected uses." More importantly, the Court of Appeals upheld J.J.'s challenge to the restrictions on First Amendment grounds, noting the importance of Internet access to the exercise of free speech:

> "Through the use of chat rooms, any person with a phone line can become a town crier with a voice that resonates farther than it could from any soapbox. Through the use of Web pages, mail exploders, and newsgroups, the same individual can become a pamphleteer . . . Two hundred years after the framers ratified the Constitution, the Net has taught us what the First Amendment means."

20

Social Media and Attorney Marketing

Imagine the potential connections for a lawyer on a site like Twitter, LinkedIn, or Facebook. Say he or she has one hundred "followers," "connections," or "friends," and each of them in turn has one hundred contacts, and so on, and so on. If that lawyer is the first to post about a new court decision, piece of legislation, or other legal development, he or she has the possibility of building and reaching a greater network than he or she ever could in person through cocktail parties, professional receptions, and similar opportunities. Gaining a reputation in one's particular area of practice or creating a niche through such "digital word of mouth" can be invaluable when it comes to growing a practice.

If you haven't already embraced social networking as a marketing tool, you're not alone, but the numbers of those who do use social media are growing. The LexisNexis Martindale Hubbell Networks for Counsel survey found that in 2008, nearly 50 percent of the responding lawyers were members of a social networking site; by 2009 that percentage had climbed to over 60 percent, and it hovered around 80 percent within the ranks of younger lawyers (ages twenty-five to thirty-five). Even the mere fact that corporate America itself is turning to advertising through social networking as a cheaper alternative to costly television and print campaigns has generated more work for lawyers. Attorneys specializing in marketing and promotion issues are busier than ever, helping clients who have taken advantage of social media platforms to directly engage consumers and navigate their way through copyright, trademark, and privacy issues. As companies continue to make greater use of social media for marketing, tapping into customer feedback, and responding to complaints, there will be a higher demand for lawyers who understand social media.

If you don't believe me, consider this. The detergent giant Clorox attracted some attention in January 2010 when it advertised for an addition to its roster of in-house counsel: an attorney whose sole focus would be on social media legal issues. *Advertising Age* called the move "surprising," but nevertheless a sign of the times. Clorox has Facebook fan pages for its products, uses Twitter as a means of gathering new product ideas, and maintains a blog ("Understanding Bleach") where it solicits reader input. The new in-house lawyer, according to the ad, would be expected to provide legal advice on overseeing and securing advertising content, "especially as it relates to social media and other Web 2.0 executions," advise on music and video licensing issues for social media and other platforms, and counsel the company on privacy laws applicable to the collection of consumer information.

For another example of the importance of becoming social media-savvy, in May 2009 a company called FMC Technologies sent out a request for proposals to law firms wishing to bid for its legal work. What made this different from any other "beauty contest" was the fact that the request was posted on Legal OnRamp, an online social network for in-house counsel, and that it required interested law firms to "state in a Tweet on Twitter (140 characters limit) why FMC should hire the law firm." According to FMC's general counsel, Jeffrey Carr, he chose this type of social media request for proposals because he was seeking tech-savvy firms that offered alternative fee structures and online billing.

In the 2010 ABA Technology Survey Report, 10 percent of the lawyers responding reported having a client retain their legal services "as a result of online communities/social networking." While that figure might at first blush seem small, it nevertheless represents a dramatic shift in how lawyers and law firms regard social media. And, it's only going to go up. The same survey reported that 56 percent of attorneys had a social networking presence in 2010 (a dramatic increase from the 15 percent reported in the 2008 survey). Significantly, it's not just the younger and presumably more tech-savvy lawyers represented. In fact, according to the ABA's report, the largest growth in social media use was recorded by lawyers aged sixty to sixty-nine; 47 percent of this demographic group reported having a social networking profile. Among all groups, LinkedIn was the most widely identified site (83 percent), while 68 percent reported using Facebook. As far as the reasons for using social media are concerned, 76 percent of the lawyers surveyed said they use the sites for professional networking. Sixty-two percent use them for socializing, and 42 percent use them for client development (surprisingly, only 6 percent said they use social media for case investigation).

As the challenges of the economic downturn continue, social media is becoming more prominent on the radar of in-house counsel. According to a 2009 LexisNexis survey of 764 private practice lawyers and 710 corporate counsel, corporate lawyers' use of social networks increased about 50 percent in 2009. The main reason given was the pressure on legal departments to cut costs, and the fact that social networking provides a way of exchanging information with peers. In-house counsel can save money on outside legal fees by networking with others for useful forms, drafting tips, case law updates, and ideas. In addition, general counsel often make use of networks like Legal OnRamp (which features some groups that are invitation-only) for a private forum for solving problems collectively; popular topics for discussion include alternative fee arrangements and how much certain tasks or projects should cost. Eugene Weitz, an in-house attorney for Alcatel Lucent, says, "Online networks are a fantastic tool for identifying expertise in the fields in which general counsel are looking to rein in outside counsel. Experts bubble up who have the ability to show their knowledge online." According to a 2008 LexisNexis Martindale Hubbell Networks for Counsel survey, corporate counsel identified the following attributes as the most important features of online networking: access to information not found anywhere else (46 percent); the ease of exchanging information and experiences (45 percent); the ability to identify, evaluate, and select private practice lawyers quickly (29 percent); finding the "right" lawyer directly (26 percent); and speed of collaboration (21 percent).

Why Use Social Media for Marketing?

The same Networks for Counsel survey revealed that 52 percent of the respondents agreed (or strongly agreed) that with an increasingly globalized economy, it's harder to stay connected with peers and colleagues; more than 40 percent believe online professional networking has the potential to change the business and the practice of law over the next five years. For many lawyers who are beginning to embrace social media, it's a matter of survival, neatly summed up in the title of a March 25, 2009, article on Law 360: "Social Networking Spurs Firms to Log On or Lose Out." Pamela Woldow, a principal in the legal consulting firm Altman Weil who is quoted in the article, says, "We're entering a time where many lawyers are being laid off and firms are barely surviving. The people remaining in the practice of law have to differentiate themselves from the other firms that are hungry for business."

There are, of course, less crass reasons to use social media. Its utility as an investigative tool for helpful information in cases is discussed throughout this book, and it's refining certain procedural and substantive areas of law. Above all, it's a great way to learn and expand your knowledge, not just your network of connections. It helps you become a better communicator. Whether it's a blog post or a tweet, brevity is pivotal when you're generating online content. Anything that sharpens your ability to express yourself clearly and concisely makes you a more effective lawyer. Besides, social networking can be fun and humanize you at the same time. Lawyers are frequently criticized for coming off as arrogant. When I chose the picture for my Facebook profile, I was tempted to go with the staid, boring professional head shot from my firm's website. My wife, however, insisted that I needed something warmer and more approachable than a photo with that "I'll crush you in court" glower. She insisted on a shot of me from a recent Disney World vacation, snapped as I put on a pair of oversized Mickey Mouse gloves and did "jazz hands." Not in bad taste (I wouldn't recommend beach photos featuring Speedos or bikinis), just something that depicts you as down to earth. I've gotten great, consistently positive reactions from friends and business contacts alike who seem to appreciate that there's a normal human being behind the pinstripe suit.

Still, most lawyers who are embracing this technology understandably view social media primarily as a platform for marketing their practice. So the key question becomes "How I do use social media to market my practice?"

How to Market Your Practice through Social Media

First, decide which social networking site or sites make the most sense to use as your platform. Here's a handy guide to some of the available options:

Legal OnRamp (www.LegalOnRamp.com)

This site bills itself as "a collaboration system for in-house counsel and invited outside lawyers and third party service providers." Membership in the 10,000-plus network is free but by invitation only, according to founder Paul Lippe, who eschews the term "social network" in favor of describing it as a "very elite" community. While you can request an invitation to join by completing and submitting an application online, this is one of those "who you know" organizations where you're better off wrangling an invitation from an existing member. The site features member profiles, discussion groups, a news and updates section, links to articles on legal sites like Law.com and InsideCounsel, as well as a collaborative wiki for posting form agreements and other helpful materials. Lippe calls the online discussions "the kind of conversation that board members have about best practices when they meet at a common board meeting."

JD Supra (www.JDSupra.com)

JD Supra founder Aviva Cuyler says her site "helps people connect with clients as well as colleagues and potential referrals where people discover they are working on similar issues." The site is largely an aggregation of articles, forms, pleadings, and briefs. It has applications that allow lawyers to post such legal documents to Facebook, LinkedIn, Twitter, and Justia.com, permitting one to reach a wider audience. Cuyler, a former commercial litigator herself, says this enables a lawyer's content to rank "much higher than if it was lost on an individual site." When people put their content on the site, it also streams out to many areas to reach targeted audiences. The site features tweets about Twitter postings in topic-specific newsfeeds, enabling lawyers to reach not only a target audience but an established one as well. Similarly, the site feeds articles onto pertinent LinkedIn interest groups. Recently, JDSupra and LinkedIn co-launched "Legal Updates," an application that showcases and distributes legal content on the homepage of LinkedIn users. It can be customized to specific legal topics.

LawLink (www.LawLink.com)

LawLink refers to itself as "the first social network for the legal community." On it, you'll find not just lawyers but also law students, paralegals, legal administrators, law professors, and even expert witnesses. Like LinkedIn, members can participate in discussion groups, post questions and answers, and link to their blogs. In addition, like JDSupra, members can post documents such as motions and briefs. In fact, Lawlink seeks to drive up participation by awarding points for postings (you could even wind up as one of the site's "featured attorneys" for the month for such accumulated posts and points).

Martindale-Hubbell Connected (www.martindalecom/connected)

This, like LawLink, is a social network specifically for lawyers. Membership is free, and you don't need to have a Martindale-Hubbell profile or subscription to join; despite this, however, its ranks are fairly thin (as of September 2009, it had only 15,000 members). As with other networks, there are blogs, discussion groups, member profiles, and legal news updates. You can even post professional announcements.

Texas Bar Circle (https://texasbar.affinitycircles.com/sbot/home)

I've included Texas Bar Circle, the social network for members of the State Bar of Texas, because I'm a member. You should explore whether your state bar, or perhaps specialty bar associations or societies to which you belong, offer a social network for its members as well. On Texas Bar Circle, members will find postings about job openings and referral opportunities, event and professional announcements, as well as discussion groups and other chances to connect. As with other social networks, Texas Bar Circle offers the chance to post questions and get professional feedback and share best practices. Groups are organized around everything from law school alumni to geographic regions to practice areas; so if you're a north Texas probate lawyer or a Houston-area family specialist, there may be a group for you.

Twitter (www.twitter.com)

Twitter is something of a hybrid—a social networking/micro-blogging site, with more than 77 million users. On Twitter, you're limited to "tweets," or messages, of up to 140 characters. Twitter is what you make of it; twenty-nine of the AMLAW 100 law firms have Twitter accounts, although a survey conducted by MyCorporateResource.com found that only nine of those twenty-nine post to Twitter on a regular basis. Indeed, some have never posted a single update. On Twitter, you can "follow" others, and find out what experts in your field or others are saying about things that interest you; you can also "re-tweet" (or forward) topics or updates you believe will be of interest to others. You can lead, and post updates or tweets about things that are of interest to you and which you feel may be important to others. For example, if you handle cases involving medical devices, you might tweet about a new piece of legislation affecting that industry, or post a link to an article on your blog or firm website discussing the implications of the new law in greater depth.

Facebook (www.facebook.com)

Some lawyers still shy away from Facebook, thinking it's for strictly a younger crowd. Not true; according to Facebook, the thirty-five- to fifty-four-year-old age bracket is its fastest-growing demographic. Others are hesitant due to privacy issues, but with proper use of the privacy settings, that concern can be alleviated. Another concern is that Facebook is too informal and not sufficiently professional. However, Facebook (as part of its tremendous growth) is rapidly gaining traction in the professional community for its business uses. In fact, a Corporate Counsel survey in May 2010 revealed that nearly half of in-house counsel aged thirty to thirty-nine have used Facebook for professional reasons in the past. In addition to having a profile, you can start a Facebook fan page or group—for your firm, for a specialty area of practice, etc. On such a page (or on your profile), you can post links to everything from podcasts and blogs to media articles in which you're quoted. As with other social networking resources, Facebook is a means not only of staying connected with existing clients and referral sources, but also of informing potential ones. Most importantly, Facebook's sheer numbers make it impossible to overlook.

LinkedIn (www.LinkedIn.com)

LinkedIn, with more than 70 million members, is known as the world's largest professional social network. LinkedIn emphasizes business and professional contacts; by way of example, my LinkedIn contacts might include not only clients in various companies and industries, but colleagues from former law firms, law school and college classmates, contacts from civic organizations, and even expert witnesses I've used. You can import your Outlook contacts after setting up a profile, see who's on LinkedIn, and invite them to connect with you. Like other sites, LinkedIn has discussion groups and you can link to your firm website, a blog, or materials you've written. If you've recently given a presentation, you can widen your audience by uploading your PowerPoint slides to Slideshare (available on LinkedIn). If a prospective client Googles that topic, your presentation just might pop up, showcasing your mastery of the subject area to an audience you never knew you'd have. LinkedIn offers attorneys access to a virtual cocktail party, where industry groups, trade associations, business owners, and entrepreneurs are all present. As one lawyer put it after a referral through LinkedIn, "Being active on LinkedIn will help you professionally, whether that translates to a new client or an invitation to give a talk or other marketing activities."

The next step after deciding on the social media platform or platforms you'll use to market your practice is to create an online profile. As with any social networking site, keep in mind that this is the outward-facing impression you're giving to the world, so carefully consider what you highlight about yourself. Don't put anything on there that you wouldn't want your grandmother to see if it was printed on the front page of the newspaper. Of course, everyone marches to the beat of a different drummer—sometimes literally. In 2008, lawyers from the San Francisco-based law firm Hanson Bridgett uploaded a video to YouTube to celebrate its fiftieth anniversary. The video depicted a band of lederhosen-clad musicians (including firm managing partner Andrew Giacomini) with accordions and other instruments marching down Market Street to a zydeco-meets-polka beat. The video has been viewed thousands of times, to the delight of Giacomini, who was inspired by "the whole social networking video-sharing culture." He says the video shows viewers "this is a firm where people don't take themselves too seriously, but they are serious about what they do."

Once you're on a social media network with a profile that showcases you and your practice, your next concern—as you are reaching out, connecting with and friending people, and following others on Twitter, perhaps—is what to put out there. It's easy to use social networking poorly, or to just sit there with a static profile. It's also easy to let your profile or Twitter account be little more than a mirror image of your firm's website. Why bother with copied-and-pasted headlines from your firm's press releases or newsletters, or the occasional media blurb about a recent award or distinction, and nothing more? Those are fine (let's face it—your Twitter feed should assume that people following you care about what you're doing), but they're not enough.

Reaching out through social media to market your practice should keep in mind one key fact: it's all about the clients (and prospective clients). Blog, tweet, or post updates about a recent case or legislation that is of importance or interest to people in their line of work. Create some targeted content that has practical advice or other value to the recipients. One consultant recommends lists, such as "Five Things to Consider When Choosing on Estate Lawyer" or "Seven Ways to Budget for Litigation," because they present information in an organized, easily digestible format with a clear takeaway for the reader. Remember, social media is not about "selling" so much as it is about building relationships. You want to deliver content that builds relationships. If you provide information about a new legal development that alters the posture of a case that some general counsel or claims manager has been sweating over, you're the new hero. Arm someone with helpful information he or she didn't otherwise have, and you'll be remembered. Also, work within the limitations of your media platform. Prospective clients may receive numerous Twitter "alerts" that refer to nothing more than, say, the name of a new piece of legislation; after all, some of those bills' titles are long. Tailor yours to focus on what's different about your take on the issue, or the theme of your content (after all, you want them to read it); like a good novelist or journalist, you should grab the reader right away.

Another crucial point with social media is that, like a conversation, it shouldn't be just one person talking. Use social media as a tool to learn about your clients and prospective clients. Keep up with what's going on in their fields, and the issues affecting them. Social media is another source of information for you to take advantage of; listen and learn. Similarly, like a conversation, you don't want to be a pest, but you don't want to be totally silent either. Chances are you are not the only lawyer sending an alert electronically to a client or potential client anyway; bombarding recipients with content that doesn't address their particular needs doesn't help you. Be focused in your use of social media—don't get caught up in a numbers game of sending out so many updates or having X number of friends on Facebook or followers on Twitter. A few genuinely interested prospective clients who find value in the content you've shared and who are, in turn, sharing or re-tweeting it to all of *their* business contacts is far more worthwhile.

If the primary source of your business is referrals from other lawyers, take online steps to set yourself apart as an expert in your field. Write a blog, and link to articles you've done or presentations you've given. Let others know about you. If you handle trucking accidents, set up Google alerts for your clients and their competitors. Don't just read industry magazines or newsletters—subscribe to their electronic updates, if available. Start or join a "Trucking Litigation" group on LinkedIn or other sites. Consider starting a Facebook fan page, where you can post updates instead of sending out blast e-mails that might wind up in spam folders. If you're on Twitter, invite your clients to follow you, and provide links to updates you've authored or seen. If you're on LinkedIn, and have done a recent PowerPoint presentation that might be of interest to the trucking industry, put your presentation on SlideShare and invite your contacts to view it.

Finally, the most important thing to remember is that social media platforms are for building relationships and aren't a substitute for them. You still need to follow up with in-person contact. Use your social networking as an entre to move the conversation offline. Pick up the phone, and set up a lunch or dinner meeting, or simply meet for coffee or drinks after work. Ask your contacts if they need speakers for an upcoming meeting or conference. Social networking is an invaluable tool to educate yourself and others, and to initiate and maintain contact—but it's no substitute for face-to-face interaction.

21

What Does the Future Hold? Social Media and Evolving Crimes, Causes of Action, Defenses, and Legal Duties

Talk to any group of attorneys about social media, and you'll find a broad spectrum of opinions on the subject. There are wide-eyed, early adopter, "true believer" types who appear to have anointed social networking as a mystical wonder that can bring in hordes of new clients and elevate its users to acclaimed expert status on a variety of legal subjects. At the other extreme are those who wonder what all the fuss is about and consider social networking nothing more than a passing fad and a mental drain on productivity.

The reality is more complex. Social media is a phenomenon that is transforming society and, as a result, the way we practice, and the legal system itself cannot help but be affected as well. While social networking can bring obvious benefits when it comes to marketing one's practice and sharing practice tips with colleagues, it is what one makes of it. Regardless of where you fall on the spectrum, two things are undeniable: social media is here to stay, and it has already affected everything from the notion of legal duty to the creation of new crimes, causes of action, and defenses.

Social Media and Evolving Legal Duties

It has often been pointed out that law does not keep pace with technology. The gradual, incremental pace that accompanies the accumulation of legal precedent cannot hope to rival the lightning speed and generational leaps that can characterize technological innovation. Nevertheless, the Internet and social media are helping transform one of the building block concepts of the law: the notion of duty.

Courts themselves have witnessed a change in attitudes toward the importance of electronic information gathering. Just a few years ago, a federal court was derisively referring to "voodoo information taken from the Internet," a vehicle the court regarded as "one large catalyst for rumor, innuendo, and misinformation" on the way to concluding that "any evidence procured off the Internet is adequate for almost nothing." *St. Clair v. Johnny's Oyster & Shrimp Inc.*, 76 F. Supp.2d 773 (S.D. Tex. 1999). Now, however, courts have suggested that attorneys exercising due diligence in getting a party served have an implied "duty to Google." In a recent Indiana decision, the court couldn't believe that the plaintiff attorney had failed to "Google" the absent defendant (Joe Groce) in the normal course of due diligence. The incredulous judge observed, "We do note that there is no evidence in this case of a public records or Internet search for Groce...to find him. In fact, we [the court] discovered, upon entering 'Joe Groce Indiana' into the Google search engine, an address for Groce that differed from either address used in this case, as well as an apparent obituary for Groce's mother that had listed numerous surviving relatives who might have known his whereabouts." *Munster v. Groce*, 829 N.E.2d 52, 62, footnote 3 (Ind. App. 2005).

In a similar case, a Florida appellate court also considering the question of due diligence in getting a party served stated that the investigative method of merely checking directory assistance to locate a missing defendant, in light of the widespread use of the Internet, has gone "the way of the horse and buggy and the eight track stereo." *Dubois v. Butler ex rel. Butler*, 901 So.2d 1029, 1031 (Fl. App. 2005). Sometimes the court even gets into the act. In a Louisiana case that revolved around the annulment of a tax sale after the trial court judge conducted his own Internet search and determined that the tax-delinquent property owner was "reasonably ascertainable," part of the appellate opinion centered on whether it was appropriate for the judge to have undertaken such a search. Although the government claimed to have performed a public records search itself that failed to disclose the mortgage, the appellate court upheld the nullification of the sale. It held that the property owner's due process rights had been violated and that the trial court conducting its own Internet search amounted to nothing more than harmless error. *Weatherly v. Optimum Asset Management Inc.*, 928 So.2d 118 (La. App. 2005).

Social networking is even showing signs of influencing legal research. A brief filed in Illinois federal court in August 2010 in a case dealing with Chicago's post-McDonald law banning gun ranges within the city actually cited a tweet by a law professor. Noting that the city of Chicago's lawyers had referenced the work of UCLA Law Professor Adam Winkler, the opposing attorneys went one better: they cited a tweet by Professor Winkler agreeing that Chicago's range ban was unconstitutional. Essentially, they refuted the city's interpretation of Winkler's law review article by going straight to the source, going to @adamwinkler on Twitter for the quote ": Reasonable gun control is one thing, this another. Chicago requires one hour on range for handgun permit but bars ranges." Just like that, the other side's argument loses credibility—in 140 characters or less. OMG!

More recently, the Second Circuit Court of Appeals ruled that a judge's conducting his own Internet search not only didn't violate any rules of evidence, but it was—in today's digital age—merely a logical method of confirming judicial intuition. In *U.S. v. Bari*, Bari (a former bank robber) was accused of violating the terms of his supervised release by committing another bank robbery in September 2008. The evidence presented against Bari included the testimony of a bank employee who recognized the robber's voice; video surveillance footage showing that the height, weight, and posture of the depicted bank robber matched that of Bari; and what trial judge Denny Chin characterized as "the strongest piece of evidence" against Bari, a yellow rain hat found in the garage of Bari's landlord that matched the type of hat worn in the video. Noting the similarities between the hats, judge Chin turned to the Internet, conducting a Google search that confirmed his belief that "there are clearly lots of yellow hats out there" and it was too much of a coincidence for the robber to have been wearing the same type of hat found in the landlord's garage. Judge Chin ruled that Bari had violated the terms of his supervised release, and sentenced him to thirty-six months in prison. Bari appealed, contending that judge Chin's Google search violated Federal Rule of Civil Procedure 605's prohibition against a judge testifying as a witness.

The appellate court disagreed, nothing that Rule 201 allows a judge to take judicial notice of facts, and that consulting a search engine was merely an efficient way of confirming judge Chin's common-sense supposition. As the court observed:

> Twenty years ago, to confirm an intuition about the variety of rain hats, a trial judge may have needed to travel to a local department store to survey the rain hats on offer. Rather than expend that time, he likely would have relied on his common sense to take judicial notice of the fact that not all rain hats are alike. Today, however, a judge need only take a few moments to confirm his intuition by conducting a basic Internet search. See *Reno v. ACLU*, 521 U.S. 844, 853 (1997) ("The Web is…comparable…to both a vast library including millions of readily available and indexed publications and a sprawling mall offering goods and services."). As the cost of confirming one's intuition decreases, we would expect to see more judges doing just that. More generally, with so much information at our fingertips (almost literally), we all likely confirm hunches with a brief visit to our favorite search engine that in the not-so-distant past would have gone unconfirmed.

Certainly, the prevalence and sheer ease of use of online resources like search engines may be leading to the creation of a "duty to Google," whether you're a lawyer exercising due diligence or a judge confirming an intuition. In a similar fashion, the all-pervasive world of social networking may be inspiring a similar evolution of prevailing notions of duty.

Consider, for example, the case of James A. Roppo, senior vice president for sales for Island Def Jam Records. Roppo was present at a mall in Long Island, New York, for a planned album signing by teen sensation Justin Bieber in November 2009. Bieber's popularity led to an overflow crowd of more than 3,000 people (mainly young girls and their parents) who were lined up to see the pop singer and get his autograph. The crowd grew unruly and aggressive, resulting in difficulty for the police in maintaining crowd control. One officer sustained a minor injury. According to news accounts, police requested that record executive Roppo help their efforts by sending a Twitter message, or "tweet," directing the crowd to leave (assuming, fairly safely, that the majority of the young ladies in attendance were "followers" of Justin Bieber on Twitter). In particular, police were concerned about the dangers of fans crowding near a balcony and the potential for fans to fall or for the railing to collapse.

Roppo refused, and was arrested and charged with felony assault charges (involving the injured officer), criminal nuisance, endangering the welfare of a child, reckless endangerment, and obstruction of governmental administration. Nassau County Police Detective Lieutenant Kevin Smith said, "We asked for his help in getting the crowd to go away by sending out a Twitter message. By not cooperating with us we feel he put lives in danger and the public at risk."

Bieber's manager, Scott Braun, was also arrested. Police claimed that Braun failed to tweet the Bieber fans to let them know the event was being cancelled due to overcrowding. On the contrary, police allege that the cancellation tweets weren't sent out until over one and a half hours later (after Roppo had already been arrested on the scene). Prior to that, they claimed, Braun had not only blocked Bieber's account to keep anyone from sending the tweet out, but he had actually tweeted fans from Bieber's account and encouraged them to keep coming. According to Nassau County District Attorney Kathleen Rice, "Mr. Braun put his own selfish desire for publicity above public safety and endangered the very fans who came to see his client, as well as innocent bystanders who were at the mall that day. By refusing to send out the cancellation tweet and preventing others from doing so, he blatantly ignored police directives and put thousands of innocent people in harm's way."

Is there—should there be—a "duty to tweet"? In the absence of a legally imposed duty to affirmatively act, most jurisdictions don't consider it actionable or worthy of a criminal charge when an individual fails to engage in certain conduct. With the ease, acceptance, and access to social networking—not to mention heightened public awareness—we may be witnessing the beginnings of a new duty taking shape. This may prove particularly true in the context of background investigations, and the potential liability that exists for failing to investigate an employee's background, or negligently or inadequately performing such an investigation.

In a lawsuit filed in December 2009 in Nebraska state court, the parents of Caitlin Marvin allege that their daughter's school district, teachers, and administrators owed her a duty to more fully investigate a teacher who eventually assaulted her. According to this suit, the Marvins allege that a teacher, John Hoffman, initially tutored the girl but that over time his interest in the fourteen-year-old took a sexual turn. Although Hoffman was arrested and sentenced to eighteen to twenty-five years in prison for the sexual molestation, the Marvins maintain that the school is liable because a "reasonably prudent school district employer" would have investigated Hoffman's social networking presence and either not hired him initially or would not have rehired him during an annual review. The plaintiffs contend that Hoffman's appearance and demeanor radically changed during his employment, including such signs of "immature, unprofessional, and bad judgment" as "tattoos, pierced body parts, and a 'Mohawk' haircut." They further allege that such changes and Hoffman's sexual proclivities should have been readily ascertainable if school officials had bothered to check out Hoffman's MySpace page, which was purportedly filled with sexual references and innuendos, including the defendant's nickname: John "Pecker" Hoffman. The Marvins claim that the social networking information was "publicly available," and that the facts were "sufficient to impart notice to a reasonably prudent school district employer of Hoffman's predatory sexual interests and predilections and propensity for sexual misconduct, but they were not reasonably observed or discovered."

Can the ease and popularity of social networking sites really lead to tort liability for the criminal conduct of third parties? While this theory has yet to be tested in Nebraska, it has already been rejected by at least one California appellate court, albeit in a different context. Plaintiffs Cody Melton, Mike Kelly, and Jesse Maldonado attended a May 7, 2007, party at the palatial Soquel Hills, California, home of Silicon Valley entrepreneur Clive Boustred. At the event, the three were allegedly attacked by a group of unknown persons. They brought a lawsuit against the host, Mr. Boustred, arguing that the attack was reasonably foreseeable since Boustred had promoted the party on MySpace. They claimed that Boustred had a "higher social responsibility" due to his active conduct, stating that a "homeowner of common sense would know that a public invitation posted on MySpace to a free party offering music and alcohol was substantially certain to result in an injury to someone." The plaintiffs maintained that Boustred owed them a duty not to actively create "an out of control and dangerous public MySpace party."

The trial judge disagreed, and dismissed the case for failure to state a claim. California's Sixth District Court of Appeals affirmed, opining that neither common sense nor hindsight determine whether a duty exists. The test is whether the harm that occurred was foreseeable. The court held that merely inviting people to attend a party—regardless of whether the forum was a social networking site—did not make a criminal attack reasonably foreseeable. In particular, the court noted that since the plaintiffs didn't know the identity of their assailants, there was no way of determining whether they were known to the host.

New Statutory Violations

Social media is also providing individuals and businesses with new ways to violate statutes, such as consunmer protection laws, in a manner never before envisioned. For example, collection agencies were quick to embrace using social media as a means of checking for financial clues about debtors. Debt collectors provide their sites, checking out residential and work addresses and even photos or statements that make reference to expensive property or other assets. The Fair Debt Collection Practices Act (which hasn't been amended since 2006) doesn't restrict debt collectors from making such investigations, even to the point of creating a Facebook account and "friending" those who owe money.

However, the FDCPA does set certain limits on how collectors can communicate with debtors and third parties. One company found itself on the receiving end of a lawsuit in Illinois after it contacted the college age daughter of a man who skipped out on his Mercedes payments (the daughter had possession of the vehicle). After the clueless daughter accepted the collector's friend request, it promptly sent her a notice—viewable to third parties on her public social networking profile—about the debt, a big violation of the FDCAA's prohibition against contact with third parties about anything other than verification of the debtor's address. As a result, the collector was sued.

Similarly, heavy-handed tactics have led to lawsuit against other collectors. After debt collection firm Mark One Financial found Melanie Beacham on Facebook to contact her about being behind on her car payments, it allegedly didn't stop there. Instead, says a lawsuit filed by Beacham in Florida, Mark One also allegedly contacted Beacham's sister and cousin on Facebook, using made-up names and allegedly harassing Beacham (who reports being called thirty-five times in a single day) and her family members. In addition to damages, Beacham's lawsuit seeks an injunction preventing Mark One from contacting "any friends and family members of the plaintiff, through Facebook, Twitter, or any other social networking sites."

And in a recent federal court case in Minnesota, a collection agency not only looked up the plaintiff's MySpace page, but used the information on it in a manner befitting the Corleone family. The debt collector's "investigator" mentioned to the plaintiff that she had seen pictures of her "beautiful daughter" online and said something to the effect of "wouldn't it be terrible if something happened to your kids . . . because the Sheriff's department was taking you away?" The debtor, Tosha Sohns, brought suit under the FDCPA, and the court ruled that the collection agency had violated the statute by engaging in harassment; by using false, deceptive, or misleading representations or means in attempting to collect the debt; and by using unfair or unconscionable means in attempting to collect the debt. *Sohns v. Bramacint*, 2010 WL 3926264 (D. Minn. Oct. 1, 2010).

New Crimes

In addition to changing the way we look at duty, the advent of social networking has ushered in crimes that would have been unthinkable twenty years ago. Consider the phenomenon of the flash mob, for example. From coast to coast, people linked through social networking sites and text messaging have suddenly, seemingly spontaneously, gathered at pre-set times and appointed locations. Often, the appearance of this "flash mob" is for perfectly benign reasons: performance art in Seattle, impromptu pillow fights in New York, a snowball fight in Washington, or a group dance number in London. But in cities like Philadelphia, Boston, Brooklyn, and others, flash mobs have resulted in violence and vandalism, prompting calls for curfews and greater police monitoring of social networking sites as a playful social experiment takes a darker turn.

Social networking's potential to be used for evil has led to the invention of new crimes morphing identity theft, harassment, and defamation. Throughout the United States, courts have dealt with cases in which a fake social networking profile has been set up to harass and defame someone. More often than not, such false MySpace or Facebook pages are created by disgruntled students in the name of a hated teacher, complete with false, highly unflattering statements and photos portraying the teacher as a pedophile. Adults are capable of this type of behavior as well, however. In Casper, Wyoming, a vindictive ex-boyfriend allegedly posted a false Craigslist ad purporting to be in the name of his former lover, soliciting sexual partners for a so-called rape fantasy. The woman was assaulted and left bound on the floor, and her attacker's defense was that he was under the impression from the ad posted that "she" not only consented to the act, but also invited it. He has pled not guilty. In February 2010, thirty-three-year-old Amanda Anderson allegedly posted a bogus job opening on Craigslist in an attempt to harass her former boss with a flood of unwanted calls.

As with so many things in life, timing is everything. Prior to September 1, 2009, Ms. Anderson's alleged action may have been viewed as nothing more than a prank. However, thanks to a law passed by the Texas legislature, such an act became a third-degree felony. Tex. Penal Code Ann. § 33.09 now makes it a crime to:

> use the name or persona of another to create a webpage, or to post one or more messages on a commercial social networking site: 1) without obtaining the other person's consent; and 2) with the intent to harm, defraud, intimidate, or threaten any person. A person commits an offense if the person sends an electronic mail, instant message, text message, or similar communication that references a name, domain address, phone number, or other item of identifying information belonging to any person: 1) without obtaining the other person's consent; 2) with the intent to cause a recipient of the communication

to reasonable believe that the other person authorized or transmitted the communication.

New Defenses

As we have seen, social networking's availability and ease of use have led some observers to believe there is a duty to avail oneself of such online resources when a reasonable person would do so. The potential for abuse of social media has also resulted in the creation of new forms of criminal conduct. In addition, though, the popularity of social media has also led to the availability of a new type of defense: the "Facebook alibi."

In October 2009, nineteen-year-old Rodney Bradford of Brooklyn was arrested in connection with a robbery. On paper, he might have made a plausible suspect, given the fact that he was already facing charges in connection with another robbery. But Bradford had an unusual alibi for his whereabouts at 11:49 a.m. on October 17, 2009, and it was one that could be verified. You see, Bradford was on Facebook at the time, updating his status to read "on the phone with this fat chick...wherer my i hop" (a reference to talking with the pregnant girlfriend and a trip to get some pancakes).

Proving the alibi wasn't simply a matter of taking Rodney Bradford's word for it, thanks to the electronic trail he'd left. Although eyewitnesses identified him in a lineup, Bradford's father and stepmother confirmed the fact that the youth was at his father's Manhattan apartment using the computer. Corroborating his story further was evidence from Facebook itself; a Brooklyn district attorney subpoenaed Facebook's records and verified that the server log-on/log-off records matched Bradford's time on the social networking site, and that the status update was posted from an Internet protocol address that matched the one registered to Bradford's father. The district attorney dropped the charges.

Robert Reuland, Bradford's defense attorney, says that Facebook verification "made the day." "What we had in hand was irrefutable proof," he said. "And that's really where it turned the trick." Legal observers hailed this as the first known instance in which social networking evidence—often used to impeach or help convict a criminal defendant—has been used as alibi evidence. Some of those commenting on the case were more skeptical, however. Joseph Pollini, who teaches at John Jay College of Criminal Justice in New York, maintains, "With a user name and password, anyone can input data in a Facebook page."

What Mr. Pollini and other skeptics overlook, however, is the fact that there was more than just a Facebook update operating in Rodney Bradford's favor. Besides the testimony from corroborating witnesses like Bradford's father and stepmother who were with him at the same residence, the matching Internet protocol address and Facebook server records would be difficult for even an accomplished hacker to fake. Although one can update a Facebook page with someone's user name and password from a remote location, the use of proxy servers, a public terminal, or any number of other techniques to hide the sender's physical location would still leave a trail more likely to *disprove* an alibi, not create one. As defense counsel Reuland was quick to point out, "This is a nineteen-year-old kid. He's not a criminal genius setting up an elaborate alibi for himself."

Ultimately, no one was more relieved than Rodney Bradford and his family. "If it weren't for Facebook, I'd still be on Riker's Island," says the teenager. Ernestine Bradford, Rodney's stepmother, agrees. "Facebook saved my son... Normally, we yell at our kids. 'Oh, you're on the computer.' It's completely different. If it weren't for Facebook, my son wouldn't be here." A Facebook representative said the social networking giant was "pleased" to be "able to serve as a constructive part of the judicial process."

With the prevalence of social networking, and an apparent willingness of people to reveal more of themselves online, there is a greater cyber trail to follow than ever before. For many, those digital footprints have led to criminal convictions. For Rodney Bradford, they led to exoneration. Bradford's case may have been the first "Facebook alibi," but it isn't likely to be the last. In a recent unpublished opinion, a California appellate court acknowledged the viability of a social media alibi. In People v. Calderon, the appellate court found nothing "implausible or bizarre" about the criminal defendant's alibi that he was playing poker on MySpace at the time of the crime. *People v. Calderon*, 2010 Cal. App. Unpub. 2010 WL 3505971 (Cal. App. 2d Dist. Sept. 9, 2010). The court held that MySpace records showed that someone was logged in to the defendant's account at the time of the crime, and that defendant had testified he didn't share his account information with anyone. While the court ultimately didn't reverse the conviction – ruling that a disputed jury instruction was harmless, and that the defendant could have logged into MySpace from another location – the language of the opinion seems to indicate that under the right circumstances and with the right evidence, a social media alibi would work.

Appendices

APPENDIX A

FORMS

CAUSE NO. _____

IN THE DISTRICT COURT OF ANYWHERE COUNTY, TEXAS
JUDICIAL DISTRICT

JANE DOE, et al,
Plaintiffs,
v.
XYZ CORP.
Defendants.

A. DEFENDANT'S RESPONSE TO PLAINTIFFS' MOTION TO
QUASH DEPOSITION <u>ON WRITTEN QUESTIONS DIRECTED
TO MYSPACE, INC.</u>

Defendant XYZ CORP. (hereinafter "Defendant") files its response to
Plaintiffs' Motion Quash Deposition on Written Questions directed to
MySpace, Inc. Defendant asks the Court to deny Plaintiffs' motion to quash
as the records sought by Defendant are relevant to the issues to be
determined in this lawsuit.

I.
<u>Background Facts</u>

This is a wrongful death case arising out of a motorcycle-truck collision on
August 31, 2009. Plaintiffs filed suit seeking damages as a result of the death
of John Doe. Plaintiff Jane Doe asserted claims under the wrongful death
statute as the purported common-law wife of John Doe. Defendants deny
that the couple were married prior to Mr. Doe' death, and dispute that
Plaintiff is a statutory beneficiary pursuant to the Texas Wrongful Death
Act.

Whether Ms. Doe and Mr. Doe were married will be a fact issue to be determined by the jury in the trial of this matter. Plaintiffs will have the burden of establishing all of the elements of a common law marriage as required by Texas law. Ms. Doe testified that the couple were married prior to Mr. Doe's death.

To the contrary, Defendant will offer evidence that Mr. Doe was not married at the time of his death. Defendant has obtained a number of records which indicate that Mr. Doe was single at the time of his death. By way of example, Mr. Doe's income tax returns do not reflect that he was married. *See Ex. A, B, C and D*, first page of Tax Returns of John Doe for the years 2006, 2007, 2008 and 2009. Furthermore, in the months prior to Mr. Doe's death, Mr. Doe and Ms. Doe ceased living together.

In order to further develop evidence as to the marital status of Ms. Doe and Mr. Doe, Defendants issued a Deposition on Written Questions to MySpace, a social networking site, for the information contained in Ms. Doe' page. MySpace is a social- networking website with an interactive, user-submitted network of friends, personal profiles, blogs, groups, photos, music and videos for teenagers and adults internationally. Any information or photographs posted by Ms. Doe on the social networking site concerning her relationships will be relevant to the subject matter of this case. As one court stated,

> "Facebook usage depicts a snapshot of the user's relationships and state of mind at the time of the content's posting."

The Deposition on Written Questions was issued on December 9, 2009. Plaintiffs moved to quash the Deposition on Written Questions. Defendants ask the Court to deny Plaintiffs' motion. The information written on Ms. Doe's web page is relevant to issues to be determined in this lawsuit. Specifically, it is relevant to the issue of whether she was married to Mr. Doe prior to the time of his death. Further, the information contained therein is relevant to the damages that she claims to suffer as a result of his death in the same way that a diary or journal of plaintiff would be relevant. Finally, any information posted by Ms. Doe on her MySpace page which concern the death of Mr. Doe, their relationship, or the injuries she has suffered as a result of his death qualifies as a witness statement pursuant to T.R.C.P. 192.3.

Because of the damages sought by Ms. Doe in this lawsuit, she has placed her marital status at issue. Defendant is entitled to conduct discovery to obtain information relevant to her claim to be the common law wife of Mr. Doe. Further, Defendant is entitled to conduct discovery to obtain information relevant to her claims for pain and suffering, loss of consortium, loss of spousal support as well as other elements of damages. For these reasons, Defendant should be allowed to proceed with obtaining the MySpace records.

II.
Argument & Authorities

A. Defendants' Request is Reasonably Calculated to Lead to the Discovery of Admissible Evidence

A party may obtain discovery regarding any matter that is not privileged and is relevant to the subject matter of the pending action, whether it relates to a claim or defense of the party seeking discovery or the claim or defense of any other party. T.R.C.P. 192.3(a). It is not a ground for objection that the information sought will be inadmissible at trial if the information sought appears reasonably calculated to lead to the discovery of admissible evidence. *Id. See Monsanto v. May*, 889 S.W.2d 274, 276 (Tex. 1994).

The party who seeks to exclude documents from discovery has the burden of proof. The party opposing discovery also has the affirmative duty to specifically plead the particular privilege, to request a hearing on the motion and to produce some evidence supporting the claim. *See Weisel Enterprises, Inc. v. Curry*, 718 S.W.2d 56, 57-59 (Tex. 1986); and *Peeples v. Honorable Fourth Supreme Judicial District*, 701 S.W.2d 635, 637 (Tex. 1985).

By filing this lawsuit seeking to recover for the wrongful death of Mr. Doe, Ms. Doe has placed her relationship with Mr. Doe at issue in the case. Additionally, her claims for personal injuries resulting from his death place her mental and emotional condition at issue in the case. Defendants are entitled to conduct discovery on these issues. Defendants' request for Ms. Doe' MySpace page is reasonably calculated to lead to the discovery of admissible evidence. Ms. Doe' MySpace page will likely contain information relevant to her relationship with Mr. Doe and the impact of his death upon her and her daughters. Therefore, this information is discoverable.

With respect to admissibility, Texas courts have allowed the admission of evidence from social networking websites such as MySpace. Texas courts have admitted this type of evidence in both criminal cases and family law cases. *Hall v. State of Texas*, 283 S.W.3d 137, 149 (Tex. App.—Austin 2009, pet. ref'd) (State introduced printout of Hall's Facebook page to show that she reveled in the role of a gangster's girlfriend and shared dark traits.); *Mann v. Dep't. of Family and Protective Servs.*, 2009 WL 2961396 at *2, *10 (Tex.App.-Houston [1st Dist.] Sept. 17, 2009, no pet.) (photographs and information from MySpace showing mother engaging in underage drinking admitted as evidence to support termination of parental rights); *In re: K.E.L.*, 2008 WL 5671873 at *3 (Tex.App.—Beaumont, no pet.) (trial court admitted a copy of K.E.L.'s father's MySpace page which contained sexually-oriented statements made by him.) Other jurisdictions have allowed parties to subpoena evidence from social-networking websites in personal injury cases. *Ledbetter v. Wal-Mart Stores, Inc.*, 2009 WL 1067018 (D. Colo.) (holding that information sought by subpoenas issued to Facebook, MySpace, Inc. and Meetup.com is reasonably calculated to lead to the discovery of admissible evidence in personal injury lawsuit and denying motion to quash); *Bass v. Miss Porter's School*, 2009 WL 3724968 (D. Conn.) (allowing defendant to discover electronic mail and information from plaintiff's Facebook account). Thus, Defendants' request is reasonably calculated to lead to the discovery of admissible evidence.

B. Ms. Doe's MySpace Page Constitutes a Witness Statement

Furthermore, any information written by Ms. Doe on her MySpace page constitutes a witness statement if it concerns any matter at issue in this lawsuit. As this Court is well aware, a party may obtain discovery of the statement of any person with knowledge of relevant facts—a "witness statement"—regardless of when the statement was made. T.R.C.P. 192.3(h). A witness statement includes a written statement adopted or approved in writing by the person making it. *Id.* Thus, information posted by Ms. Doe on her MySpace page related to this lawsuit would fall within the definition of a witness statement. For this reason alone, Ms. Doe's MySpace page is discoverable.

III.
Conclusion

Defendants' request for Ms. Doe's MySpace page is reasonably calculated to lead to the discovery of admissible evidence. Defendants anticipate that Ms. Doe has posted information related to her relationship with Mr. Doe on her My Space page. Further, it is anticipated that her My Space page contains information relevant to the injuries and damages she seeks in this lawsuit. Defendants are therefore entitled to proceed with obtaining the requested information. Plaintiffs' motion to quash should be denied.

WHEREFORE, PREMISES CONSIDERED, Defendant respectfully requests that this Court deny Plaintiffs' Motion to Quash the Deposition on Written Questions issued by Defendants to MySpace, Inc., and further pray for such other and further relief as this Court deems just.

Respectfully submitted,
Bob the Lawyer
Bobsville, Texas
State Bar No. 12345678

ATTORNEYS FOR
DEFENDANT

<u>CERTIFICATE OF SERVICE</u>

This is to certify that a true and correct copy of the above motion has been sent by facsimile transmission to opposing counsel on this _____ day of August, 2010.

_____

Bob the Lawyer

APPENDIX B

MODEL FEDERAL JURY INSTRUCTIONS

In case you haven't seen the federal jury instructions, they follow:

Before Trial:

You, as jurors, must decide this case based solely on the evidence presented here within the four walls of this courtroom. This means that during the trial you must not conduct any independent research about this case, the matters in the case, and the individuals or corporations involved in the case. In other words, you should not consult dictionaries or reference materials, search the Internet, websites, blogs, or use any other electronic tools to obtain information this case or to help you decide the case. Please do not try to find out information from any source outside the confines of this courtroom.

Until you retire to deliberate, you may not discuss this case with anyone, even your fellow jurors. After you retire to deliberate, you may begin discussing the case with your fellow jurors, but you cannot discuss the case with anyone else until you have returned a verdict and the case is at an end. I hope that for all of you this case is interesting and noteworthy. I know that many of you use cell phones, Blackberries, the internet and other tools of technology. You also must not talk to anyone about this case or use these tools to communicate electronically with anyone about the case. This includes your family and friends. You may not communicate with anyone about the case on your cell phone, through e-mail, Blackberry, iPhone, text messaging, or on Twitter, through any blog or website, through any Internet chat room, or by way of any other social networking website, including Facebook, MySpace, LinkedIn, and YouTube.

At the Close of the Case:

During your deliberations, you must not communicate with or provide any information to anyone by any means about this case. You may not use any electronic device or media, such as a telephone, cell phone, smart phone, iPhone, Blackberry or computer; the Internet, any Internet service, or any text or instant messaging service; or any Internet chat room, blog , or website such as Facebook MySpace, LinkedIn, YouTube or Twitter, to communicate to anyone any information about this case or to conduct any research about this case until I accept your verdict.

APPENDIX C

INSTRUCTIONS TO CIVIL JURY

Judge Susan Criss 212th Judicial District Court 600 59th Street, Galveston TX 77551 www.co.galveston.tx.us/judgecriss	Phone (409) 766-2266 Fax (409) 765-2610 Debbie.diaz@co.galveston.tx.us

The following instructions are court orders. They apply until the trial is over and I tell you they no longer apply. Failure to abide by these court orders will result in consequences including but not limited to contempt of court. Punishment for contempt of court will be fines or imprisonment in jail. **You can be fined or jailed for violating these court orders.**

1. Do not mingle with nor talk to the lawyers, the witnesses, the parties, or any other person who might be connected with or interested in this case, except for casual greetings. They have to follow these same instructions and you will understand it when they do.

2. Do not accept from, nor give to, any of those persons any favors however slight, such as rides, food or refreshments.

3. Do not discuss anything about this case, or even mention it to anyone whomsoever, or in the presence of others including your spouse, partner or significant other. Do not allow anyone to mention it in your hearing until you are discharged as jurors or excused from this case. If anyone attempts to discuss the case with you or in front of you report it to the bailiff at once. The bailiff is ordered to inform me of all such reports by jurors.

4. Do not post or read about the case or subject matter of the case or persons in the case on blogs, Internet news sites or social media including but not limited to Wikipedia, MySpace, Twitter or Facebook. You can post that you are on jury duty and how long you expect to be on jury duty. That is ALL you are allowed to write or text about. You cannot post anything about whether a verdict

has or will be reached or when a verdict has or will be reached or announced in court.

5. Do not read or send text messages in the courtroom. Do not have cell phones, blackberries or any other device you may use to communicate with others on while you are in the courtroom. While you are deliberating your cell phones, blackberries and any other device you may use to communicate with others will be removed from the jury room.

6. Do not even discuss this case among yourselves until after you have heard all of the evidence, the court's charge, and the attorney's arguments and until I have sent you to the jury room to consider your verdict.

7. Do not make personal inspections, observations, investigations, or experiments nor personally view premises, things or articles not produced in court. Do not let anyone else do any of these things for you. All evidence must be presented in open court so that each side may question the witnesses and make proper objection. If you know of, or learn anything about, this case except from the evidence admitted during the course of this trial, you should tell me about it at once. You have just taken an oath that you will render a verdict on the evidences submitted to you under my rulings.

8. Do not tell other jurors your own personal experiences or those of other persons, nor relate any information you obtained outside of the courtroom about any aspect of the case. A juror may have knowledge of matters such as business, technical or professional matters or he may have expert knowledge or opinions, or he may know what happened in this or some other lawsuit. To tell the other jurors any of this information is a violation of these instructions.

9. Do not seek information contained in law books, dictionaries, public or private records, the internet, television, newspapers, blogs, social media, or elsewhere, which is not admitted in

evidence. Do not research anything about this case, the parties, attorneys or any subject matter connected to the case.

10. Do not discuss or consider attorney's fees unless evidence about attorney's fees is admitted.

11. Do not consider, discuss nor speculate whether or not any party is or is not protected in whole or in part by insurance of any kind.

The Texas law requires investigation and hearings about proof of any violation of the rules of jury conduct. Jurors and others may be called to testify in open court or in chambers about acts of jury misconduct. I caution you to follow carefully all instructions which I have given you, as well as others which you later receive while this case is on trial.

When a juror violates these instructions a mistrial may be declared. Sometimes the appellate courts will order that the verdict be thrown out due to jury misconduct. Having to start over and try a case again is very expensive for the parties, lawyers and taxpayers. Trying the case over also creates stress and hardship for all involved.

As a judge I am very serious about my obligation to see that cases are tried fairly, efficiently and according to the law. I do not want to have to punish citizens who give up their time to serve on juries. But please understand that I will ensure that all laws regarding jury conduct are followed and that all violations of those laws are addressed.

You may keep these instructions and review them as the case proceeds. If you are aware of any violation of these instructions you are ordered to report it to the bailiff. The bailiff is ordered to inform me of any such reports by jurors.

In the event of an emergency, evacuation or power outage that requires the courthouse be closed, that information will be posted at www.oja.intranets.com.

ABOUT THE AUTHOR

John G. Browning is a Dallas attorney with more than twenty-one years of experience in trying a wide variety of civil litigation, ranging from personal injury and wrongful death cases to employment, commercial, consumer, and intellectual property matters. He is "AV" rated, a "Texas Super Lawyer," and a member of such prestigious organizations as the American Law Institute and Litigation Counsel of America. In addition to being a lawyer, Mr. Browning is a legal journalist whose work has appeared in newspapers and magazines throughout Texas and in regional and national legal publications and academic journals. His writing has earned numerous journalism honors, as well as the prestigious Burton Award for Distinguished Achievement in Legal Writing for 2009 and 2010.